DEAD IRANIAN GIRL

DEAD IRANIAN GIRL

A MEMOIR

ROXANA SHIRAZI

RARE BIRD
LOS ANGELES, CALIF.

THIS IS A GENUINE RARE BIRD BOOK

Rare Bird Books
6044 North Figueroa Street
Los Angeles, California 90042
rarebirdbooks.com

FIRST NORTH AMERICAN HARDCOVER EDITION

All photographs by Roxana Shirazi, except as additionally credited.
Kandovan and Khomeini posters courtesy of Alamy.
Cover photo by Beki Cowey.

For more information, address:
Rare Bird Books Subsidiary Rights Department
6044 North Figueroa Street
Los Angeles, California 90042

Set in Minion Pro
Printed in the United States

10 9 8 7 6 5 4 3 2 1

Library of Congress Cataloging-in-Publication Data available upon request

Dedicated to anyone who helps, loves, or rescues animals.

They are waiting to take us
Into the severed garden
Do you know how pale and wanton thrill-full
Comes death on a strange hour?
Unannounced, unplanned for
Like a scaring over-friendly guest
You've brought to bed
Death makes angels of us all
And gives us wings
Where we had shoulders
Smooth as raven's claws

—James Douglas Morrison

Prologue

*Border of Iran and Turkey, 2016**

**This book is based on real events. While it draws extensively from the author's direct experiences, to protect the privacy of individuals, some names and identifying details have been changed and events have been compressed, reordered, or adapted to enhance narrative flow. Readers are advised that this book contains graphic sexual and violent content and hateful language which may be considered offensive.*

Only I would find myself on the border of Iran in a small Turkish village looking for the morning-after-pill and a bottle of tequila—the pill to stop the sperm from doing its job onto my clenched reluctant womb and the tequila to combat the fear of illegally crossing into Iran on a donkey. I hobble along the sideway of a busy mountainous junction with the young revolutionary, Elijah, who is helping to get me smuggled across the border. I am dying to get to my beloved Iran, my home, my real self, so he has introduced me to Hassan, a Kurdish-Turkish smuggler who along with the other smugglers I have paid will get me on that donkey through the mountains to Iran.

Last night around a bottle of Jack Daniels smuggled in from Armenia over which he and Hassan conspired over, Elijah asked me if I would give him the experience of a male-male-female threesome. This has usually only happened to me with American rock stars, but that night my ravenousness for the erotic crumpled my knees and made me give in. I looked at Hassan and his compulsory broom-thick Turk moustache over his gleaming gold teeth. He was kind about my pitted acne scars and my lusty belly with three tiers of blubber, all feta cheese related.

I had wrapped my Islamic headscarf tight to feel safe and cozy against the contrast of the gossamer linen dress. My eyes were streaked in kohl and my gold Egyptian bangles jangled over my furry arms. Then the first brush of Hassan's bristle moustache felt tickly against my crotch as he leaned over me, his gold teeth aglare, and I cringed that the reek of my garlic and onion breath overpowered the bubble-gum smell of my lip gloss.

Quickly, though, the kisses and the strokes of the two men gave me comfort, anaesthetizing my fear of the imminent illegal smuggling into Iran with a fake passport and new identity, the sandwiching cementing me between two centurions.

It was then I had realized that I had started to like Elijah. A bit too much, recently. In this lonely land, totally alone from Amman, Jordan to Cairo and then Istanbul and now Eastern Turkey, I had been so lonely, held in place only by the beautiful fact that I would finally be in Iran, ready to be peeled like a lychee, glistening like new-born yolk. It was all so close: the singed vermillion of the ancient Persian culture, of extended families gathered at each other's homes singing, dancing, banqueting, reciting poetry late into the night; bazaars at midnight and myriads of humans picnicking on the grassy knoll, sizzling meat and guzzling hot tea next to their samovars; the whispers and shrieks, gossiping and songs when there are stars.

I came hard. I came with the trailing baggage of busy Tehran streets of 1970s, of prison visits with my mum to political prisoners, of upsets and rain, of chalk streets, of ancient Persian dusk and a climate of fear on the streets of Tehran, and of the Shah's secret police, SAVAK, raiding homes and executing political activists. I came hard with an aura of child loneliness in a foreign land, of fear and not belonging. I came with moldy pomegranate pulp. The aura and energy from me, although inherently loving and maternal, has rage lodged in the pit of my core, too exhausting for most people to process.

Being on some form of 'list' in Iran for being a person of moral turpitude was something I of course knew would happen when I published my memoir *The Last Living Slut: Born in Iran, Bred Backstage* in 2010. It was perhaps an act of self-sabotage, something which I have a supreme talent for. But this illegal journey is not yet another act of self-annihilation. It is because I have nothing left in England.

My family have cut me off. All of them. The ones in Europe. The ones in Canada. In the US. Because of my book. And I don't have any friends since I ditched the misogynistic fundamentalism and homogeneity of rock 'n' roll, supposedly a bastion of anarchy and sexual freedom, but only for men. I cannot understand how the world of rock 'n' roll celebrates and worships men who are legendary for having had sex with underage girls, who boast in their memoirs about degrading women, and then demonizes me for writing *my* rock 'n' roll sexual memoirs. Rock 'n' roll has felt more like a religious fundamentalist country ever since. A place where the worse the behavior you engage in, even sex with underage girls, the more of a rock God and icon you become—as long as you are a man.

And whereas those around me idolize these musicians, as well as male writers—Bukowski, Henry Miller—who are iconized for their sexually graphic memoirs of a working-class identity and the degradation and abuse of women, they instead vilify *me* for my book.

I have been blacklisted by everyone and every place I know. I don't have a job, can't even get one since my book came out in 2010. Employers tell me I don't fit the "safe" and "correct" category of Iranian woman: "we love your journalism experience, but we googled you, and as an Iranian woman you are too controversial," or "you are not "brand safe."

And apart from my self-sacrificing mother, who has taken a vow of martyrdom since birth, my immediate family in the UK is too "left-wing" to sully their name by associating with me—all while maintaining a posture of militant activism at meetings and marches for women's and refugee rights, at rallies protesting Islamophobia, and in their rhetoric. My writings on sex, Iranian identity, rock 'n' roll, and my body isn't the "correct" anti-imperialist narrative. It is not palatable for their champagne socialist circles.

I have nothing left to lose if I get caught by Iranian officials and sent to prison for being me. I go into this knowing that if I die, at least there will be no more feeling of alienation, that at least I will be where my soul is, my real self, a self I was forced to leave behind as a child and lost overnight along with all my friends, family, and a father I have never really known.

Though I have always missed Iran achingly, I have only gone back to visit once, and I didn't want to leave. There has been a void—a *canyon*—since I was forcibly sent to England in 1984 at the age of ten in the middle of the Iran–Iraq War with only my heavily asthmatic and heart-failing maternal grandmother as a chaperone. My mother told me that it was just a holiday when I begged her not to send me away from her, my siblings, my sociology classes at school, my cousins, and my many friends—when I begged her not to send me away from my life. I didn't speak English, and I was all alone and terrified in this new country. My mother must have viewed England through a Disney/Mary Poppins lens and thought a ten-year-old kid would be instantaneously swept into the embrace of chic, sylph-like erudite intellectuals as she stepped off the plane and into a world of Jane Austen novels, piano recitals, and ballet classes within some Georgian manor where English people inducted exotic refugee kids into a new life in the utopian West out of the pure goodness of their genteel hearts.

I never have fitted in. *Nigger* and *Paki* were just a bee sting when I was ten.

This alienation because I wrote a memoir has annihilated me.

Recently, out of desperation, I took my book into the Iranian embassy in London and asked them to tell me if I would honestly be safe were I to go to Iran. Honesty from them was wishful thinking but I wanted to trust them like they were the village elders, the scholarly clerics of wisdom and grandfatherly love. The bearded men with no ties (the tie is seen as a Western and counter-revolutionary symbol, thus not permitted by the Islamic Republic) took me into a room, looked at my book, and asked me if I had ever had sex outside of marriage—adultery is punishable by stoning—and I said "no," as I had never been married. They asked me why I had the Islamic symbol on the cover of my book next to the word "slut" and a photo of me in my Islamic headwear as a kid. *It was the designer who done it—not me, guv—but isn't it fucking cooool?* I wanted to say.

I don't know why I went there. What were they gonna say? "We pardon you, nothing will happen"?

Their gazes as they flicked through my sexy photos burned me, but I wanted to know if I was still considered a human being in the Islamic Republic of Iran. The elderly men were embarrassed, and I felt really bad, like this feckless creature who had swaggered in with her book and photos. Flustered and disturbed, they shot me intermittent looks of stupefaction and pathos, as if I were an artefact in the little cabinet of demented curiosities. Combined with their faux syrupy assurances and the excessive, florid adulation so typical of our Persian culture, it was clear they were not be trusted.

"We'll find out for you if you are on a blacklist. Come back again in a few weeks." They regarded me with the same suspicion reserved for nonces at a playground.

I have traveled far to find smugglers here in Eastern Turkey. I have trawled Kurdish cafes in north London to make the right contacts with human smugglers. So many people including some of my family escaped Iran after the revolution on horseback through the Turkish mountains. Why couldn't it be done in reverse?

I was put in touch with a Syrian pilot in Amman, Jordan, named Farid, whom I was told was crucial to meet in person. I thought I would make it a bit of a Middle East holiday. An appetizer, a warmup to the main event. In an Amman café, the blond pilot put me in touch with an Egyptian family in Cairo I would travel with, and so on to my smugglers here in Eastern Turkey, where my fear and loneliness has made me suction onto Elijah like a crustacean. He is a bit scared of me, I think—of my sheer chutzpah. It somehow does not make the ponytailed twenty-something revolutionary with Rumi poetry tattoos feel like the Turkish man he ought to feel. He suggested the m-m-f *ménage a trois* when he read about my first book online just after we met in Istanbul. It was to make him look audacious, fearless, rockstar-y, and I realize that if I want my intellectual revolutionary poet from a far-flung village in a far-flung land so that his blood and sweat from fighting for change is pure and authentic, it will also come with the tinge of fresh-off-the boat rube-ish ness. All those poets and writers and activists I have known from New York and London are all smudged with gourmet coffee and health food emporium produce, trapped in social media and the grip of first world "problems." They covet suffering like an eco-friendly designer satchel, which renders their revolutionary poetic-ness null, void. I, too, do clichés.

Elijah is passionate about getting me to my homeland. He knows I face prison and torture if I go the normal route via my passport: I'll be arrested at the airport or clamped and pronged at 4 a.m. on my dad's floor as I lie in slumber, waiting to be taken to prison and interrogated for hours on end about being a heretic; a *mortad* (apostate), which is punishable by execution; and *mofsed-e-filarz* (someone who has spread corruption on earth that threatens social and political well-being). And I have been told by many official contacts that I am well-known in Iran for embodying these capital crimes and it would be dangerous for me to go there. I guess the contents of my first book and my photos would have made that obvious anyway.

On this leg of my journey, Elijah has let me fake-join his tourist group, a herd of "alt" travelers from all over Europe and Canada who think they are achingly cool to be teetering on the edge of the Syria border, full of warm lamb and sugared tea, taking selfies at terrorist-ravaged sites. Their nosiness at our fucking and room-share is a constant. In Urfa, a town near the border of Syria where the hotel staff wanted to alert the police of our trysts so Elijah would get arrested because as an unmarried couple we were sharing a room together and thus "disrespecting Turkish legal and cultural codes of conduct," the group practically broke into applause.

Elijah finds me the bottle of tequila and more miraculously the morning-after-pill in this Kurdish populated Turkey/Iran border. My mouth, full of mince, falls open in shock. It makes me like him more.

He leaves the group and takes me to Hassan again.

"Hurry! Hurry!" Hassan motions me over to a small truck and I get in. "Will I see you again?" I ask Elijah.

"Yes! Yes! Drink the tequila. You're only going to meet the contact."

"But I'm scared." I hold him tight. "I want you to come with us."

Elijah takes a step back and eyes me concernedly. "Are you sure you want to do this?"

"I miss Iran." I pout and stamp my foot like a toddler.

"Well, you should have thought about all this when you wrote that book."

It's a bit harsh but totally true.

Meanwhile, Hassan is revving the engine, gold tooth gleaming in the metal.

"It's okay. He knows good people." Elijah holds me like my mum would have done were she here. "You will meet with them and come back tonight and go in the morning."

"Okay, you hold onto the tequila then." I take a last gulp—I'm a bit pissed already—and swallow the morning after pill. "Take this empty packet, too," I tell him, "just in case the revolutionary guards find it."

I know he is lying, that I won't be coming back. That this is it. I kiss his beard, his dark broody heroics. It's like he's my husband. Elijah closes the van door after me and waves goodbye. I hand him the rucksack of clothes, books, and cosmetics I've had with me thus far. My life is in Hassan's hands now. He seems kind, but his black sunglasses could be hiding malicious intent. I tighten my Islamic *chador* wobbly with liquor.

I have wished to remain inconspicuous. The lemon-yellow tent that housed my body from the doorsteps of England was frilly with époque-esque squiggles at the chest, and that was the only scandalous feature about it, like showing a bit of ankle in old porn. The mustard leggings underneath were from a supermarket bargain bin and my cream plastic slippers were bought from the over-sixties ladies' club. When I got on the airport bus in London with my straw hat, the driver proudly branded me Shirley Valentine. The observation was true. My deliberate downtrodden housewife make-under had been a success. I then slept until Istanbul, where I was changing for Arabia, somewhere in Arabia. The desert and then the Nile.

And then what?

The blistering late afternoon sun streams through the windows of Hassan's baby-blue pickup truck and melts down our backs as my white face, a half-moon, peeps out from my shrouds. We speed away from towns and villages toward the mountains as darkness sets in, the fizzing sherbet of the orange sky now rinsed into a jaundiced haze.

"*Evin harda*?" (Where is your home)? Hassan barks like I've just got into his Uber, paralytic after a night on the piss and I can't remember where I live.

Never have I been so grateful that Azerbaijani is my mother tongue. The language that glued my maternal grandmother and I together. "Tehran," I manage to stammer.

The night is coming, and I will need to get on a donkey or horse to cross the border. I just know that when I finally reach the border of Iran, I will gain new life. The child in me will come out all flushed and giddy. The earth there is mine. Should I really be getting on a donkey and go without thinking, without analyzing?

Whatever happens to me will happen. Death. I don't know. Imprisonment.

Maybe not. Maybe my presence in the country won't be detected. Maybe I'll trickle and seep into the landscape to be as one with the concrete and bazaars, the mountains and mud alleys, the sweaty humans and sabzi and the unbearable pollution.

I know the smugglers are going to be giving me a fake passport to travel around with and eventually use to get back to England with, and surely being in the possession of a fake passport in Iran is utter madness. I would be accused of spying, as many Iranians from the West who have been imprisoned in Iran are. But this is me, with a platinum subscription to self-sabotage that has been my life: the Death Drive taken to extremes. Some people are addicted to drugs; I'm addicted to the adrenaline of danger. Perhaps it's because my childhood was a flood of constant adrenalin, of fight or flight situations: revolutionary demonstrations in front of armed soldiers, political activities with my family, the Shah's secret police raiding our neighborhood and family home, destroying socialist literature, prison visits to see my political activist family and seeing their torture scars, then the Iran/Iraq war, the fear of being bombed, air raid sirens. I was always on high alert, and my body was hooked on the adrenaline. *Proper* hooked.

We get out for a cigarette break in a busy main road. At an ice cream stand facing a perfume shop, I hear a gaggle of Persian women with colorful clothes and thick manes of hair, their low laughter velvety, maternal, like warm milk to my veins. Persian women converse as if they are telling tales of the *One Thousand and One Nights* even when they are talking of mundane things, their descriptions poetic, the rhythm of gossip lulling, textural.

"She has fox eyes—slanted, jade. It is as if she purrs!!" the older lady wrapped in sheathes of petal pink says. I look around expecting to see a pre-Raphaelite painting they have gotten their hands on or even a Fellini film poster, but she is just talking about some woman in some tacky perfume advert poster. Western women do not talk this way in ordinary conversation.

My body melts. I weep. I miss my homeland. I weep because it's like being back in the womb, but I can't have it. Nothing fits like Iran. Nothing clicks for me like Iranians. The twilight, reciting Persian poetry, the mountains and fruit trees and big families all gathered on long dusky nights. The ancient culture. I ache like I am being cut. No, not cut, because that's too clean. I splinter. A thousand paper cuts saturated in lemon juice and salt swish in my veins. Would death be more painful than this? I walk over to Hassan.

"Okay, Hassan, let's go find me that donkey. A one-way donkey ticket to Tehran please. Forever."

Amman, Jordan, 2016

I had woken up in Amman, Jordan. I was treading the Middle East carefully in order to cement my relationship with the chain of contacts and to meet them face to face instead of flying straight to Turkey where I would be taken by horseback to Iran. But also because I wanted to travel a bit first in the Middle East as a "warm-up" to being smuggled through the Turkish/Iranian mountains. My contact in London had given me the name of a tourist café where I would find Farid, a Syrian pilot refugee whose connections to smugglers were a network of people I'd have to connect with; first in Cairo before going on to Eastern Turkey. There was a fee, four thousand US dollars, which I would have to pay to the smugglers in Istanbul, Turkey, before the onset of the journey. Of course, it crossed my mind that the smugglers could take the cash, abandon ship, gang rape and murder me in the mountains and leave me to be pecked at by some ravenous vertebrate. Shit, I was gonna risk it. What did I have in England? Nothing, nothing. A terrifying emptiness. A palpable loneliness.

I would treat the first leg of my journey in Jordan and Egypt as an appetizer, dipping my foot in the waters and I would try to relish it, the Middle East, to relax and soak up the Arabian nights.

On my first night I slept in a motel crawling with insects and curtains that smelt like soup. Black roaches peeped over the hem, drunk on the searing heat and I let it go, for this was not the time to appalled by critters. In a residential alleyway next to a mosque, it was inevitable that at the crack of dawn the mournful call of prayer—led live by the Muezzin or from a tape recording—would abruptly splinter the salt-deep black of the neighborhood, twirling around sleeping heads in the pre-dawn silence. My childhood, my grandmother, sleeping on flat rooftops under the stars, the Persian twilight, it was all wrapped up in that mournful wail of prayer blaring from the mosque. *Your lost soul is somewhere inside that sound, it's what you have traveled here for,* I thought when I felt pissed off at being woken up. Groggily I pulled on my *hejab* and stumbled into the crisp inky dawn and went and stood staring at the mosque in my slippers. I was more determined to get to Iran now. That dawn I ate feta cheese and fresh bread with sweet black tea and put on my yellow flower chador—the full-on Islamic cover—with rose oil dabbed on my wrists and walked to the downtown bazaar.

The chockfull of flat roofed white houses clustered together reminded me of Tehran. The cars' incessant horn-beeping in the bowels of the city with doddering motorbikes clumsily weaving through the narrowest alleys over-laden with whole families balanced on top, children placed on laps and wrapped up bundles balanced on heads mirrored street scenes in Tehran. Wedged through all this were fruit juice booths on every corner selling for pennies cantaloupe melon muddled with brown sugar, crushed pomegranates poured into soured iced mugs, and creamy milk with banana pulp.

In the dusty alleyways of the bazaar someone was selling a pack of Saddam Hussein playing cards complete with photos of all his government and the Tikriti family. I bought a pack to pass the time. Alone in my room I had been watching fat turbaned Arab men host game shows as I read Bukowski write on repeat about women's saggy cunts and drinking and fucking, so this pack of cards would be much needed relief.

Vendors and peddlers sitting outside the bazaar vaults and archways chain-drank a constant stream of hot black tea in tulip glasses delivered on trays by prepubescent boys weaving though the crowds. The sweet pungent whiff of rotten garbage whistled down the dark cobbled alleyways, and flies buzzed on animal carcasses displayed behind windows like mannequins, their white and crimson marbling split open like watermelons. Some of them draped in shrouds of white muslin exhibited like little murdered bodies as the flies dined.

I navigated my way into a catacomb of souks lodged deep inside the old town walls weaving through a tumult of traders displaying hessian sack-fuls stuffed with saffron, sumac, turmeric, pistachios and dried fruits. Silk traders sold gold, boy apprentices sewed suits and barbers shaved balding elders late into the night under the warm whir of fans and glow of halogen bulbs. Dirty and love-starved dogs and lazy lady cats lactating, flopped listlessly by the wayside and shoeless children scurried under washing lines hanging from balcony to balcony in cramped alleyways chandeliering the narrow skyline.

I wanted cuddles. Not soup, nor henna tattoos or warm lamb. Nor the soft drizzle of the Arabian dusk and musk. I was getting worried about the smuggling over the border now.

Even with the full length Islamic hejab, I was getting grubby stares and soft heckles muttered under the hot breaths of men. I was relieved to reach the dark cool shadows of the tourist café, an Italian themed place offering the exotic Western cuisine of pizza and lattes. My instructions were to say *I'm looking for a tour guide to show me around town*, and when I was handed the menu, I saw that along with starters, mains and desserts there was also a section for ordering a tour guide priced by the hour (a half a day cost about twenty US dollars). I told my name to the man who took my menu and whose face slightly twitched like I had just uttered a spy code. Immediately he disappeared into the back and was back with Farid, a blonde, blue eyed Syrian.

"We are all Alexander the Great's descendants in my country. His men did a lot of breeding with our women when he conquered Syria," Farid began.

Farid was a pilot in Syria but had to abandon his home country now because of the civil war.

"So we'll walk to the old town and we can talk on the way," he said.

Farid spoke English like a Merchant Ivory aristocrat. He must have learnt English from 1970s cassette tapes or from mimicking old movies. He gave me the address of a lantern shop in Cairo with instructions on who to meet when I got there. I was ravenous for every tiny detail, to bolster the feeling of security. Arabs, strange men, illegal men, smugglers. It had seemed like an exciting adventure in my head but this was real. These might be dark times and hurting.

"Why you want to do this?" Farid spoke kindly but made me embarrassed at my own naiveté and lunacy.

"Because I miss Iran so much. It's my home. I need it."

Walking alongside a man was very different to walking alone as a woman. No prolonged stares or harassment. No lewd comments or hissing. I was the property of a man so my existence as a woman was legitimized; I was a complete woman.

The great jaw of sunset spewed the onset of crowds, cinematic in their haggling, hobnobbing, eating and drinking and socializing in the nightlife of the bazaar. There was no need for a pub in this world, where social activity consisted of sitting and pickling your liver because you need alcohol as social lubricant. These were people revved up by the lusty night, by the dusty vaults, by the traders' eerie lullabies. These families came alive under the Arabian night as if they had just woken, along with pavement cafes open way after midnight, a kaleidoscopic thrum of life, instead of stuffy pubs and clubs with people obliged to get paralytic, go home, throw up, shag and repeat, hardly ever seeing their family or enjoying the beauty of life without alcohol.

In the town square mosque, people rushed to the ablution fountain in its courtyard for the pre-prayer cleansing rituals.

"Let's go talk in the courtyard," Farid said.

The tormented wail of call to prayer whirled eerily around the mosque courtyard enveloping the Qur'an-engraved stones and cherub-carved water fountains, swooshing around the throngs of men huddled, engrossed in the pre-prayer ritual washing of toes, hands, foreheads before heading inside the mosque. Burnt wood singed the air and the sound of *azan* (prayer) sizzled and lulled me into a warm trance.

Farid explained to me how the smuggling would take place. I would have to go to Cairo first to meet his friend and the friend's family in an old lantern shop. We would all need to travel to Turkey together as a group, with me posing as their British friend, an English teacher. Farid said they needed a woman with a British passport. For whatever reason, he didn't disclose and I didn't want to know the details. Once in Istanbul, I would be taken to meet the Turkish contact, transfer the smuggling fee, and go with the Turkish contact directly to the smugglers in Eastern Turkey, who would then take me to Iran through the mountains. I would be given an Iranian passport with a new identity but once on Iranian soil I would have to go it alone from there.

I stayed in Amman a few days, just so I wouldn't be in and out like a spy. I thought about my life in the West, the severance of my childhood overnight, the knicker-soiling from the name-calling and racial violence, the isolation and loneliness, the never belonging. The sense of fitting in that only came when I became a companion of rock stars.

I missed the real me.

Then there were my biological father and grandmother. I would get to them soon enough, but not in daylight. It would come knocking later in the inky haze of night, when I slipped into slumber, the guilt trying to push its way through, jerking me awake telling me that I should have made an effort to be part of their lives, as they sat day in day out, lonely and wretched with no one there for them and only satellite TV blaring that drivel from Iranian Los Angeles. All those wasted years when I shut out the noise by swinging and trapezing from stadiums backstages to tour buses whilst existing in the sticky albumen sac of rock stars, shutting out the noise of my father gnawing at my insides, tapping me on the shoulder, calling and calling, begging to see me in Iran. I should have been at one with their splodges on their sofa, breaking bread with them, giving them smiles, warming up their lonely and desolate lives. This dark drilling guilt, this monster that came knocking in the scotchy amber haze of night in hotel rooms as I lay awake, some famous rock legend or other sleeping soundly next to me making it a bit easier to manage.

Only there and only then could I gloss over the faces of my father and grandmother, of my mother, ex loves. Of those I have loved and betrayed.

But not anymore. I am alone now.

K
IZZAT IBRAHIMAL-DURI
RCC Vice Chairman

A
UDAY SADDAM HUSAYN
National Assembly Member/
Olympic Chairman/
Saddam Feyadeen Chief

5
WATBAN IBRAHIM HASAN
AL-TIKRITI
Presidential Advisor

A
QUSAY SADDAM HUSAYN
AL-TIKRITI
Special Security Organization
(SSO) Super visor/ Baêth Party
Military Bareau Deputy Chairman

A
SADDAM HUSAYN AL-TIKRITI
President

8
TAREQ AZIZ
Deputy Prime Minister
RCCmember

A
ABID HAMID MAHMUD
AL-TIKRITI
Presidential Secretary

J
IBRAHIM AHMAD ABD
AL-SATTAR
MUHAMMAD AL-TIKRITI
Iraqi Armed Forces Chief of Staff

K
AZIZ SALIH AL-NUMAN
Baêth Party Regional
Command Chairman
Respo nsibleofr West Baghdad

ONE

2015

It's early 2015 and I am scraping the toilet bowl of a home in Kensington for a bit of quick cash. The household's grandma insists on the hand-scraping as "it's the way to get it properly clean." Then I have to go do webcam sex work. I am saving up to fly to Alabama to interview the Ku Klux Klan. Every penny from cleaning houses, stacking shelves at supermarkets and webcam sex work goes to food, bills, and being able to continue to do what I love: investigative journalism.

Since my memoir *The Last Living Slut: Born in Iran, Bred Backstage* came out in 2010—a title chosen not by me, but by my editor Neil Strauss, and one I fought bitterly hard against in favor of *Sex, Iran, Rock 'n' Roll*—I have applied to hundreds of jobs in my field, even at the intern level, and been rejected every time, always getting a response along the lines of: "We googled you and you have written a book on sex and Iran. You are not brand safe. So it's going to be no." Year after year, job application after job application, despite my writing experience, education, and skills, I am told the same thing: as a Middle Eastern woman you are too controversial.

I am the "Other," so not treated equally to the white Western women I see in the media who have written sexual memoirs, even ones who have written about being escorts, like Brooke Magnanti, be given platforms to promote their book at big book festivals, give talks at conferences and speak on daytime TV about their book and life experiences.

And it is just a continuation of how it was only the UK media who blocked interviews with me and stopped the book being publicized when the book came out. I had been all over US and European media, giving interviews to promote my book but when it came to doing the same in the UK, my US and UK publishers' requests during the promotional campaign had been shut down by many women's magazines and national newspapers, some initially accepting and then hastily withdrawing.

"Nobody will bite!", I kept getting emails from my publicists. "Nobody wants to promote the book or interview you!"

UK bookshops requested that my book cover, a photo of me as a ten-year-old in my headscarf coming to England be changed if they were going to stock my book in their stores. So my publishers changed the cover to a cartoon drawing of a pair of tits.

Female sexuality is icky if not filtered through a perfumed, educated middle/upper class lens. And a lot of the book's readers were grossed out by my raw unvarnished human condition—STDs, body odors and fluids, disease and illness, hunger and poverty, council estates, pregnancy and abortions. Is the human condition not natural to the human female?

And it also makes people uncomfortable because it's not couched in trauma. Because there always needs to be a *reason* why women are sexual, a reason for this "anomaly"—the female pursuit of sexual activity and pleasure and the boastful expression of it. Childhood sexual abuse? Mental instability? Drugs? Low self-esteem? Unlike men, women are not allowed to have raw sexual experiences purely as human beings.

I think all of this as I sit in front of a journalism diversity funding panel of six people. I am here as their ethos of "diversity" has given me the green light that they will be on my side and help me get funding for my journalism.

"Even if you had a NCTJ [national journalism qualification] it wouldn't mean that anyone would hire you," two of the panel speak these words to me.

I feel like a sex offender sitting in front of a parole board.

"We googled you and you are *Iranian* but you write about sex and rock 'n' roll?" a woman with a buttery bouffant asks, looking positively befuddled.

"Yes," I nod politely.

"Hmm…that's *different,* isn't it?"

"Well we *are* a diversity panel, and she is diverse!" an Asian lady gently rebuts.

Another lady winces like I am soured milk, a bit too icky for her M&S/South of France sanitized air. She says, "You know, your personality is so very different from your sexy photos when we googled you."

"How can you tell my humanity from photos?" I ask.

"Well…" She stiffens in her chair and looks away.

"Look, I am going to be honest with you: just because you have a journalism qualification and lots of experience as it is evident on your CV doesn't mean anyone will give you jobs," says one guy, repeating what they have already made clear. "They'll google you, and in spite of all this journalism experience you have had, which you have done unpaid and on your own initiative, they won't hire you. You'll probably get the same rejection from employers—because they'll google you."

"And what? I haven't killed anyone or committed a crime. I literally just wrote about my life," I state.

I had not realized that in the UK media, "diversity" required rigid categories, was not fluid. As a Middle Eastern woman, you need to stick to the behavior codes and uniform of those categories to "qualify" as diverse. It must be either oppressed refugee, someone escaping their home country, or an academic and activist talking of the human rights violations of their country. I was all of those: vocal and active in speaking and writing about Iranian politics, human rights violations and gender and cultural issues, but I was also was very vocal about my sexuality and the rock stars I had fucked. Furthermore, I wrote my human experiences like a "man," in a raw, unglossy. and graphic way. Sex, rock 'n' roll, abortion, and abuse were all mixed in with memories of my beautiful Iran and Iranian politics, and this was not the "safe" stereotype of Iranian woman that the UK media required. Women can't be self-endorsing embodiments of sexual prowess, fuck champions, *and* be academic and political. If I had been a man, I'd be Russell Brand.

I don't fit the "correct" and lazy stereotype I am supposed to be. Through the lens of the Right, I'm an eternally passive, oppressed victim. It feeds their anti-immigration, Islamophobic agenda, demonizes Muslim countries and maintains the Middle East as problematic. And for the Left, I'm just a tool in their backlash against the racist Right's symbol of Middle Eastern woman as oppressed and "victim," weaponizing her attire and her body in order to fight Western imperialism and Western sexualized femininities.

My humanity operates outside both these frameworks and doesn't benefit any agenda, so it is invisibilized and deemed illegitimate. I am in love with investigative journalism, so the only thing is to do it on my own, unpaid. For my own blog.

I have already interviewed serial killer Richard Ramirez through letters from death row and gone to court cases of high-profile criminals and interviewed women who are victims of violence and abuse, and women who were political prisoners and FBI agents and strange aristocrats with tales of Thai brides and wildlife rescuers and... Sometimes I do the odd interpreting job for minimum wage, but those jobs need to be quick cash so I can dedicate most of my time to my journalism.

I nourish my brain and soul, continue to acquire knowledge as constantly being rejected for jobs for writing a book is killing me. When I clean toilets and show my butt crack on the old webcam as some man wanks, I feel suicidal.

Why was it so different in the US when I publicized my memoir? So many interviews on radio and magazines, TV and newspapers, book signings and promotions—so many welcomes. Diversity did not have such rigid categories there.

The only thing that gives me comfort is the thousands of adoring and supportive emails I have received from across the world since 2010. Women write to me about their own experiences of abuse, of abortion, of being political refugees in countries. I am over-spilling with the gush of love and gratitude. I can't believe how much love and support I get from people who understand my voice.

Simultaneously, I am choking on my education and knowledge. When I scrape kitchen floors or stack shelves in a supermarket just so I can investigate archaeological digs or prison inmates bribing officers or neurologists and psychiatrists about criminal psychology, I wonder if sending me away as a child to live in England did more harm than good.

The journalism "Diversity" panel all look at me in silence.

And what? What am I supposed to do?

I feel the same alienation I felt when I first came to England.

Back then, I was Negar.

Me, my grandmother, and mum
on my last night in Iran, August 1984

TWO

After leaving the "diversity" offices of the journalism funding group, I go straight into Marks and Spencer and buy a pinstripe suit with blue earrings that dangle madly and sparkle like magic as I stride along High Street Kensington clutching my files. My phone buzzes. One of my street contacts is telling me there is a child abuse ring going on around London. He doesn't know exactly where these trafficked children are, but he tells me they are drugged to the eyeballs and in a catatonic state as clients abuse them. So many things that traumatize me and make me murderous as a human, galvanize me into action as a journalist. I buy a burner phone and upload a couple of sexy photos under the name Isabella to a sex work site where those looking for anything-goes-sex can contact me. This is the starting point for an investigation which right now seems more like undercover detective work than journalistic.

Sure enough, after a few days and a slew of requests from men who want to pay me to do everything from the anodyne (outdoor sex) to the eye-watering (stamping on their bollocks repeatedly), to the medicinal (feed them a concoction of thick and savorous glop of multiple-sourced semen), someone asks if I have any daughters or little girls I work with, that he'd like to procure them.

"Little girls of how old exactly? Twelve? Thirteen?" I ask.

"No, seven or eight years old," he responds.

I keep him going, questioning his requests and his history with children, until I have a catalogue of texts with evidence. Then I go to the police with his address and phone number and texts. He and a gang of pedophiles are arrested shortly after and the case goes to trial. I think what a loss it is to all those places that haven't wanted to hire me as investigative journalist.

At most times in my life the only narcotic I can reach for is the Rock Star, whose shots of adulation, praise, and attention yank me out of slumping into the Sunken Place. Even though I squirm with unease that he, such an adored rock star would want someone like me.

I go to see my mummy so she can feed me. All our lives, my mother has pushed down all the domestic violence, all the pain, abuse, and suffering, by pushing food onto us. My frustration and anger at not being able to get any job is buried for now by my mother's onslaught of eight or nine different sets of Iranian stews and rices—*zereshk polo, sabzi polo*, lamb, saffron chicken and plum, garlic yogurt and pureed aubergine with *kashk*—all designed to stifle heartbreak and smooth down the jagged edges of life. To ensure my pain is totally smothered, there is saffron ice cream and trays of persimmons, watermelon, mango and pomegranate.

She flits around light-heartedly in the kitchen, breathless because of her failing heart and devoted to me, her first-born, conceding that I can't get any jobs because of my book. She stays silent, broken-hearted, seeing herself as a mother who failed (how did she end up with such a problematic creature for a daughter?) and wishing I had done a PhD like every other normal person in my family instead of writing a book with such sexually graphic detail.

My mother sees a daughter difficult from birth, her head too big to push through, oxygen-starved, taken away from her and isolated at birth for two weeks by Soviet nurses in a military hospital. A Soviet hospital because it aligned with her socialist beliefs. A place where they kicked and slapped her and took away her baby with no physical contact. She sees a sleepless child with epileptic brain waves, angry, fatherless and bookish—always reading and writing. She sees a daughter she sent off as a ten-year-old to a different country to be bullied, first at a school in England, then by her violent stepfather. A difficult teen, isolated from others, always singing jazz and swing, Monroe-obsessed, acting-obsessed, but friendless. Then a sudden world of men with tattoos and eye liner and jettisoned into a world of tours with rock bands. Abortions aplenty and trauma, bloodied and broken by love, sexy pictures on the internet, ass pushed up, arched, back and mouth agape. Photos that she hated, a sexy book and a title she was gutted by, so embarrassed and crushed at how exploited she had been by her editors but proud at her academic achievements and writing, her kind heart and unbroken spirit. It has all been part of what life/pain must be for my mother.

"Vy yoo are getting so fat? Yor bum is so big. Yor face is fat too, not the delicate high cheekbones yoo used to have when you ver nice and slim," she says, still a typical Iranian mum as she presents the banquet of foods, enough to feed thirty people.

Then without a beat she scuttles off to the kitchen to bring me more food and when I am so full that I risk her wrath by refusing any more she says, "Vy yoo don't like my food? Yoo never eat my rice and *ghormeh sabzi*. Yoo never like vat I make. I go to so much trouble for you. I work so hard in the kitchen. Yoo never appreciate. Eat more cake, eat more rice. Eat, eat, eat."

"You *just* said I am getting fat." I laugh. "You're so funny, mummy."

"Yes, but in my food there is no fat. Eat, eat, eat."

"Oh is that so?" I giggle. My mum would be brilliant for a Scorsese-style documentary about Iranian mums.

Then there is a sermon about how everything in cosmetics and detergents is carcinogenic. "Roxana, yesterday I read in newspaper that shampoo is full of chemicals. It give yoo cancer. So now you have to use natural herb to wash your hair. Washing powder is chemical too. It give yoo cancer too. Only use herbal product. Your sister has not vashed her hair in years and it is very shiny and healthy."

"That's just grim." I wince. My younger sister: successful, PhD-educated (a prerequisite for making you a whole human being in Iranian culture), and husbanded.

She sees that my spirit is down. She knows I can't go back to Iran, but she doesn't understand why I would miss it.

"Don't think about these things," she gently chides. "Ve can vatch film together. Yoo choose," she says.

My mum has always taught me about amazing films, starting with the *Deer Hunter* when I was eight and still living in Iran. As a kid she educated me all about the Vietnam War and it was important to her that I watch educational films.

Her council flat is full of socialist literature, political books, Ingmar Bergman and Ken Loach films, broken furniture and organic herbal products. And even as her body is flailing, fading, her militant revolutionary spirit is *blistering*. It's combative, heroic.

She hates anything too "Hollywoody" but loves English comedies like *Only Fools and Horses*—or as she calls it "Only Horses and Fools"—and *Keeping up Appearances*. She laughs a lot but always falls asleep in the middle of films and forgets any films she has ever seen because of the many epileptic seizures she has had in life.

As long as I can remember my mother has refused to take any medications for her epilepsy or blood pressure—not even painkillers for a headache—instead dumping and concealing in tissues under her bed any medication in favor of frequent violent, epileptic seizures, strokes, heart attacks, and pain. And it is pain and suffering, life as hardship, that my mother has fanatically subscribed to all her life; a smooth sailing and serene existence makes her a fraud. A die-hard socialist since her twenties, her belief that chaos, hardship, and dark challenges is the only authentic way for a socialist to exist is hardwired into her. She has a complete martyr complex. A bit Joan of Arc, really. Her fervent embrace of altruism means she must embrace chaos. Self-sabotage and the drug-addled and violent husbands are a natural by-product of it all, as well as staying with drug-addled or violent husbands to "fix" them, fervently pursuing council housing since she came to the UK in 1985 when there are better more comfortable options available, and only taking jobs that involve strenuous physical activity and mental anguish such as working with violent homeless kids who pee on her head or kick her in the stomach or adult with physical disabilities all while she has heart problems and constant seizures. Oh, how I am exactly my mother's daughter, especially in our common love of rescuing and healing cats, obsessing over animals and nature, and having mini breakdowns if we learn of anything animal cruelty related.

Eating her food and watching films is our bond. Always has been. To push down the pain. To anaesthetize the blows of my stepfather. She churns out dish after dish, and we eat and drink tea, and I try to be light and happy for her. My mama, who is warm and uber maternal and annoying and loves Azari music and left-wing politics, her curves and film star looks still there under all that zealous need for suffering.

"Have yoo done something to your lips?" She's noticing my collagen-enhanced lips. "They look sooo puffed up, like you've been punched in the mouth."

"No, it's fine," I mumble. She loves critiquing every inch of my body in that typical Iranian mum way.

I tell her delicately about the rock legend that I have been seeing.

"Vy yoo do these things again, Roxana?" She looks horrified and shakes her head. "All these man with tattoo, these rock stars, they are uneducated louts, hooligans. Your brain and education is so much more than these men! Alvays deez famous rock stars you alvays date. Vy yco do this?"

She has said this many times about the many rock stars I have had entanglements with. She couldn't be more disappointed.

We can talk without fear when my stepdad isn't home. It is liberating.

I watch her put food out in her London garden for the city foxes that visit and gather seeds and scraps to take for the birds in Brixton.

Photoshoot for Vice *magazine, with my sexy hejab attire in Brick Lane, 2011. Photo by Aziza Shadenova*

Mummy in her late teens/early twenties

THREE

Tehran, 1973

My mother was milk-soaked when they came for her. The damp blotches spread like water lilies across her blouse which annoyed her more than being taken to prison for freedom of speech.

I was six months old. Soft, useless, squinting into the bright slap of the day, unaware I was being taken to prison.

The Shah's secret police, SAVAK, had raided my grandmother's home bashing down the front door and ripping apart furniture in search of anti-Shah literature one afternoon as my mother nursed me. They arrested her for anti-Shah political activity and before my grandmother's terrified eyes the five of them bundled her into a car. But not before she had insisted on bringing me and my nappies with her. Once inside the interrogation room, she had been blindfolded and braced for the torture that was fate of all political activists while I was handed over to the guards. She was questioned about her friends' and family's political activities but she had refused to talk, so after twenty-four hours they had snapped, telling her to get out. She had grabbed me and run.

Being a socialist revolutionary in resistance to the Shah's totalitarian regime, a dictatorship with little social and political freedom, was more important to her than anything else in the world, and she continued her activism even when she took me to the school where she taught literature. She was twenty-four years old, with ironed hair (with an actual iron) that for years had reached past her buttocks but was now hacked to a shorter, more modern vibe.

She had had an army of suitors since her late teens, coming far and wide from villages and towns to ask for this graceful well-bred beauty's hand in marriage. It was her Tabrizi porcelain skin and come-hither cat eyes and mermaid hair and the fact that she was from a noble class, her family being educated, cultured landowners.

But she aggressively pursued the anarchic and the antagonistic to societal norms, the nice safe doctor husbands she was supposed to settle with like all her cousins and friends, and hooked up with a tall silent poet, Nasser, whom she had met at university, both studying literature and psychology. With her short skirts and poker straight hair (all her friends still wore their hair in the outdated 1960s puffed-up bouffants and backcombed beehives) and he with his bell-bottoms and platform heels and tinted eyewear, they made for a handsome couple. Except his allegiance was to opium and poetry and not to being a political activist and revolutionary like her.

Before I was born, he'd completed the compulsory military training, with them living in the barracks and she had lain awake at nights, anxious that this man—distracted, sluggish, pacified by poppies—could be anyone's father. The opium made him so mellow and laid back that it transitioned into being apathetic and uninterested in parenthood.

He had been absent on the day I was born in the Soviet Military hospital in Tehran in September 1973. Pain relief was considered bourgeois indulgence and the nurses slapped and kicked her when she didn't push hard enough, as if cruelty would expedite dilation. In keeping with the stoic philosophy to childbirth, she had been deprived of water for hours to experience extreme and prolonged thirst and left on the table—perhaps to inspire maternal grit. At one point she had even thought about running away from the hospital.

In line with the institution's dogmatic minimalism, mothers and newborns were kept apart. For seven days, nurses wheeled me in like a dairy delivery, granted her a few minutes of breastfeeding, then wheeled me out again convinced that that their strict, almost militaristic routine was in the patient's best interest.

She named me Negar , meaning 'beloved' and 'sweetheart; and we lived with my maternal grandmother Ashraf, who everyone called Anneh—meaning "mother" in Azari dialect, because she was a mother to everybody who met her. A bright sunny energy, almost celestial in aura, people far and wide flocked to her home, which was the hub of food, love, gatherings and afternoon siestas for neighbors, relatives and even my uncle's political activist friends, hiding from the SAVAK.

My father who was never around and was mainly hanging out with his own mother and siblings in a house not far from us, had taken to stealing some of my mother's earnings, sometimes hidden under the rug, for his addiction, and so my mother did the unspeakable. A divorced woman in 1970s Iran had massive social stigma, let alone one with a young child, but my mother went ahead and got a divorce. This probably added more cachet to her trendy identity as a revolutionary-poet-feminist-teacher with a young daughter. She left me with Anneh when she left to go to work teaching all day to provide for me and my grandmother, just like she had done before I was born for her parents- all her wages every month had been handed to her father who was crippled after a stroke. Life was meant to be hard, otherwise you weren't a real socialist.

Manijeh and Nasser during his time in the army, with me in her belly.

FOUR

So in my grandmother's ancient two storey house in Narmak, a working-class neighborhood in Tehran, with a vast flat rooftop for sleeping on, on hot summer and a huge garden filled with a grand pomegranate tree, apricot and morello cherry trees and fishpond, I clung on to Anneh, speaking Azari. My mother's family were from the northern city of Tabriz and spoke Azari, the Turkish-rooted dialect of Northwestern Iran.

I ran around, copper ringleted and sleep-deprived, mimicking Azari songs that whirred around the alley from the warm hum of Anneh's swooning love songs as she ran a modest kingdom out of her ramshackle kitchen, making a plethora of stews and rices, garlic yoghurt dips and aubergine lamb, while gossiping with the neighbourhood women, often while sat outside their house cleaning herbs as street traders filtered in and out selling their wares.

"Come on over, bring your family," she'd implore the neighbors and relatives, even my uncle's activist friends who dipped in and out for secret meetings upstairs. And she'd busy herself stacking fresh sheets and bedding, picking fresh flowers and fruit from the garden.

"I bought this cream bag. It's Armenian, so chic. Shall I buy you one too?" she'd coo softly at a random visitor reaching for the clasp of her wallet.

Her lungs wheezed and crackled, her hefty frame dragging breathlessly, wracked by years of asthma that had worsened along with her brittle bones, faltering heart and eyesight, because since her thirties some charlatan quack had been dishing out large quantities of steroids to supposedly fix her asthma. After twenty years of the incompetent doctor's lack of knowledge which insanely no one had flagged, the steroids had caused high blood pressure, weakening of sight and weakened bones along with heart and kidney problems.

And she still managed to laugh and dance more than anyone else, leaving her front door on the latch to have people wander in for food and company. The alleyway outside buzzed with the noise of us kids playing hopscotch and of street traders: The salt seller would be the first to arrive, bent double, with hunks of rock-salt in a hessian sack on his back:

Namaki! (Salt seller!) he'd yell in the middle of the alley.

"Has anyone got any scraps of bread for an old man?" he'd croak.

The neighborhood women would rush out from their homes, bringing out scraps of dried bread, leftover food, or old rags to exchange for a piece of rock salt. And his leathered face would break out into a toothless and grateful smile, as he grabbed the goods and hobbled off into the next street.

A weathered old maid (she might have actually been in her thirties but poverty and hardship would have made her look frail and old) with two jet-black braids down by her waist and a gold tooth would come in every morning to give a hand. Masha Baiim would prepare breakfast with Anneh and we would sit on the floor around the *sofra* (large oil cloth) with Morello cherry jam, feta cheese, fresh bread from the alley's bakery, hot tea from the samovar, thick cream and honey. I could be very cranky, maybe because I was perpetually constipated, sometimes not having a bowel movement for a week, or because I was a shitty sleeper (both still apply), and for some reason, the things she did pissed me off. I would pull her braids from under her headscarf and bite her arm hard.

The kids in the neighbourhood spilled out from dawn to play outside till the smudge of twilight, filling the alleyways with shrieks and dusty bare feet. Every district had its designated maidoon—essentially a grassy oval with a number assigned- and in the bright sunshine of the muddy alleys we played group games or make-believe scenes as we picked fruit from the persimmon or mulberry trees. Motorbikes zigzagged past us like dragonflies, coughing smoke, while men with sun-wrinkled faces wheeled carts piled high with sour-salty tamarind or dried sour cornelian cherries for us to snack on. A man wheeled in a in Ferris wheel, and we rode in cabins creaking with such arthritic menace that it was unclear whether the thrill came from the height or the sense of imminent collapse. In the winter, when there was deep snow, the beetroot seller wheeled his cart in to sell steaming hot beetroot which we peeled to find glistening newborn flesh that stained our fingers and dripped sweet juice down our chins. And in the spring came a man with a barrow full of fresh *gojeh sabz*—unripe sour green plums—which everyone would sprinkle with salt and eat until our tummies hurt.

A unique and joyous treat was the Mutoscope man, who would wheel in this movie machine. For a coin slotted into the machine, we could peep with one eye and see *What the Butler Saw*, a Victorian-era film reel of a woman undressing in her powder room shot through a peep hole. In her boudoir, the "butler"—the viewer—watched her peel away her feather boa, corsets, pearls, and French knickers to reveal plump translucent skin and bouncing curls which she brushed with an ivory hairbrush. This film machine was called *shahr-e-farang* (foreign city) and showed an exotic world belonging to the oh-so-fairytale-like West. It was a secret world that I longed to escape to.

"Allah-O-Akbar, Allah-)-Akbar!" Throughout the day, the sound of mournful prayer from the loudspeaker of the local mosque wailed. A deep respectful silence fell onto the streets at noon as people faced Mecca to pray with their prayer mats and *mohr*, a chunk of clay that came from Mecca.

My grandmother was not religious, but like everyone else in her generation she was traditional, so she would slip on her chador, a floral and light cotton tent-like coverall and whisper the *namaz* under her breath; at one with Allah. This would be followed up with an afternoon siesta like everyone else.

On the layers of hand-woven carpets that adorned Anneh's home—the ground floor was mostly open with a wall dividing it into two— was a dizzying kaleidoscope of motifs: paisley, tulips, peacocks, and gazelles, and scenes of turquoise water gardens and Weeping Willows, all from different provinces of Persia. On these carpets, people snoozed and ate.

"Stay and sleep, we'll have early evening tea together," Anneh would get relatives and friends who dropped by to have a nap. Sleep, in general, was a communal experience. Bedding was piled in corners. Floors became mattresses. Guests, relatives, strangers—everyone slept on the floor on the stacks of rose-pattered bedding my grandmother provided. Work would continue into the evening after an afternoon siesta break. In the scalding hush of the siesta, when the city slowed to a crawl, I played in my grandmother's huge fruit tree garden, picking sour cherries and apricots, inhaling tea roses. Sometimes alone and sometimes with my boy cousin who was my age. Together we'd make shelter with the huge fir tree's pines and play mummies and daddies or lie inside the fishpond in the middle of the garden, slithering naked with goldfish and coated with slimy green moss. I would lie there, loving the slime against my chest and tummy, holding my breath, letting my bronze ringlets get soaked through before letting it dry in the burning sun as I lay on the concrete slabs of the garden.

"Azizam, put some underpants on!" my grandmother or mum would scold me if they caught me from the window of the living room. But I never liked clothes on my body even though I was crazy for fashion. I loved the feeling of my skin being at one with nature, in the elements.

The blistering cracked concrete of the garden courtyard was also perfect for washing the carpets, which in the summer I pulled and dragged with Zahra Bajii (another weather-beaten home-help lady from the provinces with gold-capped teeth), getting out the garden hose and mountains of laundry powder on the carpets, to stamp, slip and slide my little feet along with her big bunioned ones to get it cleansed of dust and dirt.

Masha Baiim had stopped coming and Zahra Bajii, who was anywhere between thirty to sixty, had taken her place. She helped my grandmother and our other relatives with cleaning herbs, washing the carpets, cooking, and washing. Like many of these ladies from the outskirts of town, she was illiterate, destitute, and living in a shack in a shanty town. She had to marry off her child daughters, so she had to save money for the dowry. Anneh and my mother, along with our relatives, lavished gifts on her every night before she went home: cuts of cloth, meat, shoes, cosmetics…

She had a thirteen-year-old who was getting married.

FIVE

I would run out to line up outside the neighborhood bakery as a chain-gang of men by the clay oven prepared the dough and threw it in the pit to bake *nooneh sangak*, a long triangular bread with tiny stones embedded on its underside. When it was my turn, I'd carry the stack of burning bread in my arms back to the house where my grandmother had woken up and was busy lighting the samovar.

"Are you my golden girl or my princess?" Anneh would embrace me in her lap after and I breathed her in, pressing my ear against her giant tummy and hearing the clutter of her insides, her heavy bosom dressed in a floral pattered cotton dress, warm and perfumed against my breath.

"I'm both of course!" I'd say innocently and Anneh would fall into fits of giggles as she set about brushing her honey French-cut bob and slipping into chic cream or beige skirts and caramel tops for the evening's *mehmoonis* social gatherings and parties, which are a core part of Persian culture. She also embraced tradition by wearing the chador when she went outside, although only the light-colored floral ones and never the ultra-conservative thick black version.

"I want a bride doll, I want a bride doll," I'd stamp my foot like a spoiled brat. And Anneh indulged me. If I wanted another bride doll to add to the living room doll army, she fetched her wallet and took me out to the shops to buy one.

Early evening, as the city emerged from its slumber, people threw water on the pavement to keep the dust down. Shops had re-opened and the city streets heaved with families out for the night, buying cakes to take to mehmoonis, shopping for new shoes, gold, or textiles, past sizzling kebab stands or melon and cherry juice sellers, snacking on saffron ice cream, sticky syrup confectionary, or sour dry cherries.

Eating a sheep's brain sandwich in Haft Hoz

When it was our turn to host a mehmooni, Anneh, panting and wheezing, popped her antiquated pills as she set about in the crumbling kitchen preparing dishes of lamb and aubergine stew, barberry rice, yogurt and garlic, koofteh Tabrizi, and cinnamon and rose-water rice pudding, her failing eyesight sometimes mixing up salt with sugar and the womenfolk of the party would swoop into the tiny kitchen to help her out. Persian pop songs blared from the cassette player and we danced. I had begun to mimic famous Persian singers—male or female—and relatives and neighbors would pop in as I put on a cabaret of my best learned songs. My mother, who was deeply involved in her political activism, was a bit hostile to such "Shah-centric" activities and would be off to another anti-Shah meeting.

"Negar! Why don't you sing that new Googoosh song?" someone would shout, or "Please, do the new Leila dance!" When performing for an audience it felt like everything clicked; I had found my real true calling in life.

"I want flared trousers and platform heels, lacy ones!" I'd winge and moan through gritted teeth and stamp my foot at my mother to get me the latest 1970s fashions when she went out at night. I'd say it over and over until my exasperated mother gave in and bought them for me. Even aged six, fashion, along with books, were my top priorities.

Like many girls of her generation, my grandmother had been a child-bride, married at the age of twelve to a man twenty years older than her. Because she was premenstrual, my grandfather, who was educated, acknowledged her as a child and waited until she started her period before any physical intimacy took place, unlike many men who chose to have sex with their child brides on their wedding night. Living in a dilapidated ancient house in Tabriz with huge antique iron gates, they had many children, some of whom had perished at infancy. The first-born, Youssef, had died as a toddler from an illness which could have been easily prevented if there had been doctors in their town. Between my uncles there were two more, and then came the death of their stunning blonde, blue-eyed Nahid, the youngest girl, from eating cement as builders did work at their home. Anneh's and my grandfather's weeks of gut-wrenching wailing and chest-beating had broken the family and put the town in mourning at the loss of this beautiful doll.

My grandfather passed a year before I was born, but Anneh's mother, my great grandmother, had come to live with her and I would peek at her sitting on the bed, bony, vacant with Alzheimer's, crow-black braids down to her knees. She stayed silent, but her hands remembered and her fingers twitched with muscle memory, still convinced she was still working as a seamstress as she had in her youth. Curtains, bed sheets and table clothes: nothing was safe; constantly subjected to her scissors and sewing machine. She'd cut, sew, stich and pleat any fabric in sight and my grandmother and mum had to keep pulling her away gently tugging her away from her unfinished creations. But she'd always find her way back to the fabric. She lived in the folds and seams now, stitching meaning into whatever scraps she could find.

I was cocooned in and smothered with love. With no father, a community of people were raising me: neighbors and relatives, friends and activists. My mother's younger sister , who had given birth two months after my mum, had breastfed me when my mum was at work, and now with her husband in prison for anti-Shah activity, she came to stay with us. My boy cousin and I played intensely but also wrestled and got into physical fights with me winning as I was bigger. My aunt was ten years younger than my mum and not at all interested in activism so her young vibrant personality lightened up the house. My cousin and I bounced around with her, making theatre and dance routines copied from TV. Then, after supper in the courtyard with lots of singing and night stories, we'd get the pash-e-band out to sleep on the rooftop.

Eat, party, and sleep on the rooftop.

My mother and aunt rolled out the white gauze tent and rolls of sheets and on hot summer nights, as the indigo smudged into kohl-black, under a night sky convoluted by the sound of prayer and gunfire, we climbed up to the roof, leaving Anneh downstairs in her bed, and pitched two billowing gossamer tepees to keep out the night's crawling mischief. A sea of rooftops under the star-studded night beckoned as neighbours slept in the crackling crisp of night air. Beneath the thick velvet of a summer sky, with one pash-e-band for my mother and aunt, and another for me and my cousin, people whispered stories, and my cousin and I giggled by torchlight, listening to other neighbors from adjacent rooftops. There were tales of people rolling off the roof mid-asleep to their death or like one of my father's brothers, to a slower, more infantile brain.

Left: Anneh with my grandfather who I never met. Right: My beautiful Anneh.

My father dropped in to see me. Tall and shy, he held my hand and took me to his sister's house where I sat an scowled like a cage animal. These folk were different to my mum's family. They used street words, crude and sweary, sat in their pajamas all the time and farted for jokes. They watched films with women's wiggly bottoms in short skirts and heckled and jeered at the telly. It was an alien and unsettling environment compared to the conveyor belt of political activism and burning anti-Shah literature at my grandmother's house. This house with my father's family was filled with talk of cabarets and nightclubs, lots of boorish men with smutty mouths and women who scraped and bowed. My dad's sister let me put makeup on and wear her high heels and tops that plunged at the chest. They were fervent Shah lovers.

I never knew when my dad would show up. I'd wait and wait at grandmother's doorway to be picked up, and he forgot. I wasn't interesting enough for him, pretty enough, glamorous enough. I was a shy, nerdy bookworm. On the occasions that I saw him, I was shy and quiet, horrified if he took me to the toilet to try and get me to have a bowel movement, and I cringed that he, such a tall handsome fella, should see me in such odious circumstances.

"You get a prize!" he'd applaud triumphantly at times when I was finally able to go to the toilet and bought me a Scalextric set for putting in the effort of pushing so hard.

He loved me in his own way: gently, silently, the seductive pull of opium his primary concern and child responsibility a bit of an inconvenience.

Hours turned to days and weeks of ghosted doorways, me standing, bags packed till dusk waiting for a sign of him to come walking into our alley, then turned to months of longing, tall, good looking, tinted sunglasses, an absent fantasy figure I could never have.

I started to grasp the fact that opium was a deep-rooted Persian tradition, like tea from the samovar, the hammam, afternoon snoozes, and Persian carpets. My father needed opium more than he needed to see me.

Fatherhood, for me, was always an abstract idea—an absence dressed up as a title. What I got instead were a series of male stand-ins. My mother's brother, for one: a man who filled the gap with books and political debates. That didn't last. The SAVAK raided our house, and he disappeared into the same system that had already swallowed half my family. And so, I looked elsewhere for the authority figure I didn't have. Soldiers, for instance. They were everywhere—posted on corners, leaning against alley walls, guns casually slung over their shoulders like accessories. I was five years old and already mesmerized. Their uniforms, their blunt masculinity, the cold restraint—it was intoxicating. I didn't just want their protection. I wanted their attention.

It ignited something in my tummy and something shifted in my insides, filling the void of a father figure. And then, right about that time, Bakhshi, my grandmother's upstairs lodger started having sex with me.

SIX

We moved through the city in orange Peykan taxis, my mother and I. You didn't book them. You stood on junctions to shout your destination at passing windshields until one who was going your way stopped. They were shared, always. A rotating cast of characters. Strangers climbing in and out at intersections, conversation snippets bouncing between windows like loose change : the latest rice cooker advert or a foreign perfume, the best uptown confectioner's for an upcoming courtship ritual, a quiet child's shyness, expletive-filled rants at the Shah. With the windows open and the cacophony of the street life whizzing past, the taxi driver's radio whirred sentimental '70s pop songs: Hayedeh, Mahasti. Googoosh, Dariush.

We were going to Foozieh, the part of town where my mother's younger sister and my cousin lived at her in laws' palatial two-hundred-year-old home. Her husband who was also her first cousin, had been released from prison and she was back at her in-laws'/uncle and aunt's home. Winding alleyways led to a huge antique gateway, through which a luscious vineyard chandeliered with village lanterns led through to a catacomb of floors and rooms with many of my mother's cousins living there.

With every mehmooni, which could be every night, aunts, uncles, and about thirty to forty cousins and relatives spilled in and out of the home, paying their respects to the head of the family, The Don, my aunt's father-in-law Haj Agha- an honorific title meaning Master, or Chief (Agha) and haj, derived from the term "Hajj," which refers to the pilgrimage to Mecca. Haj Agha, a much honored and respected man, was in his eighties, bed-ridden, and perpetually reclined on an ottoman full of *motakkahs* (giant tubular cushions sewn with intricate Persian rug covers designed for lounging on) and kilims, surrounded by visitors. As well as being my aunt's father-in-law, he was also her and my mother's father's brother. The two brothers had been powerful landowners in their village in the north of Iran, with Haj Agha taking multiple wives of all ages across the land and sprouting a multitude of offspring who didn't know each other as they grew up. It was customary for first cousins to marry in Iran, so many in laws were also the bride or groom's aunt or uncle. Haj Agha and his second wife had had nine children, so there were a huge amount of second cousins I could play with as well with as neighbors' kids who dropped in.

Everyone danced in the middle of the reception room as kids screamed and chased each other. In a circle around the dance area, some declined to join; mainly the older men of the family, the 'ugly girls', or that rarest of creatures; the older unmarried woman, curdled and soured and past her prime which was over 25 years of age. They sat clapping and watching before being aggressively pulled up to join. Music from the cassette player blared Persian singers and in another room a TV was on. Often, someone would sing a solo song, recited a poem or played an instrument as everyone sat in silence and respect. I was expected to give one of my performances and my mother would glow proudly, acknowledging that this performance-loving side of me was definitely inherited from my father's side, the Shirazis.

Food and eating in Persian homes was a theatrical and biblical affair, whether you were rich or poor and it naturally involved lots of loud voices talking over each other over the sofra on the floor. A banquet at every mehmooni which could be every night was normal. Stews of every kind came with saffron and barberry rice with melting butter. Salads drowned in lemon juice and dried limes with herb stews and pomegranate molasses with crushed walnut were added to meats and poultry.

Then there were fruit plates. Colossal trays piled with mulberries and Loganberries, sour plums, oranges and Morello cherries. Mini cucumbers peeled and sprinkled with salt and apricots and peaches.

And in the midst of all that—of war, and politics, and family theatre—there was Bakhshi.

Top: With Anneh in Haft Hoz. She had started wearing the chador after the revolution.
Bottom: With ma in Haft Hoz as usual

SEVEN

Bakhshi was moustachioned and white-shirted and had a blue Citroen 2CV like most people in 1970s/80s Iran. It prattled and purred, wobbling its tinker box shell and . I felt like a spoiled princess riding around in it eating candy. A man living in our home made me feel more secure.

He slipped his penis along my vulva when we were upstairs in his room with the door locked, when my grandmother was having her siesta and my mother was at work. Although I was dying to play with my friends in the alleyways, picking fruit and flowers and playing pretend in the maidoon, I walked up the hulking stone steps to his quarters in my plastic slippers. I was scared and thrilled. I was a bad girl. This was *our* thrill. Our secret.

Slowly, I climbed the heavy steps, dark and silent, to see Bakhshi. It was my fate, my identity. I was a bad girl. I would go to hell with other tainted, sullied scarlet women. The ones I had seen on TV. I felt a pull with them in my tummy.

Upstairs was shadowy and dark. Slivers of sunlight trickled through, and I could hear the war hum of the projector in the bedroom. Bakhshi had closed the curtains and blinds, and although it was siesta time, he was not asleep. He waited for me to come up and quietly took me into a drawing room where two prayer mats and mohrs were set out. He had started teaching me Qur'an recitals, the shorter child versions, and he would tell me to kneel in silent prayer, facing Mecca with a clay mohr, which I loved to lick as it gave off the smell of the damp just-rained-on ground in summer. Throwing on the little chador all over my body, I felt blanketed in a cozy safety—closer to God. I had learned all these shorter child prayers by heart and knew God would reward me for being a good girl.

When we finished praying, Bakhshi took my hand and led me to where the projector was in the bedroom. It almost always played Bugs Bunny on the wall. It was a boy cartoon. A golliwog always sat on the shelf with exaggerated features—bulging eyes, sausage lips, and tight curls—nodding its head. The bedroom was dark, its curtains also drawn, and Bakhshi closed the door and locked it with a key.

He sat me on his lap to face the cartoon on the wall. I fixed my eyes on the wall, frozen with fear, feeling icky, responsible for being this ruined woman. Bakhshi's fingers slid between my, legs rubbing all along the place I weed from. How unhygienic. Didn't he know that place was full of germs? His fingers were going to stink.

I felt Bakhshi shuffling around and then heard a zip. As the hyper bunny and company went *boing! zap! boom! pow!* and dreamy music filled the screen, Bakhshi's "thing," what my boy cousins had, was rubbing along my "down there." His breath against my neck got more rapid, whispering things I had never heard, faster and faster—some words sounding Arabic. This thing between my legs was terrifying. We were doing something bad.

I would go to hell. I would definitely go to hell.

Bakhshi, breathless, finally stood up and unlocked the door. He went to the bathroom, washed his hands, came back, and put some socks on and told me to go downstairs. The cartoon was over, and I was allowed to go.

And I kept going back up to the second floor.

EIGHT

I felt more grown up than the other kids. I felt special. I started crawling under the *korsi* (a low table with a blanket over it and a heater underneath for people to sit around to warm up their feet during snowy winters) and I would squeeze my eyes tight and fantasize about the soldiers. They "turned me on". Danger and threat became my muddled insides' mating call. I imagined them giving me attention and love. I was naked and lying on the ground, and they loved me and found me pretty. It gave me such a thrill. I fizzled with warmth and happiness at the gang of men in uniform. I was a little girl, but I felt loved, and I felt attracted to these men, to their power and authority.

I slid my hand in my panties and touched myself where it throbbed. I felt like I had found the key to a magical world. I felt like a queen. From then on, I loved having the boy neighbors and cousins give me attention. It made me feel special. I began to pay attention to prettier dresses and putting on girly airs and graces, aloof but coy, especially when the older twin boys next door chased me. I loved playing street games and being as sporty as boys, but I found that acting more "girly" got me what I wanted: attention, a.k.a. love.

The attention from the boys in the neighborhood "turned me on" even though I was only about five years old at the time. It felt like a water ride in my tummy, one that swooshed around and made my body tingle whenever my bare skin touched theirs or whenever they leaned over me, their hot breath against my neck.

Bakhshi had moved in so my mother and grandmother could get some income into the household as my mother wasn't earning enough to take care of the three us. When I went in search of his company in the afternoons, I knew what might happen—and yet I did it, again and again. I saw him as my friend and was mostly just irked that he didn't even have the courtesy to show me girlie cartoons like Cinderella instead of the Bugs Bunny he always put on. With soldiers everywhere and my mother's fight or flight existence, taking me to demos where soldiers tear-gassed people or shot them I started to get a rush from dangerous situations, so much so that during power outages in the city or during raids by soldiers I got urges to rub myself down my knickers with twigs from trees.

I felt I was a bad girl. Tainted. I knew then that this was my destiny, and my child body was a bit muddled: my sexual chakra had been ignited and incorrectly charged up to dangerous men. The absence of father replaced with sexual abusers of children, armed soldiers and marauders and then later, a violent stepdad. At the ages of eight and nine years old I would get the boys my age to touch me even though I knew nothing about sex or orgasms. I just knew that my tummy triggered a whooshing whirlpool of "forbidden feeling" whenever I touched and played naked with boys and girls my age. It was exhilarating.

NINE

I sat between my mother's knees while she scraped me raw with sefidab, the white powdered exfoliator that with a pumice stone unclogged pores, deep cleansed, and removed dead skin cells. I was left pink and raw and shiny new. She wasn't gentle. She never was. But there was something safe in the way her hands moved—like she was sanding me down to something better.

In the day or at twilight, when the sun softened and shadows stretched long across the alley and the mosque's cry poured from the loudspeakers, Anneh and my mother bundled up loofahs and washcloths with fresh folded clothing and took me by the hand to hammam.

The centuries-old public bathhouse, which was open until midnight, was a ritual of the medicinal, social, and spiritual. Separately, men and women socialized, drank tea, and exchanged gossip as they squelched and exfoliated in the fug of rose steam.

Inside a giant hall with cracked mosaic and stone pedestals glistened with water and soap, where every echo of water splash and murmur pinged from the glass ceiling, women of all ages lounged naked or with flimsy sheets around their waist. In circles, hammam workers scrubbed with coarse loofahs, slathered hair in towers of rose foam, removed body hair with sanding pads and rinsed off with cool silky water. There were hot rooms for peeling old skin and your sins and cold rooms for shocking yourself into resurrection.

Rumor and shock drooled: marriage proposal ceremonies, Western beauty creams, clothes from Armenia, an old crone's salty eye, as the clinking of ice cold Pepsi or Canada Dry glass bottles, ordered by a loud holler from private cubicles by parched customers fizzed in the building.

On the way back home, my mother and I would stop by the neighborhood's main shopping square- Haft Hoz (Seven Ponds)- a park surrounded by the buzz of traders and shops, the social hub of the Narmak. Families brought their samovars and ate on sofras on the grass as people walked around shops munching *balal*, (charcoaled corn on the cob plunged in a bucket of cold salt water) bought from street vendors who also barbequed liver, fanning the sizzling grill, the singed meat

mixed with traffic fumes. I scowled as I chewed the tough piece of meat, but my mother insisted it was good for me as she got me tall glasses of fresh carrot juice to wash it down with or marched me to brightly lit sandwich shops to get me sheep's brain sandwiches with gherkins, which were spreadable and creamy which she said was packed with vitamins. In my flared jeans and curly hair I watched people brawl in the guzzling traffic and barter for gold. The cacophony of honking horns and petrol fumes, miniskirts and catcalls was muted by my mother's indefatigable mission to overthrow the Shah's regime, marching me from pillar to post to revolutionary meetings, all the while trying to provide for her child and mother.

From the way the adults talked at home, I was beginning to understand that something dark and prophetic loomed. A tumultuous storm was brewing, sparking danger and a threat to all, and adults talked frenziedly, plotting in homes and universities and the unrest and gunfire in the streets was becoming more frequent. Students teargassed, arrested, and tortured in prisons. By the thousands, people marched again the Shah and his oppressive, brutal, corrupt regime—a puppet of the United States.

The Shah had established himself as a monarch and planned a speedy Americanization of Iran. But his "Westernization" of Iran was more concerned with superficial aspects of the West: the sexualization of women and promoting a culture of partying, promiscuity, and nightclubs instead of an actual concern for the population's lack of proper housing, food, education, and freedom of speech. Iranians dismissed an Americanization or Westernization that blindly mimicked the most vacuous aspects of the West but continued the medieval practice of imprisoning, torturing, and executing writers and journalists who dared to criticize the Shah's dictatorship. The system made a mockery of its people, taking the wealth of an oil-rich country and pouring it into the monarchy and its chosen elites while the workers of Iran lost their livelihoods and the poor and illiterate were more and more marginalized.

People were bitterly angry at the alarming widening gap between the wealthy and the poor. Tehran's hip vibe had the rhythm and swing of New York city and the Shah wanted to keep pushing religion out onto the fringes but rampant government corruption ensured that wealth remained concentrated among officials and the Shah's inner circle, leaving the majority struggling.

As job opportunities and housing became scarce, sprawling shantytowns emerged on the outskirts of Tehran, packed the with out of work and disillusioned. Growing unrest among the people led the ruling regime to tighten its grip, transforming into an even harsher military dictatorship. The Shah responded to dissent with mass arrests, stripping away civil liberties and banning strikes. Freedom of speech and the press were systematically dismantled, and opposing the Shah became a dangerous act, punishable by torture, imprisonment, or execution. His secret police, the SAVAK, intensified their reign of terror, raiding homes suspected of harboring anti-Shah materials and arresting anyone deemed a threat.

Amid this volatile political climate, numerous resistance groups emerged, each with its own factions. Though their ideologies varied, they shared a common goal: to overthrow the Shah's military rule and establish freedom and social justice in Iran.

As protests and anti-Shah demonstrations escalated, so did violent clashes in the streets. Gunfire became a familiar sound.

TEN

My mother, naturally, was at the centre of it. We visited her cousins in prison—sometimes through bars, sometimes in open courtyards. Flowers were thrown. Cheers erupted. The performance of resistance had its rituals, too.

The guards, however, were less poetic. They hurled graphic sexual slurs at my mother in front of me—words I didn't fully understand but understood enough to feel shamed by proxy. She never dignified them with a reaction. But later, her face would drain of color, and more than once she collapsed into seizures when we got home to Anneh. It wasn't the fear, exactly. It was the chronic state of alertness that wore her down, a kind of psychological dehydration.

Left: Mummy at university.
Right: Birthday where I was stroppy even though I was spoiled

A suitor that had been mooning around my mother for years worshipping her, came forth to ask for her hand in marriage. Doctor Hosseinchi was also Tabrizi and infatuated. He brought her flowers and showered her with gifts while I stationed myself on the stone steps behind the front door waiting for him to pick my mother up as she got perfumed and ready.

"Please, ma, he is nice." I tugged at my mother's skirts and begged her to marry this refined, well-dressed, plump doctor. But after a few meetups my mother finally bristled to my grandmother: "He is too simple and not at all political! That would never work for a militant revolutionary like me who wants a like-minded man to marry."

My grandmother and I were gutted. Anneh, like me, had a weakness for the trappings of luxury: velvet dresses, perfumed gentlemen, a life less precarious. Marrying a fragrant debonair gentleman might have anchored us to something reassuringly dull.

However, my mama made up for rejecting the poor lovesick man by throwing me a lavish birthday party in our house. Relatives flooded our reception room, and she splurged on a lilac crushed-velvet frock with floral trimmings and a cake. My ringlets were crowned in white flowers and stacks of gifts were piled high on the table.

I was grumpy as always because I hadn't gone to the toilet in a couple of days and was pissed off that someone had dared give me a toy bear that beat its attached drum when you wound it. It was a boy's toy, and I wanted dolls and my best girlfriend who I had lost to the SAVAK.

Only a few night before, walking home from the bathhouse with my mother, we saw that the SAVAK had raided the house at the end of our alley. Huge iron gates and towering trees shrouded the house and its secrets. A man and woman, rakish, with dogtooth caps and huge tinted shades would dodge in and out from their parked coupe.

*They're friends with the Shah…they throw dirty parties…they do drugs and sex….*The word in the neighborhood was that they were secret service, America-loving degenerates. But their daughter, Parya, was a little older than me and had become my playmate. I admired her extra-long hair and green eyes but always felt on edge around her parents. Unmarked cars had pulled up outside the house and men were bringing out Parya's parents, along with boxes and piles of books. That night as we cuddled up in our rolls of sheets and blankets, neighborhood whispers talked of the couple storing weapons and drugs.

Parya had been my friend of sorts—the first girl that had shown me the pink secret between her legs on our doorstep. I had stared, fascinated not by the forbiddenness of it but by its delicate strangeness, its vulnerability. And then she was gone—disappeared as if she'd never existed, folded neatly into the revolution's growing catalogue of missing people.

It was the eve of the revolution, and my mother was absent from home a lot, either at demonstrations or secret revolutionary meetings. I would hear from neighbors and activist friends of my uncle stories of the way the guards tortured the prisoners: not letting them sleep for days with bright bulbs in their face and excessive noise in their ears, binding their legs and arms in metal crushers, flogging their feet with electric cables, leaving them hanging upside down for days. It was horror as wallpaper—normal, steady, even oddly comforting in its predictability.

At night, throngs of people hollered anti-Shah revolutionary chants from the rooftops—"Marg bar Shah!" (Death to the Shah!) The pewter skies rumbled with gunfire and people's rage, hidden safe from slabs of light in the city's power outage. The curdled muddled sky, crisp with salty terror gave me a head rush more and more as I watched people in the alley disperse, all running back to their homes.

But I didn't go in. I stood still, gushing with adrenaline. I wanted to stay outside, it was giving me a thrill. I loved the air at this time, how the shadows hid you in dark corners. My mother was somewhere in the streets, caught up in some brawl, arms linked with the wall of people marching toward armed soldiers. I feared for her all the time. My grandmother was inside, cooking, worrying about her and me but I didn't make a sound, didn't let me grandmother know where I was. I wanted the panic, the thrill of danger, the smell of burned wood.

ELEVEN

My mother rushed in and told me that she wanted to take me to a prison called Ghasr to meet someone. She had, despite his continued romantic pursuit of her, shunned Dr Hoseinchi and met a man, a political activist, through a friend. Through the prison rails, I shook hands with a dark surly rake-thin man with tinted glasses. He was a revolutionary, a socialist, and the brother of my mum's friend. He had spent time in a cell with my uncle and mother's cousins. He was practically family.

She could have had anyone, but she was thirsty to play out life as a Greek tragedy, so after an opium-addicted husband it was essential that she hook up with someone equally unsuitable to enter the next chapter.

Saeed scowled a lot and didn't make any eye contact with my mum when he spoke. In prison for anti-Shah, left-wing activity his arms were cobbled ravines of mauve and chartreuse torture scars, and he told us he had escaped prison and slashed his wrists with razors in the public bathhouse cubicle when he heard the SAVAK had found out his whereabouts.

This sealed the fucking deal for my mother, A bit Che Guevara, a bit rock 'n' roll. She decided she'd marry him there and then. Also, she was exhausted from having the stigma of divorced woman with a child hanging around her neck.

When the Shah fled Iran in January 1979, a lot of political prisoners were released and Saeed came to our home to stay. On the first night home from prison, I waited earnestly at the door to greet this man. My mum and grandmother had dressed me in my best cotton flower dress and had scrubbed my face raw to make it all shiny and new. It was a formal dinner, which my mother and grandmother had spent five hours preparing. There was a power outage, and we ate by a gas lamp as the soldiers patrolled our alley outside. I may have larked about or been a bit reluctant to finish my dinner, so a huge thwack suddenly landed on my face and sent me flying, my nose dripping with blood. Then more slaps around the head until my curls were matted with snot and blood. Stunned, I scrambled to get up, and it was only after a minute's dumbstruck silence I began to shriek.

“Come on, soldiers, come on, SAVAK—come and take this bad man back to prison!” I wailed between screams and snot bubbles. No one came to comfort me. My mum and grandmother had to respect the man of the house now.

Soon after that, there was an official marriage ceremony in our home with people sitting down in the reception room and talking political things. There was no music, no fun. Saeed looked sullen and did not look at my mother once.

“Stop calling him Saeed,” my grandmother told me. “You must call him dad now.”

I had really wanted a daddy.

TWELVE

I think it was snowing that day. It was definitely drab and gray as I stood on the doorstep on the day of the revolution, February 11, 1979, and heard the blare of car horns in the city and people dancing in the streets celebrating the fall of the Shah. Saeed and my mother had been on the streets every day with hundreds of thousands of people, marching toward tanks and troops and being shot at and tear gassed and now with them, I proudly belted out revolutionary songs I had learned by heart and strangers swooped me up and applauded me for memorizing all the chants.

My new daddy came with a dark silence not from opium but the brink of wrath. At any given moment he could pounce and whack me. It was never expected, and I was always braced to get slapped. He also came with grisly tales of torture and raised scars on his back from being flogged, and night terrors where he would jolt up and scream in the middle of night from some bad dream, probably a nightmare about prison.

I was given children's books on the class system, the gap between rich and poor, the evils of capitalism, and how socialism was the only way human beings could live in equality and harmony. But I was peeved that the new Supreme leader Ayatollah Khomeini, this divine holy imam, the Iranian people's savior, forbade mixed genders at school. I was dying to go to school with my boy cousins and neighbors. Suddenly, I didn't like this white bearded Mullah. I didn't understand why girls were segregated from boys.

We settled into an apartment a ten-minute walk from my grandmother's house. It was a new building block at the bottom of a small alleyway with mulberry trees and a maidoon at the top end. Along with these new neighborhood friends I walked to school with, came a whole new family from my stepdad. Brand new cousins, aunties, and uncles who hailed from the holy city of Ghom. They socialized in loungewear and chadors, used tasbih beads as they whispered recitations from the Qur'an and dipped torn bread into sopping wet stews and sucked out the marrow from bones. They were laborers and truck drivers and not very educated, their words loaded with slang that made my mother squirm. But they were kind and generous and she was loved and embraced, especially when Saeed hissed: "You're secondhand goods. I've married damaged goods."

I took to school like fish to water, sucked it in like it was second oxygen. This new world of education was what had been missing from my life and it was perfect. From seven in the morning with my best friends Mahin and Mojhgun we walked through the alleyways, past the maidoon to huge sky-blue gates. There, along with hundreds of other girls we lined up before classes began to have our fingernails inspected for any signs of nail polish and be reprimanded for any stray strands of hair that might have escaped our dour navy or black compulsory head scarf. At noon we came home and it was the turn of afternoon students; you were either on a morning shift or afternoon one.

I devoured science, maths, Mark Twain, Samad Behrangi, books about Palestine, political fairy tales and Persian history. Books were my soulmates, and getting dressed up for mehmoonis nearly every night, my happiness, although adults spoke in more fearful hushed tones not quite believing that our country had gone from bad to much worse.

Khomeini announced a system of governance called *Velayat-e Faqih* based on the rules of Shia Islam formulated by himself and other clerics earlier in the decade. In the absence of Allah, this would represent his word. The people of Iran were no longer considered citizens but merely followers, and anyone in opposition to this rule was considered an enemy of God and subject to be imprisonment, torture, and execution. Women were forced by law to cover their hair and bodies. Items such as makeup, nail polish, perfume, ties, and cologne were viewed as symbols of Western depravity and wearing them was deemed counterrevolutionary, leading to severe punishment. Renouncing Islam carried the death penalty. Adulterers faced stoning, while those engaging in extramarital sex were subjected to flogging. Women needed permission from their father or husband for nearly all activities, and due to strict gender segregation, public spaces like buses and offices were divided.

The revolution had risen as the result of years of tyranny and oppression by the Shah. The people of Iran—politically repressed, economically exploited and broken by his repression and autocracy—yearned for democracy. Khomeini, a resolutely anti-Shah, anti-communist figure, exploited this social unrest oppression and repression as well as social anxiety in people losing their sense of identity and Persian culture by presenting himself as the savior of the people. An opportunist who utilized Islam as a political tactic and a weapon for ideological justification, he was backed by the West, which feared a Leftist government in alliance with the Soviet Union. Leftist groups were very strong in Iran and posed a threat to the West, especially as they were the most likely to get in power. The backing of Khomeini was a strategic move by the West, a force against a possible communist regime, but what began as an anti-dictatorship revolution soon turned into an Islamic Fundamentalist power grab.

A climate of fear accelerated. The Revolutionary Guards, the *Basij*, and the morality police, strong-arm thugs from the "Army of God—roamed the streets in jeeps and unmarked vans to stop and pounce on and assault anyone displaying any sign of "anti-Islam" activity or attire. Showing a strand of hair or wearing lipstick in public for women was met by flogging, assault, and hidden razor blades in tissues handed out by the morality police. Arbitrary arrests, executions, and confiscations of property became the norm, as did kidnapping, torture, and rape of women and men.

There were many political groups, organizations and parties that had been united with Khomeini in overthrowing the Shah. But soon after the revolution, Khomeini ordered the mass arrest and kidnap, torture and execution of anyone of any age suspected of being in allegiance to any of these political groups, even though they had helped him become supreme leader.

With my new baby brother in Haft Hoz

THIRTEEN

Even though I was fully aware of the escalating horrors escalating under the rule of Khomeini, I was blissfully happy. We lots of parties, and soon I had a wardrobe full of beautiful dresses and accessories, especially once my stepfather ditched his taxi driving job and started his own construction company. We ate at mountain top restaurants, and drove around town at night, mainly to fancy cake shops and toy emporiums.

At night, the roads dark and jammed with beeping traffic, angry drivers got into fights. On the side of the road by kerosene lamps , vendors sold wet walnuts from jars, the skin of which I would peel in the back seat of the car, totally entertained by the city and the characters we passed.

My brother turned up fat and wobbly in March 1980 as I sat around the *eid-e-nowruz haft sin* (seven Ss for the Persian New Year, the first day of spring). Around a goldfish bowl and big mirror with garlic (seer), coins (sekkeh), sumac, senjed, sabzi (wheatgrass grown in dish), samanu (a sweet wheat pudding), vinegar (serkeh), or apple (seeb), I waited with my cousins and aunts and uncles whilst my brother was born.

"It only takes a twinkle in the eye from me for her to get up the duff," I had heard my stepfather say to people. "We'll call the boy Mohammad." My stepfather's family celebrated with a feast, ululating and burning ruse seeds, its sweet pungent smell wafting all over the house to ward off the evil eye. My little brother was swiftly circumcised and brought home for me to play with. I delighted in washing and changing the poo-streaked rags of this happy, smiley, blubbery baby.

I was always drawn to anything with a high vibration, so I fell in love with my stepdad's family who were earthy and prayed at least three times a day and fasted during Ramadan. It made me feel not only holy but *whole* to learn the Qur'an and recite the namaz as taught by my new silver-haired grandfather, who sat me down for our incantation as he lit up his opium lamp. Pewter ashes dusted the tray and resins he'd melt were sucked up into his pipe as he smoked and puffed as I slowly got hypnotized breathing in the thick smoke, the smell of singed opium just like the smell of burning ruse seeds to ward off the evil eye. I'd melt on the motakkas as he told me stories of prophets.

During Ramadan I fasted until dawn, then woke in the dark before sunrise to throw on my vast cotton chador and eat a snack. The morning hung crisp and hushed, my mum and stepdad slumbering deeply as I peeled myself off the floor thickened with warm blankets and pillows and tiptoed to the apartment opposite ours to join Mojhgun's family in prayer.

In September of 1980, the Iran–Iraq War began. Droning air raid sirens drilled into the air and into homes where on TV there was a constant spool of young men getting ready for battle. War anthems urged every male citizen, even teenage boy, to prepare. One song that constantly blared on TV sang: *Oh army of Imam-e- Zaman* (Mahdi, the last of the twelve Shias who has not emerged on earth yet) *get ready! Get ready!* The footage showed young men in combat fatigues and backpacks in the field putting their red band of courage around their heads and tying bayonets around their waists. Khomeini called fighting the satanic forces of Saddam Hussein a blessing and promised martyrdom, an automatic free pass to paradise for any boy and man who went to war, and so they prayed and cleansed themselves, making themselves "fragrant" in preparation to meet Allah in death.

I took frequent walks to my grandmother's house. In the dark, loud war songs mixed with the sound of prayer from the Mosque's loudspeakers. More and more shrines appeared on every street to pay homage to the neighborhood's martyrs: teen boys or middle-aged fathers, grandfathers and sons. Death hung in the air, and fear gripped us all. It was the revolution's infancy, and terror and death were what the people of Iran had been presented with. Mistrust swept through the country and everyone started to speak in whispers, even at home. Anyone, even your neighbor, could be a government spy listening to your conversation and gripes about the new regime. The consequences were deadly. Desperate street vendors, shoemakers, soup distributers, florists with their shops crammed full of funeral wreaths—they all became potential spies for Khomeini's regime, ready to rat anyone out for uttering anti-regime sentiment.

I would press my head against my grandmother's heaving bosom and breathe deeply, inhaling her love. It was a small, safe place in the world. I no longer missed my real father: My new dad taught me how to ride a bike, holding on to the back and running behind and letting go only when I told him to. He taught me how to dine like a lady, but he also slapped me when I was bad. My real daddy would make fleeting appearances in my life. A tall, dark shadow, silent and sullen, looming at the end of our alley, staring at our building. He still wore flares but was now sporting a stubble, having turned his allegiance to Hezbollahis. Every time I saw him at the end of our alley, he was alone, as if he had been standing there watching me.

"Negar, put your headscarf forward," he'd instruct, wanting me to follow the Islamic law of the country.

I'd stiffen awkwardly and walk past him. I didn't really know him. He was my biological dad, but I didn't have any emotional connection to him. He was a stranger. Different to us, to our class of people. To me, he was a vagabond.

One day he strolled over to our yard when my stepfather was teaching me to ride my bike. He talked with my dad, not even coming over to me or looking at me once. I heard him say, "I am happy for you to have her."

I felt worthless, like damaged goods. My dad didn't want me because I was of no worth. I was not good enough. Not clever enough, pretty enough, interesting enough. I sat glued to my bike. My new streamers blowing in the breeze made me proud. My new daddy made my nose bleed all the time, but at least he wanted me.

FOURTEEN

In between tons of playtime with my friends and cousins, I spent my time reading and performing.

"She is so beautiful and such an amazing performer," my mother's friends announce, shaking their heads in wonder.

I felt special. I was the center of the extended family unit and the neighborhood princess. I wore beautiful dresses and shoes and learned as many songs I could, imitating Bollywood singers and their dances as well memorizing from black market cassette tapes all the songs of the now forbidden1970s Persian singers who had fled Iran for Los Angeles.

My stepfather somehow managed to procure black-market films from local corner shops. My favorite, without question, was Gone with the Wind. Scarlett O'Hara embodied everything I aspired to: imperious, arrogant, unapologetically gorgeous, forever making men dance to the snap of her fingers. High society and low morals—an irresistible combination.

Of course, my stepfather had other ideas. Every time he caught me gazing glassy-eyed at Scarlett's latest tantrum, he felt the need to inject a dose of realism. "You don't want to end up like that spoiled brat, do you?" he'd sneer, as if the cautionary moral were the only thing worth salvaging from four hours of plantation melodrama. "Look how she ended up."

Meanwhile, I dedicated my afternoons to more immediate concerns: sneaking makeup, staining my cheeks and lips into the approximate pinks of adulthood; shrieking and chasing Mahin and Mojhgun through the streets; plucking persimmons and marigolds with religious zeal and strewing them at the feet of the forbidden boys like some fertility ritual. It was as close as we were going to get to romance before the morality police started arresting children for smiling at the opposite sex.

Back inside, the grown-ups were less whimsical. My uncles paced the cramped living room like caged animals. The new regime was cleaning house with an efficiency the Shah could have envied—executing anyone they deemed a political inconvenience. Leftists, monarchists, dreamers, cynics, university professors, students, whoever had the misfortune of appearing literate. The slogans promised paradise; the streets promised a bullet.

Mass arrests by the Islamic Republic just after the revolution refilled the jails with political prisoners, including Marxists, intellectuals, liberals, thousands of members of the pro-Soviet Tudeh party and the Mojahedin-e-Khalgh (MKO), the regime's most powerful opposition group. Those who didn't agree to abide by the new Islamic rules were tortured and executed by makeshift improvised revolutionary "courts" who had tried and convicted them and sent them off to firing squads.

June 20, 1981, is a turning point in history. Tens of thousands of executions took place in Iran. Any human displaying a hint of "un-Islamic" and/or anti-revolutionary behavior, even teenage boys and girls distributing leaflets, were imprisoned and held in solitary confinement and subjected to daily brutal rape and torture, sometimes in front of their families.

The Islamic Republic had hired a couple of serial killers with a fetish for torture, mutilation, and rape. Assadollah Lajevardi, nicknamed the Butcher of Evin Prison, was appointed Tehran prosecutor after the revolution and head of the State Prison Organization. A psychopath and sadist, he was known for the pleasure he took in torturing and raping prisoners, including high school students, in front of their families. He was responsible for the execution of thousands of political prisoners. His sadistic torture was so bad that even Islamic clerics complained about him leading to him losing his post. The other, Davoud Rahmani, the head of Ghezel Hesar Prison by order of Lajevardi, invented and employed a multitude of torture methods, relishing in keeping young women in isolation "graves," coffins or tiny toilets for seven or eight months as he tortured them.

My mother's brother and his wife (who was also his cousin) started planning their escape on horseback to Turkey. It was only a matter of time before my uncle would be executed as he had been a left-wing activist during the Shah's time.

We waited till dead of night and got into the car. Then we drove to the deep dark waters where from atop a bridge my stepdad and uncle dumped boxes of left-wing literature into the river. Some nights by the gas lamp we sat in my grandmother's garden by the fishpond and burned books and pamphlets. We'd smell the fire and smoke from other neighbors and know that everybody was getting rid of anything that hinted at anti-Khomeini sentiment. I would hear about what was happening, the thousands that were being raped, tortured, and executed by Khomeini's regime, and to me, at nearly eight years old, he became the devil. A white bearded old imam who was evil and executing everybody.

One day on our street, a young female Mojahedi strapped herself with explosives, and ran to embrace an Islamic scholar, killing them both instantly. *Shahid*: martyr. The cult of martyrdom became the beating heart Iran post-revolution Iran. This life-after-death and automatic entry into paradise propaganda provided the Iranian state with waves of volunteers. Teenage boys wore slogans that read "Imam Khomeini has given me special permission to enter Heaven." Martyrdom meant suicide missions like strapping explosives to the body and running toward Iraqi tanks. The martyr's death meant a grandiose and elaborate funeral, an instant elevated social status for his family, which included an abundance of normally rationed foods and other special treatment by the state, including having streets or schools named after him. Portraits of the deceased martyr lined the streets and murals of him with Qur'an verses were painted in his honor and installed above junctions and at mosques. Every day in neighborhoods across the land was a funeral for a shahid killed in the war. Popup shrines appeared at the end of every alley crowned with framed photographs of fathers, child soldiers, elderly men festooned with colored bulbs, flowers and passages from the Qur'an. Giant murals of war Generals killed in war were plastered across junctions of the city and the side of buildings with white doves and the gates of paradise with Khomeini's slogans scribbled over it, like: "War is God's great gift." Alongside them, Khomeini scowled down on the city from billboards with slogans like "America can't do a damn thing" and "We shall export our revolution to the whole world. Until the cry 'There is no god but Allah' resounds over the whole world, there will be struggle."

FIFTEEN

"He's wiggling his bottom again." My stepdad giggled at my little brother, all nappied up and jiggly, butt shaking to any war anthem that came on the telly.

We sat in the middle room, bemused and entertained by my baby brother, who was always smiling, his fat body wobbling as he went on all fours to move up and down, up and down to funereal war songs, gurgling with glee.

"Oh martyrs get ready get ready for paradise," boomed the nasal mourning. One by one, teen boys went up to the battlefield to get blown up to pieces so they could get their key to heaven.

"They're getting actors to appear as Imam Mahdi now," our neighbor said, sitting in front of a silver platter of pistachios, sunflower seeds, and dried mulberries and shaking her head. "To get the poor boys to believe he is appearing to them, to urge them to carry out a suicide mission."

After a while we'd switch off the telly and put on a black-market Bollywood film my stepdad had gotten from under the counter of the butcher's.

"He's disappeared up her leg now!" My mum would roll into fits of giggles as my baby brother loved the feel of ladies' stockings and nylon tights, and we'd find him crawling over to feel up any woman's legs who was wearing those.

As much as I loved films, I'd mostly be in my bedroom lost in a book or two. Literature came easy to me, and I soon got the top grades at school: maths, literature, history, science, and religion—the concept of heaven and hell being a daily part of our Islamic indoctrination. Whatever I did that was "bad," such as fibbing or being vain in front of the mirror, was instantly met with a doomed voice in my head from God: you're going to hell!

So my innocent meetups with Mahin and Mojhgun, the lipsticks and eyeshadows stolen from our mum or grandmothers' purses and boy-talk curdled from child's play into the a dirty feeling of deviancy. We were sinners bound for hell. My own small rebellion didn't stop there. I wallpapered my bedroom with oversized posters of 1970s glamour queens — women mid-pout, mid-pose, mid-orgasmic-stare — and then sat cross-legged on my bed, studying them with a baffling mix of admiration and longing. Naturally, it didn't take long for my mother to notice. Her reaction was predictably apocalyptic: not only was I risking my neck by flaunting forbidden Western icons under a regime that had already outlawed hairspray and open-toed shoes, more egregiously, I was a moral failure.

The posters came down. The shame, however, stayed up, invisible but permanent wallpaper. I was officially indoctrinated: chic was filth, elegance was betrayal, beauty was corruption. Any instinct toward glamour — the silks, the scents, the sly tilt of a wrist — was something to be buried, deep and ignoble, like a mutinous thought you didn't dare finish.

What I craved most — the shimmer, the danger, the power of it — was exactly what I was meant to despise. Symbols of chic, elegance, seductive femininity were a burning shame to be hidden away in the pit of my core. All things that I felt drawn to and identified with, so all of me.

I would then go get ready to see my mum's family at Haj Agha's manor for the night's mehmooni, where we now talked of the new regime's crimes against its own people. Hair scraped back into a tight pony, pearl combs sunk into my crown and face scrubbed harsh with soap, I was cleansed. But Khomeini's crimes against the humans of Iran made the women's makeup more garish, the perms even puffier and music cassettes and videos of films, now highly illegal, listened to and watched more than ever. It just drove everything underground; everything, now taboo, was done in secret.

We would take trips with my cousins to the Caspian Sea—*shomal,* which literally means north. The north of Iran was divinely luscious and green with stunning villas and snakes and lizards. We'd drive past majestic mountains towering over us in craggy junctions and rocky dirt roads, past farms and villages to the beach which was now segregated by a makeshift wall. The new Islamic regime forbade mixed genders, so the women and girls swam fully clothed on one side of the sea, and the men and boys in the other side.

On one of the trips, my mother had put me in a swimming costume as she continued adhering to the compulsory beachwear of headscarf and *manteau.* I was only eight years old, so my mother thought we could get away with having me swim in the water without an Islamic cover. Suddenly a male revolutionary guard ran toward us, grabbed my mother by the arm, and screamed obscenities at her, including calling me a child whore. I was told to cover up my body and stop showing my skin. Suddenly, my body had become a sexual thing. Women's bodies and their hair became highly sexualized to me. I was always a sensual child but in an innocent way, and even Bakhshi's sexual abuse had not managed to defile me as badly as it should have. But by now, having the "dirtiness" and "shamefulness" of the female body combined with heaven and hell propaganda suddenly snapped me into being highly aware of how I as a female was "impure" in the eyes of God, my face, hair and body a demonic temptation to men's piety.

I was nearly seven years older than my brother, so I constantly babied him, washing his rags, looking after him, and one afternoon when I was home alone after finishing school for the morning—schools were attended either as a morning shift of 7 AM till noon, or as an afternoon shift of around noon till 5 PM—I watched him take his first wobbly steps.

Soon after, my brother got scarlet fever. Neighbors gathered around his bed burning rue seeds to ward off bad spirits as he burned in a semi-conscious state with fever on the bed. My mother, in a state of delirium herself, screamed and howled with terror as my stepfather brought a doctor around.

I had recently had scarlet fever and knew how ill he felt. My mum and stepdad had thought I had been faking it to bunk off school and had sent me off marching, even as a rash crept up my neck and I nearly fainted. But this was my baby brother. My everything. I bathed him and cooled his brow with wet cloths until the medicine worked its magic. I put on my chador and prayed and promised to God that I would cover up my body and not show skin again.

But the air raid sirens droned, and night after night we and our neighbors found ourselves seeking shelter in the underground car park of an apartment block. Saddam's bombs would hit towns across Iran and I would sit in the dark, hearing the explosions and knowing that at any moment we would be hit. We'd cower in the shelter in the dark, the adults in panic and us kids terrified. I held Mahin and Mojhgun as we prayed, our hands slithering in sweat, our dolls clutched closely. I thought of my grandmother all alone in her house, the windows shaking, the sirens ever closer, the bombs nearing, and I would want to leap out and go to her. To me she was more my mother than my mother. She was from heaven, an angel.

How we left her on her own in that house. How she must have been terrified.

SIXTEEN

When the bombs weren't falling the underground car park became a place of naughtiness. I started skateboarding up and down the neighborhood in my hejab, but it was standing up on the red skateboard and rolling down the wide concrete slope into the car park that gave me a thrill, one borne from the smell of the dark cavernous space. Of petrol and fear, of dark deeds which would surely confirm my place in hell.

At about eight or nine years old, I took some of my same-age male cousins, female and male childhood friends to the underground car park, threw off my Islamic hejab, and lay down in my flimsy dress with my arms spread out on the cold car bonnet and made them all touch and stroke me all over.

During afternoon siestas, when all the adults were napping, I got together with my cousins or Mahin and Mojhgun and played games—grown up mummy and daddy, doctor and nurse. We would show each other our *down-there*, each of us examining, touching, and rubbing. This secret game playing was the most delicious euphoric feeling. It made me feel like a goddess, immortal, invincible.

One day, as the war anthems played in the next room, I shut my bedroom door and got two of my boy cousins to play a game of master and slave. I lay down naked, pretending to be a princess dozing off, and got my cousin who was my age to command the younger boy, the slave, to touch me all over my body.

I kissed girls my age full on the lips and licked their tiny rose-bud labia. I was always "turned on." The intensity of the excitement and the erotic charge that swooshed in my veins made me go dizzy with ecstasy even though I didn't know what sex was or the facts of life.

My baby sister arrived one day as I was doing my art exam at school. Dark skinned and shriveled like a prune, she was moody and scowled a lot. I was nine years older, and like I had done with my brother, I babied her all the time.

Owing to my stepfather's new role as owner of an architect design company, we had a roomful of shiny new toys, including my play tent, which smelled of fresh plastic. If I was on the morning shift at school, I would get home to play in this little tent and create imaginary worlds. My mum and stepdad would be at work and my brother at nursery. All was silent. With Mahin and Mojhgun we'd create a "wives club," and after we had gathered herbs from the maidoon, we'd bring them back to the tent and pretend to cook and prepare dinner for our husbands, gossip about the neighbors and look after our babies.

But sometimes the games turned sensual. I would take my cousin who was a little younger than me into the tent and kiss him and get him to touch me all over in the secrecy of the tent. I knew God was always looking down at me and keeping score of all the bad things I was doing.

At school, not only did I get top marks but I was Miss Popularity, and everyone was my friend. In girl gangs, we'd get together in the playground and walk home. Even after school we'd get together in the alley and next to the latest martyr shrine of colored bulbs, whisper about boys, the thrill of it all making us giddy. The morality police would crawl past in their jeep, checking us out for stray hair, or a deviation from the Islamic uniform of headscarf, black or gray manteau, and trousers. They even examined our nails as they passed.

A few months before, the revolutionary guards had stopped our car with me and my siblings in the back. These uniformed thugs surrounded our car and screamed at my parents. Under my manteau, you see, a bit of my leg was peeking out, and it took a cash bribe from my stepfather to get them to leave us alone.

Meanwhile, hot whispers in the middle of night rose to screaming matches between my mother and stepfather.

Bitch, bastard, mother fucker, cunt, gutter-trash ..

My little brother and sister would wake up screaming and look on in terror when the fighting got physical—my mum hitting him, him punching her. I would comfort my siblings and take them back to bed, all the while praying my mother wouldn't have a seizure as it would traumatize the babies even more.

Despite all of this, I had the happiest, most fulfilled life. I was loved by all: the sea of relatives that we saw every day, my friends, our neighbors. The air raid sirens, the power cuts, the two other neighbors who molested me like Bakhshi had-my tender and sore breasts has started to bud and puberty had given me a full afro bush which made these new pedophiles' breast grabbing and crotch fingering so much more repulsive to me than when I as pre-pubescent—none of it made me hate my life. I was a happy child. Cerebral and creative, I was around so much love and family, so many parties, and I had even taken interest in a green-eyed boy a year older than me called Ali, the brother of a family friend.

Ali had invited me to his birthday party, and that morning I had gone to the shops with my mum to choose a pretty dress. My hair was scraped back, and I wore earrings and a bracelet that my aunt had given me. It was a party filled with all of Ali's male friends and every boy wanted to dance with me. Ali liked me, I knew, and I really liked him. Looking at his photos now, he looked a lot like River Phoenix. We danced and talked, and he made silly boy jokes. I felt I was growing up.

And right then, right in the middle of the harmony and stability of my life—the stability of school and friends and loved ones and safety—my mother decided to send me off to England.

SEVENTEEN

It was the summer of 1984 and my stepfather had managed to bribe someone in some tourist visa office to get me and Anneh a visitor's visa to England. I was told I would be going for just a visit and be coming back. It was a lie, and it was a whopper.

Everyone in Iran, including my family and especially my grandmother, saw *kharej* (countries outside of Iran; mainly the West) as Utopia, a place straight out of the pages of a 1950s society magazine. It was a cream tea and beige land in which coquettish ladies and gentlemen in elegant Vogue attire were dotted around a land of manicured lawns and purified breeze.

So I was taught which knife and fork to use and how to sprinkle salt on food in a genteel manner. It was all a bit of a lark, a bit of jaunt to a pastel-hued world where I could buy French face creams for my friends as gifts and learn English before I came home all Anglified.

I had taped myself, my mother, and grandmother as I voiced my concerns to my mum.

"Will I come back soon?" I ask in the tape.

"Yes, it is just a trip," my mother says.

"Will I be able to study sociology in England?" I ask.

"I am sure you will," my mother replies.

Then I sing an old Persian song about hunting deer.

In the tape my voice sounds so innocent, constantly pleading with my mum to tell me if I can continue my education for sure in England. I loved school and I wanted to keep learning, especially sociology.

My grandmother also speaks, constantly reassuring me that I will be able to study in England. My mother tells us that we are just going for a visit first, then we'll come back and decide if we should all go to England as a family.

"Well, I am going to kharej." I swung back my hair with a pout showing off to all in the neighborhood who had gathered around in their excitement to hear of the local popular girl's trip to England.

What a spoiled princess she was—so privileged, so spoiled.

"Ooh, will you buy us perfume and bring back bananas?" the amassed crowd cooed.

Bananas were scarce in Iran.

"Can you get me some Crème Vichy?" Baharak shouted from the upstairs window of her house.

"Yes, for sure! I'll bring everyone a gift." I'd raise an eyebrow and swish my headscarf like a lady going to kharej. I thought I was going temporarily, and my grandmother thought so too. Everyone thought that.

Everyone except my mum.

So on a balmy August night, the whole neighborhood spilled into our apartment bringing gifts and trays of food, burning rue seeds around my head for luck, and wishing Anneh and I safe travels. Everyone laughed and whooped, took photos and cried. There was even a professional cameraman who took a video of me on the sofa, singing, dressed up in a new spaghetti-strapped floral cotton dress and sitting on my bed, waving coquettishly. The overhead camera lights were bright and burned hot on my skin, but I felt like a film star.

Mahin gave me a small photo to remember her by while I was away. Mojhgun couldn't talk for crying. My aunts had bought me a gold bracelet, and a neighbor gave me a crucifix so that I could fit in. We were given silk scarves and I got a brand-new red nail polish to wear after I got there, as I would have to rub off my polished nails before I got to the airport on account of the morality police.

My uncle and aunt, intellectuals and activists during the Shah's rule, had already escaped to England via Turkey on horseback, and my grandmother sat by our suitcases, which in addition to our clothes was stuffed with an assortment of gifts: pouches of dried sour cherries and saffron, *lavashak* (fruit leather), dried mulberries, *ajil (*a mix of nuts and seeds), and boxed sweet snacks like *gaz* (nougat with rose water and pistachios). Hand-embroidered fabric and silk tablecloths tucked safely away at the bottom of the case for whomever, my grandmother sat amongst an adoring congregation of neighbors, in-laws, and relatives. She'd see them again soon enough, after this pilgrimage to the shiny slick West for her granddaughter to be dipped in Western social graces and upper-class education. She was giving up her home, her family, her neighborhood, her whole life for now, and she was doing it for me. To accompany me.

She was laughing and joking with everyone. She thought she'd be coming back in a couple of months.

My mother stood in a corner watching us, eyes red as I cooed bedtime lullabies to my baby sister. She was quiet amongst the throngs of people, batting a hand to whoever approached her. My four-year-old brother knew his big sister was leaving and shyly bit his lip and giggled as I bearhugged him, taking in his smell and warmth, his little Zorro outfit all buttoned up.

Everyone filtered out around midnight, and we snatched a couple of hours of sleep before my mother shook me awake at 3 a.m. to go to the airport. My stepfather drove as my aunts and uncles followed behind.

A navy manteau and orange head scarf was wrapped tight over my cotton dress and in the back of the car, I looked out at the sleeping neighborhood and my school, which would start again in a few weeks. We'd all be learning big history books and literature as I hit eleven years of age in September.

I clutched Mahin's photo tight.

It was still dark when we reached the airport, and I posed for photos with my sleepy relatives and attempted a polite smile. It was exciting to go on a trip, but my mum was crying and I wanted so much to tell her that we would be back soon. I didn't understand why she was being so sad. I was distracted by the Revolutionary Guards inside the airport, and I rushed my goodbyes, promising to write letters to everyone.

We were taken to a cubicle and interrogated about our trip, and my grandmother told them it was a holiday. Then we were searched so thoroughly that my grandmother's shoes were slit open at the sole to search for any hidden items. In the terminal, I saw a man's cigarettes snapped in half one by one as the Revolutionary Guards searched for—well, something.

I remember that as soon as we entered British Airspace, I took off my headscarf. It was what I had been waiting for and it felt so exciting, so wild. I could now legally show my hair in public. Then I applied slapdash streaks of paint to my nails.

There. Now I was ready for this new shiny world.

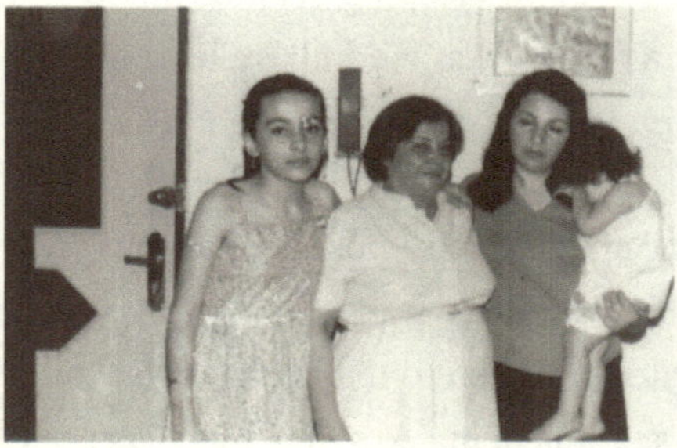 

Last night in Iran, August 1984

EIGHTEEN

England, 1984

By the time we staggered off the plane at Heathrow, it was abundantly clear no one was coming. No uncles, no cousins, no hastily scribbled signs with our names, not even a second-hand friend of a friend sent out of politeness. My grandmother and I were on our own, a ten-year-old with no English to speak of, and a woman whose lungs were already working on partial capacity, dragging a lifetime of possessions crammed into cheap suitcases.

We would have to find our own way to get a flight to a city called Manchester without knowing a word of English. My uncles, Anneh's own sons who lived in Manchester and Reading, had not bothered to come greet us at the airport and Anneh and I had been walked to customs by a man we had met on the plane so he could translate the immigration officer's questions. When it was my turn in the line, I stood in front of a uniformed man who looked at my birth certificate and papers and asked me things I didn't understand. Luckily, being raised on fight-or-flight adrenaline had equipped ten-year-old me to arrive in a new country, push around suitcases, and find a connecting flight. The Iranian man we had met on the plane instructed me to run around the terminal and repeat "gate tree, gate tree, gate tree" to anyone who would listen so that we could get a connecting flight to Manchester at gate three.

"Gate tree?" I ran around in panic repeating this to anyone I could.

A Japanese man threw up his arms and shook his head.

"Gate tree?" I asked a lady waiting by a check in gate. She also shook her head.

Gate tree, gate tree, gate tree. I repeated it to everyone I could, but perhaps my pronunciation of *three* was not comprehensible.

I walked out of the terminal where I had told my grandmother to wait while I went inside to find our gate and plane. When I ran back outside, Anneh was crumpled on the pavement, wheezing violently. Her lips were blue and she was struggling to breathe. Her asthmatic lungs had started to seize. The stress of landing in this new world with no one to greet us and having to find a connecting flight was terrifying for both of us. She was scrabbling about in her cream leather bag and finally got out a blue Ventolin pump to pump a few puffs into her mouth as I stood back and willed it to work. A muffled raspy whistle escaped her throat as she choked, fighting for breath, her bulging eyes pleading with me to help her.

I ran back inside the airport and tugged at the arm of anyone I could, but all they saw was some crazed child. Back outside I watched helplessly as my grandmother had gone purple in her lips and keeled over clutching her chest right outside on the pavement.

With all our worldly goods packed around her I tugged at her arm, *Wake up, wake up*.

She'd been a mother to me since birth, more than my own mother had, and she had wheezed and panted out of her little home and all its fruit trees in Tehran to fly to the chic and elegant stratosphere of the Western world clutching her cream suitcase which housed all of her most beloved treasures, gushing with loving pride that she could keep her little granddaughter safe. She was dying right before my eyes.

Someone must have called an ambulance, and I remember sitting in the back of a big van with tubes, all our luggage squashed next to me. I was a big girl now. A proper adult. Then it all goes black, and my memory has been wiped out. No matter how much I try, everything from sitting in the ambulance to waking up the next day in a bed somewhere is a total blank. All that comes to mind is an image of a shiny white bowl for doing my toilet instead of a hole in the ground and not knowing how to use it

Then I remember sitting in a car being driven to Manchester.

NINETEEN

Manchester, 1985

My grandmother and I found ourselves on a large council estate in Hulme, a zone packed with high rise government housing blocks, where discarded syringes and piles of dog poo adorned the grounds. Gloomy pewter skies veiled over council tower blocks and a perpetual yeasty brew belching from the beer factories nearby sank into our damp living as we sat in the living room of an eighth floor flat looking out at all the other tower blocks. My young uncle and aunt who had been political prisoners in Iran had a few short months ago just managed to escape Iran on horseback via Turkey with their one-year-old son and been given this social housing flat in a building filled with other asylum seekers and Indian and Pakistani residents.

We never talked about how my grandmother had suffered a heart attack at the airport and was now subject to violent asthma attacks and being constantly hospitalized. But I had been sent to this country to become a glossier version of myself, so I believed this was the best place to be in, this utopia. I got busy playing in the corridors of the tower block, fresh with the stench of council-grade disinfectant and drizzled in stale piss and amused myself by zooming up and down the juddering lift, where used sanitary pads and smashed glass bottles proved a brand-new concept after playing under fruit trees with neighborhood friends. Outside the tower blocks, I jumped over gates as livid Alsatians chased me and boys and men with shaved heads and tattoos on their forehead heckled funny words and flicked a flash of their pen knives.

Food was things out of tins and rice-puffs from a box and never-ending sacks of potatoes that were peeled, sliced, mashed, and fried. I was sent off to get things from the shops around Moss Side, and I hopped and skipped over singed grass to corner shops full of Indian men with turbans and smashed windows with boys in "bovver boots."

"Take walks all over the streets, you're bound to find a penny here and there," my uncle would urge me. "It all eventually adds up to buy food."

Day and night, under the glare of a lightbulb, my uncle and aunt chugged on an old sewing machine, cutting, stitching, picking, and pressing denim parts for a Pakistani factory owner who popped in every other day with a fresh batch of denim pieces bundled on his back. In exchange for a few quid, they made stacks of jeans every two days, so washing the dishes round the clock was demanded of me and the cooking and cleaning assigned to my grandmother, when she wasn't having a blue-lipped, choking asthma attack.

"Now you make sure you do it spotless," my uncle and aunt normally stood over Anneh and me as we did house chores to make sure we earned our keep.

"It's a strange place we have come to," my grandmother whispered to me. "Sitting in this room day in, day out, no family, no life."

We gazed outside at the concrete scratching the gray skies. Smoke chugged from factory chimneys as we sat with our belongings from Iran, the smell of home still clinging to the fabric. Flower-pattered skirts my grandmother had sewn especially for her new life in England, gold bangles and earrings the neighborhood had gifted us on our last night sending- off party and packages of hand-embroidered silk tablecloths from the bazaar we had bought for this new world pooled around us, along with bags of pistachio nuts and pouches of saffron and dried cherries.

"Don't tell your mother anything," Anneh cautioned me quietly. "She'll get upset and worried. Tell her everything is great here."

So in the evenings, my grandmother and I washed our faces and buttoned ourselves into our best full-skirted turquoise and fuchsia homemade dresses to wander into the living room. We watched the telly blaring about MFI and Argos, which seemed to be what everyone in this new world was desperately after, along with a man named Boy George, who dressed like a lady, and an important woman named Maggie Thatcher, who hated poor people and wanted to destroy all the miners.

I missed playing with dolls and daydreamed about my school and all my friends and family. There was no food or friends, school or warmth but there were new creatures: punks. From our room we gazed down onto the estate at plumages of acid-yellow and fuchsia, neon pinks and lurid greens, to where these hair- sprayed lorikeets lined the fences, hair standing up and stiff, spitting and drinking from bottles with names too hard for me to pronounce. I started writing pages of letters to my mummy about the social injustice in England, how much poverty there was in this utopia; the punks and their Mohicans, and the working classes of England. I wrote about how I was not getting any education and how kids with strange accents shouted things to me and how dog poo and people sleeping in the streets were so common everywhere. I wrote about how much I missed my school and friends and studying and her, my mummy. My letters were then read by my aunt, who frowned and crossed out bits that made my new life sound sad.

The loneliness and depression mixed with the starvation was taking its toll, and my grandmother's health declined rapidly. Her asthmatic lungs, aggravated by the damp, wheezed and whistled and she regularly gasped for breath until my uncle called for an ambulance and she was wheeled away to the old Victorian infirmary, where in a mixed dormitory she would lie on her own, staring at the ceiling and think of her home back in Tehran, full of grandkids and family, the sunshine and her neighborhood.

Day in, day out, I looked for pennies on the ground. Pennies so I could buy a bar of fudge to eat. One time, after yet another stay in hospital, my grandmother hid a couple of pears for us in her bag. That night with the lights off in our room, we lay in our beds, munching and crunching on themand felt like queens; haughty and superior.

In order to learn English, I had started going to a big library in central Manchester, where with a cassette tape and headphones, I listened to words and wrote them down in my clunky English spelling. In the morning, I walked to the local school, Ellen Wilkinson, where because I didn't speak English, I had to have special lessons. I was dying to know what the teacher was saying, what the other pupils said, and the first words I learned were in the playground were "fooking" and "cow."

No one seemed to like learning. These kids in England cared only about being naughty and acting like louts. I spent my time in the science lab, English/Persian dictionary in hand, trying to understand squiggles and words. I would carry my Farsi-language Mark Twain books everywhere: *Tom Sawyer* and *The Prince and the Pauper* to keep me from getting bored. I also had my Samad Behrangi books, which were full of tales about social injustice and which I read over and over. They reminded me of home, my friends, of learning.

As my aunt and uncle worked at the sewing machine, my one-year-old cousin was loaded with sugary drinks and chocolate eggs, and he'd bounce off the walls shrieking like a monkey.

"Calm yourself down!" My aunt Perry would grab him, and he'd smash a gooey egg splat in her face. I busied myself stuffing envelopes with hair clips and teddy stickers to send to my siblings as I hid their photos my mother had sent me under my pillow. "Wallop!" "Bang!" would go the pots and pans as my cousin whacked them together running up to Anneh having a lie down on the sofa. He bashed her skull with the frying pan and blood spurted out from the gash where it bled and drooled onto her face. I rushed to clean her up; my aunt was too young to be burdened with a mother-in-law and kid niece whose bosoms had started to bud and was mumbling something about a stretchy bra for school.

Stacks of letters were written to my mum, cousins and friends. Mahin and Mojhgun sent me photos and notes about what they were learning at school, and I tried to memorize it all, drink it in, so they could live inside me along with council estate skies and Mohicans.

Dear Ma,

Hello. I hope you are completely well and my brother and sister also. How is dad? I am really missing you. I wish you were here. Mum, you don't know how many different types of toys there are here and what beautiful toys they are. Everywhere you go there are toys and clothes. Clothes that a person wouldn't even dream of. There is a doll here called Barbie and she has everything, lots of shoes, clothes, makeup table, lipstick, eye shadow, kitchen, car, wardrobe, a husband. I wish you were here so you could buy me things that I want. The clothes are very, very beautiful here. The shoes shimmer with beauty. There are lots of beautiful things here but only the rich can buy them. The rich areas are really nice but the rest of the areas are so bad. For example, there are gangs of children who go around stealing and smashing car windows and no one says anything. I live in a really poor area. But at school I am learning the piano. I see mums holding their kids' hands and I wish you were here. I am really upset that you're not here.

Some of the men here have tattoos on their arms and wear earrings and their hair is long and messy. It looks horrible.

Write Back Soon,

Your daughter

In the classroom, when I couldn't understand anything, I began writing. I wrote furiously about the Iranian regime, the bad man Khomeini and what he had done to the Iranian people. My political writings were interrupted by lists of singers I liked:

<u>Pob Stars</u>

Duran Duran
Teena turner
Boy jorj
Mikel Jakson
Maddona
Wham
Prince

TWENTY

"Karma, karma, karma, karma, karma chameleon" rang in my head as I walked to the shops in Moss Side, trying to dodge the Alsatians. It was winter 1984, and I had made a great discovery: charity shops. Jumpers were ten pence and skirts were five. I got the pennies from an uncle (Anneh's other son) who lived in Reading. He had been in the UK since the seventies and had a giant afro. Anneh was bought a meal in a café, and I was taken to a charity shop, where they bought me a jumper, skirt, and bra. Even though I would have preferred a doll to play with, clothes were a necessity—especially as my body was sprouting and expanding with all sorts of lumps and bumps.

My uncle and aunt in Manchester had no money and were trying to place me and Anneh elsewhere. We were a burden and they wanted their own space. This trip was starting to become a permanent arrangement which made me feel uneasy. This Jane Austen West was all smoke and mirrors; a scam. My life in Iran was like a princess's compared to this. It was me and Anneh against the world and we sat in our room keeping quiet and out of sight, me reading or writing, and she lying on the bed, wheezing, lost in thought.

Her home was far away. The cherries from the garden trees would have come and gone by now and the mulberry bushes would have shriveled. Her pride, the goldfish pond, would need to be filtered and cleansed of debris and algae, and her curtains and upholstery, hand-stitched by her mother and passed down through the generations in Tabriz, would need to be dusted down. The hessian basket that she took to the shops for strained yogurt, bread and meat would still be waiting by the door, just as the butcher and vendors waited for her to come by. Her family and neighbors would be gathering around for food and song, Islamic regime vexations said in whispers, and rooftop sleeps under the stars.

Sitting on her doorstep under the bright sun before the sound of azan, the evening prayer wailed out into the neighborhood and chatting to other neighbors about powder and rouge, lip cream and brow plucking and stuffing *dolmas* the right way. It must have all seemed like a rose-hued vintage postcard to her now.

Anneh's sons were all in *Kharej*. She had three in the UK, and her eldest, a heart doctor she hadn't seen in a decade, lived in California. Despite his wealth, he didn't seem to want to help his own mother or me. He hadn't seen her in a long time, and still, he didn't seem interested in coming over to England or helping her dire medical condition. It seemed none of her sons in England cared, either, and when I tried to tell my mum in Iran, my aunt who always stood next to me, glared and cut the conversation short.

I watched Anneh clutch the doorways of the living room more and more.

"*Oluram*...I am dying."

She was struggling to breathe, and ambulances were called again and again. This burdensome woman was consequently banished to another high-rise flat by her sons and issued a box full of brie as food. But the damp of England racking her lungs was only a trifling offense to feeling utterly bereft of living life, her home, her identity, her family and community. Even within a war-torn country, we had had a huge, warm, loving neighborhood of relatives and neighbors, and we missed the cradle of that all-consuming love. It drilled a hole in me that could never be filled or put back together.

TWENTY-ONE

Dorset, 1985

I too was packed off to a foster family in Ringwood, Dorset, where I attended a Steiner school called Folly Farm. The family, Doris and Pete had their own little boy, Keef, and had adopted a three-legged dog called Tommy and a three-legged cat called Flower Pot, so I guess they decided to add a child refugee to their menagerie of wretched things. I was given my own very room and plastered the walls with Duran Duran and Wham! It was here that I soaked up English like a sponge because there was no other way to communicate. My trustee English/Persian dictionary with me wherever I went I learned how to get by.

We lived in a stone cottage and every morning I went to school in a pre-fab building with four rooms and a kitchen. Ours was a class of children aged eleven through fourteen, and because this was Steiner education, emphasis was given to individualism, the arts, working with nature (woodwork, pottery, crafts), and physical movement, such as eurythmy. There were no uniforms, and we called the teachers by their first names.

The kids were different too. Well-off. Glossy. They came with perfumed mothers and jovial fathers and went skiing over Christmas as casually as you might pop out for milk. Unlike Manchester, where the air practically crackled with the combative energy of Indian girls and disaffected black boys, Dorset was aggressively, hermetically white. It smelled of milky tea and horse stables, and you learned to say "lovely" with three extra vowels or risk social death.

This was it; this was the land of coquettish hellos and croquet that had to get programmed into my human self in order to become a better, shinier me.

How I missed my Anneh, my friends. But I was totally on my own now and had to do what I was sent to England for.

Soon after starting Folly Farm School, I picked up a new word I could not find in my dictionary. Four girls in my class—Julia, Rachel, Christiane, and Tracey—had started constantly calling me "nigger nuts" and "nigger."

One night, as Pete was giving Keef a bath, he told me, "It means black man."

"Vhy they call me dat?" I asked.

"Because it sounds like your name, Negar."

I blushed crimson. What an embarrassing name I had.

"Who calls you that?" Pete asked.

"The girls at school," I replied.

Pete looked at me with sadness in his eyes. "That's not very nice."

"And *Paki Paki Paki*, like a song," I added.

Pete turned back to bathing Keef.

I wasn't yet Roxana.

I excelled at school, earning top marks in French and a prize in the form of a Dairy Milk chocolate bar, which only made the four girls even more angry; at lunch time I was cornered in the classroom and beat with a broom stick. I had a moustache and wore woolen peasant clothes my mother had knitted me in Iran and boxed over to me for the cold and damp of England. I was a geeky bookworm.

So I started to pee myself every morning before school. I was terrified of those four girls, each of whom were a year or so older than me but in my class nevertheless. I was petrified of being bullied by them in everyday situations, and whenever they felt like toying with me. I was stressed out every second, knowing they might call me nigger and have the class laughing at me. I was eleven years old, and having stolen Doris's Stuyvesant cigarettes, I began puffing and blowing on the cigarette, trying to find something to take off the stress.

"No, Negar, no! that's not how we do things in England," Doris had come bounding down the stairs in her Dutch clogs to catch me smoking next to my Duran Duran poster. I was duly sent to have a lavender bath to get rid of the toxins.

One day I opened my desk to find that Tracy, Rachel, Christiane, and Julia had placed dog shit inside. All the kids howled and cheered, and I pissed myself instantly. I dove into Huckleberry Finn in a corner of the classroom, where the wee continued to drool a little more.

I briefly went to Manchester to see Anneh. She was living in a flat and getting by on bread, tea, and eggs. We sat together and reminisced about home. It felt like it was compulsory for us to live in England, like we had won a golden ticket to paradise and leaving it would mean giving up the Promised Land, the key to utopia—even if utopia was full of hunger, poverty, racial bullying, sickness, and loneliness.

But we had to shove it down and fucking enjoy it. After all, it was the West.

In the morning I said goodbye to her and made the train trip back to Dorset.

TWENTY-TWO

I carried my stacks of Farsi Mark Twain books everywhere with me in case I got bored in class when I didn't understand what was being said in English. Anneh had made me sandwiches with the slabs of brie she had been given, and I kept them to eat at school. At lunchtime, I sat at my desk and bit into my stale but lovingly made sandwich as Tracy, Julia, Rachel, and Christiane made cross-eyed, jerky, "retarded" gestures and spat.

"It's piss she is drinking," a boy named Danny joined in as I sipped on my apple juice. I was scared but ignored them. I wanted to be fluent in English so me and Anneh could live together and I could get a job doing translation work to make us money, so I continued with my reading. Most of my English language skills were swear words and racist slurs, along with pop music lyrics. The girls in class were obsessed with George Michael, John Taylor, Nick Kershaw and Paul Young and I had to recite their song lyrics if I wanted to get past them.

Soon it was the Easter break and I rushed to Manchester on the train only to find my grandmother's flat empty.

"She is ill." My uncle batted a hand. "In hospital resting."

I begged to see her.

"No visitors allowed," came the reply.

I waited a week, not reading my books, unable to do any homework. I sat in my grandmother's empty flat and clutched her dresses, the sheets and her belongings still warm and smelling of her. I longed to hear the familiar sound of her whistling chest, smell the elegant vial of her Armenian perfume. I waited and waited to see her in hospital until I was sent to my uncle and aunt in Reading, where they sat me in front of piles of Betamax tapes of *The Rocky Horror Picture Show* and *Kane and Abel.*

"Is she still ill?" I asked my uncle. "When can I see her?"

He said nothing for days and I kept being told that she was ill. I missed her so much.

One afternoon as I was doing the washing up my English aunt crept up behind me.

"Anneh is dead," she announced.

I didn't cry but focused on scrubbing bits of dried egg yolk from the frying pan.

I knew, somehow. I knew she wouldn't be suffering anymore and inside me was relief for her. She had struggled to breathe since we landed in England in August of the previous year. Nine months of hell, and not even sixty years old.

It was all because of me. I was the reason she came to England, she had died because of me.

This demented creation, this insult to nature—I had killed my grandmother.

I gazed hard at *Dynasty* on the telly. I liked Crystal but not Alexis. I focused on the glitz, the outline of the shoulder pads and the glamorous women. It masked *everything*. In the shower, I scrubbed my body with rocks so that I wouldn't feel. I'd murdered her. I was evil, Satan's spawn. She had died because of me. And that me, that kid died, too.

I will always remember how no one, not one of her children in the UK or the US, ever did anything for my beautiful angel grandmother. They left her on a hospital bed, alone and terrified, not speaking English, not knowing how to ask for food or the toilet or to communicate her pain. And then she died all alone in the middle of the night in a strange country—her child-bride scars; her ten children, some perished at infancy; and a lifetime of memories reduced to a statistic on a Manchester city council spreadsheet. She was not even sixty years old.

Anneh's body was sent to Iran for burial, and I mourned for her alone. I would wake up at 4 AM every day, light a candle, say prayers, and talk to her. To my uncles, it was like she hadn't existed at all. Talk of her was forbidden and happened only in hushed tones, as if she had been a virus and not the heartbeat of our whole family. All signs of her were erased from my uncle and aunt's home and if I mentioned her name or cried that I missed her, I was quickly told not to be so emotional. This was the torture and murder of a celestial soul.

Shortly after, I found myself bleeding from my vagina. I looked for cuts, but there was nothing. I checked my panties to see if something had caused the blood. Maybe someone had done it in my sleep. I carried on with life until people started noticing my blood-stained jeans as I walked around. Doris pulled me to one side and explained that this was what was called periods, menstruation, and that it happened to girls from my age every month. I was freaked out. Why had no one ever told me this? I was issued with a small pad which I stuck sticky side up to my pubic hair, thinking the adhesive would stick to the vagina and stop the bleeding. It took me days to figure out that the sticky side went on the panty and that I had to keep changing it.

I had also figured out how to stop the bullying: stop being a book worm and get sexy like the singers in the pop videos. I stopped reading books, wore my skirts super short, shaved my legs and wore kitten heels. I also started bleaching my skin with hair bleach. Instead of white ski, it became red raw. The girls showed me a bit of respect from then on.

Class photo at Folly Farm

TWENTY-THREE

Bristol, 1985

Doris and Pete were old school hippies and decided to drag me along to Glastonbury Festival. Predictably, it rained, and I got lost. The entire field turned into a pit of viscous mud, impossible to traverse without a full-body slide, and by midday I looked less like a child and more like a creature that had crawled out of a swamp.

By then it had been almost a year since I'd seen my family. So I decided, quite rationally, to run away and live by myself. Plan A: wander into the mud and disappear. Plan B: improvise.

But life, with its infuriating tendency to keep moving, had other plans. Toward the end of the summer term at Folly Farm word arrived: my mother had escaped Iran. She was coming, with my brother and sister. For once, reality outperformed fantasy. I was giddy, nearly deranged, waiting on the doorstep of Doris's cottage that morning. I had been up since 4am.

She stood there, gripping my brother and sister by their small hands. My brother blushed crimson with the bashful grin of recognition while my tiny sister scowled and told me to get lost. My beautiful mother — who had sacrificed her country, her job, her dignity — had crossed the world to come and rescue me!

We moved into a student hall of residence in Manchester. My brother, five years old, was still in war mode, and all his drawings were of bombs and devastation. He'd run around the room making the *"Pow! Bang! Boom!"* sound of machine guns and explosives, spray-gunning the Iraqi enemy with the imaginary Kalashnikov shuddering in his little arms. My sister, who no longer recognized me, took weeks to stop treating me like a stranger who might steal her biscuits.

They were both bewildered and confused by this new upheaval in their life. No daddy, no friends or food, and my mother, with a platinum subscription to altruism readily took on the role of martyr, selling her wedding necklace to buy us food and began cleaning rich people's homes as I babysat my little siblings. It was a big step down from being a teacher with a degree in psychology, and it must have been very hard to become a cleaner and having just lost her mother. Moreover, she was now a single parent of three as my stepfather, who not having been able to get a visa, remained in Iran.

Reunited with my baby brother and sister.

Billie Jean, *Thriller*, and *Get into the Groove* blared into our lives as we visited the council flat of my mum's sister and my cousins who had also managed to get out of Iran that month. Our sofra was packed with sugared cereal and spaghetti hoops and we longed to find pomegranates and cherries from shops. My cousin, who was my age, began loitering with me around the Arndale Centre, a shopping center in the center of Manchester, smoking, shoplifting, and looking at porn magazines. It was so crude, so primal, that it made me have my first squirting orgasm as I played with myself, first reaching for a bicycle pump to rub along my vulva and then using my fingers. I did not understand what had just happened. It had been a crescendo to something urgent and explosive, and then a rush of relief. I was not yet twelve years old, and I thought it only happened to me. It was a secret, and I was a freak.

Two things happened that summer before I turned twelve: I spent the summer learning English from reading the Marilyn Monroe biography *Goddess* by Anthony Summers, dictionary in hand as ever; second, my mother bartered her way into a community in Bristol for adults with learning disabilities, exchanging labor for lodging — one room, four bodies, no questions asked.

I was sent to another Steiner school along my brother and sister. The school allowed people to pay what was in their means, so as my mother had no money, we paid nothing. Held inside an old cathedral, our days were filled with woodwork, making art from dried leaves and grass, exploring caves, spinning raw wool into yarn to make clothes for ourselves, and making pots and bowls from clay. It was a hippy school, and all the kids wore handmade rainbow knit jumpers and had names like Sunshine, River, Leaf and Moon. We spent days weaving wicker baskets and singing folk songs.

As the Steiner ideology centered on the arts, the finer points of math and science were left to rot.

I wrote a novel on the street kids of Brazil called *The Secret Garden* and got all the main parts in all the school plays. I smoked every day by nicking my mum's cigarettes and drank Guinness in the park's toilets where I'd hid a bundle of clothes I'd change into: fishnet tights and gloves, short skirt, crop top and heels- out of my mother's sight. I memorized "Papa Don't Preach," "La Isla Bonita," and "True Blue," and danced around in my underwear hoping I would have sex with a boy like Axl Rose from Guns n' Roses but marry a man like Al Pacino, as I was obsessed with him in *The Godfather II*.

My stepdad couldn't get a visa to England, so instead he escaped to Germany during the Iran–Iraq War, leaving all our belongings behind, and from Germany he eventually got a visa to come to us in England. I had envisioned his arrival as unshackling of us from the chains of poverty, my mother finally freed from being a refugee single parent, cleaning houses all day whilst trying to feed, school, and shelter three kids.

I had glossed on the red lipstick and trowelled on the rouge on my bleached skin, bleached with a whitening cream bought from the local Indian shop. We met him at the train station with a bouquet of flowers and brought him home.

A kind lady called Jane had let us live in her basement flat for free so we could leave the community center. In the mushroom rooms- dry rot sprouted and bloomed mushroom-like growth on the walls- my mother and stepfather and my siblings and I all slept next to each other, all of us stuffed in there for sleep like a can of tuna. We had head lice and a video camera to cheer us up. On-loop video footage of my stepfather getting off a train from Germany to come join us in England played as entertainment; a day we had celebrated.

My schoolmates were kinder and there was no name calling apart from the odd "you look jaundiced" and Jane the upstairs neighbor had come down to relieve me of head lice and screaming little siblings by offering me lotion and her spare room for free. In my own space I discovered Dylan Thomas and shut off in my room, listened to Richard Burton read *Under Milk Wood* over and over. Then I auditioned and got a part in a local production of *Under Milkwood*. Theatre, poetry, and acting were my natural path. I started acting classes at a kids' club and learned how to do impressions of Marilyn Monroe in front of my teacher, Nick Flores. He would get me to stay late and take me to a small room with a stage where I would dress up as Marilyn with a blonde wig and do my most breathy kittenish impression of "I Wanna Be Loved by You" and "Diamonds Are a Girl's Best Friend." There, late at night, he would pinch my nipples to stiffen them to groom me to stardom. I was confused and frightened and felt disgust, but I wanted to be a movie star and listened to my mentor. I was obsessed with Marlene Dietrich, Greta Garbo, Louise Brooks, Clarke Gable, Theda Bara, Ava Gardner, James Dean, and all the old movie stars. I lined my wall with every poster I could find, especially ones of my idol, Marilyn Monroe. I desperately wanted to be like them, full of old Hollywood glamour.

Always surrounded by Marilyn. Always trying to look a bit vintage

TWENTY-FOUR

Finally, we reached the top of the council waiting list and moved out of the mushroom room and into a high-rise block in Bristol spilling with Kurdish asylum seekers, Bengali families and bashed-up teen mums. Laundry slumped over washing lines in the gray concrete corridors soaked in the fumes of curry and tamarind from the Bengali flats. Dirty nappy bundles slipped under feet. Our estate had international flags billowing out of its windows like an asylum seeker hotel. The green and white of Nigeria, the green and red of Bangladesh, Kurdish and Turkish emblems, Somalian and Rastafarian flags amongst the St. George's flags.

Ground View was next to a brothel called "The Happy Hand," which offered wonderful sandwiches as a temptation to customers. Its most famous alumni, Genevieve the prostitute, whose Satsuma sheen polyester cycling shorts had been a constant fixture of the parlor, was now working from home in our block. She knelt outside her door in the narrow belt of the corridors doing press-ups in green stilettos, her long, jeweled corn rows clinking together. Her exercise bike would be whipped out in a flash onto the middle of the landing whenever she saw visitors arriving to see neighbors. In her thong and green stilettos she began to pant and heave theatrically on the bike as she lapped up the trauma on the Sikh and Hindu faces.

The initial novelty of seeing my mother after three long years quickly soured for my stepfather and the daily beatings began where they had left off in Iran, when runny egg and air raid sirens during the war blended with thwacks and wallops leaving my mum with seizure after seizure. Regular vicious violence to me and my mother was meted out from my stepfather, whose indignation stemmed from the rage and shame of begging for dishwashing jobs in pizza restaurants after having been the CEO of an architectural company. In Iran, he was lauded and held in high esteem by a wealth of high-ranking peers and friends, enjoying a rich social life and networks of relatives and friends in every city. In England he was just a brown asylum seeker, jobless, living on a shitty council estate. Gone were the lavish parties with our wealthy relatives and family friends, the hospitality of the Persian culture, and any money we had. Even his stepdaughter, who used her fluent English to ask for dishwashing jobs on his behalf, was more advanced than him. It made him feel even smaller and triggered his inferiority complex. Anything his stepdaughter did was a trigger for his barrage of abuse.

"Her clothes look like homeless people's," he'd loudly shout in front of the neighbors when she proudly wore a new floral River Island dress she'd bought with money she had saved.

"It's like an animal being strangled," he'd heckle at the finale of a song she had prepared to perform in front of her family, and her ears would burn with shame and embarrassment.

My mother gave all her energy to day and night shifts at a children's home for violent teens from dysfunctional families. The kids had disturbing pasts and frequently urinated on the staff. Depleted of all her reserves of love and energy, she'd nevertheless rush home, catching a string of buses, running home to the kitchen to frantically prepare a plethora of Iranian dishes for us kids. This was to choke down any residue of malevolent energy that might still be lingering around from recent beatings launched onto her or to me, our family pain, the children's terror and tears buried under —aubergine, rice, lamb and garlic, and chocolate treats and watermelon, all of it meant to anaesthetize the daily abuse my mother and I received from our stepfather, abuse witnessed by my little siblings.

"It's not his fault," she warmly provided logic and reason as she put away the dishes and folded laundry after a beating or verbal onslaught. "He had a horrific childhood, having to work as a kid, and mum dead when he was seventeen No one gave a shit about him, you know?"

My mother and stepfather continued their political activities from Iran, hosting meetings and rallies, our flat again full of literature on socialism and Marxism and intense debates on social and political theory with relatives. Relatives who, although equally educated and intellectual, knew nothing of the violence in our home. Domestic violence was taboo in Iranian culture, and immense shame and indignity attached to it so tightly that my mother hid it from all, instilling the same in me. If a relative saw me in the aftermath of a beating, I would lie and say my face was puffy because of too much sleep. This culture of taboo and shame, alongside my mother's epileptic seizures (another taboo) and our poverty, created a secret dark existence known only to us. We were shut out from close relatives, neighbors, and friends, and all the outside world saw was a bright-eyed, bouncy trio of kids.

Even though my brother and sister were still little, every Sunday the five of us would go to work cleaning a big law office in Bristol City Centre. We were all assigned a chore: hoovering, dusting, bin changes, or the toilets, with the heavier work going to me, my mum, and stepdad. We got paid £30 which was spent on food for the week.

At school I played Antigone and Adriana in *Comedy of Errors* and at night I read my Chekov and Strindberg plays or watched Coppola and Scorsese films.

"You think you're so special, don't you?" my stepfather would hiss to me in the passenger seat of the car when we were alone. "You think you're SOOOOOO. FUCKING. SPECIAL! Do you know that everyone laughs at you behind your back? Your clothes, your hair?" he'd sneer. "You think you have an English accent? The neighbors have told me your accent sounds foreign, thick Iranian." He'd honk. "You think your English is soooo good, don't you?"

My sense of self-worth had become that of something feral. I'd blush furiously as I made excuses to go to my room.

"*You*"—he'd come quietly in my room, out of earshot—"need to leave home. Staying here, living here, doing nothing. You're a dead weight. You need to leave." I was accused of eating too much of the food, using too many lemons to squeeze on my chips or salad. "These lemons are for cooking. If you are gonna use them, give us the money." It was a hefty task to process this vitriol as a young teenager.

When my stepfather tore into me or my mum it always ended the day for us kids. A wallop and howling followed by another punch. On the occasions I ran away from home, my modus operandi became buying giant teddies from charity shops for my brother and sister. We would daydream from the upstairs window looking at the swaying of the trees where a lone metal horse see-sawed on a square patch of grass.

Our neighbor Mike would come around with a bottle of milk. He'd bring the *Morning Star* and other left-wing literature to discuss with my stepdad. My mum didn't understand why English never took off their shoes inside the home, but she never said anything, bringing dish after dish of stews, rice, salads and desserts she had managed to hastily whip up in the kitchen. Persian hospitality stipulates that you must do this even if the postman pops around to give you a letter. And the guest can't say no. Ever.

At night if she wasn't doing night shifts, my mother sat mending our clothes and watch Fellini and Ingmar Bergman films. I'd be terrified the lack of sleep would make her have a seizure but she refused to listen. Exhausted from working in the children's home, looking after three kids and cooking, and taking bashings from her husband, she nevertheless had a voracious appetite for literature, for history, for politics and for the arts. Her intellect bordered on genius, with the ability to discuss Marxism, Freud, Andy Warhol films, the Vietnam War, the history of Persian poetry and even medicine. Her intellect didn't extend to leaving an abusive husband.

At fifteen I put my face in a gas oven and breathed it all in, but after going dizzy and getting sick, I stopped and switched off the gas. I was eternally enraged that my childhood narrative had been interrupted virtually overnight. I was enraged at being made to feel different and being poor, having no friends and constantly on alert for my stepfather to snap, to launch himself on me or my mother. At night my ears would sharpen, straining for any sound of either my mum's screaming epileptic seizure or a vicious punch.

My escape was old movie stars peeping down at me: Greta Garbo, Norma Shearer, Theda Bara, Louise Brooks, Rita Hayworth, Ava Gardner. And masturbation gushing furiously on the linoleum toilet floor.

A kitten my little sister had brought home had become a beloved pet. One late night during a vicious exchange with me in front of my siblings, my stepfather took the kitten and dangled its body from above our thirteenth-floor balcony. "I'm gonna chuck her down," he screamed, chalk white with rage and trembling, ignoring my little sister's screams and my mother's pleas for him to stop as we snatched the kitten from him. I knew that my stepfather had been through a lot in his life. From being tortured as a political prisoner in Iran during Shah's times to slashing his wrists in a bath when he was an escaped convict. Sometimes at home he would repeatedly bang his head on the wall to protest my mother's bickering until the neighbor next door complained about the loud thumping. Most nights he let out a sudden loud cry in his sleep from nightmares.

By the time I had turned ten years old I had been fully educated on the many strains of Iranian political factions, and become an expert on the torture practices deployed in the Shah and Khomeini's prisons, having listened intently to the accounts by family friends and seen the scars first hand on my uncles and stepfather. In my last year in Iran when I was ten years old, I had sat watching one of my stepfather's dear friends, the commander of the Iranian Navy, beg for his life on TV. He had been arrested along with thousands of members of the Tudeh party (a pro-Soviet Union Communist Party) to which he belonged to.

Bahram Afzali had been tried in front of a military tribunal in 1983 and had been sentenced to death for being a Soviet spy. I had remembered our visits to his lovely home which had a swimming pool and security guards outside the apartment. We had watched him begging for his life in front of a kangaroo court on life TV, his tall frame, tinted glasses and chiseled jawline making him look more like a film star to me than someone who had supposedly done "bad stuff." Our family's friends and relatives were being executed rapidly since Khomeini came to power. That does something to a guy. Watching my stepfather dangling our kitten above the balcony, I suddenly saw how damaged he was. He was gone.

Getting angry at home life would get my mum to pull out her ace card:

"If you talk about these upsetting things, I'll start having a big fit right now. You'll make me ill. Is that what you want?" , the risk of having a stroke, a heart attack, or even sudden death worked beautifully as a pacifier. Everything was taboo to my mum and she was perpetually in denial of anything "bad" and did not want to hear it in her presence because it would cause/seizure/heart attack/death.

A strangulated prolonged scream from her throat was the kickoff to her epileptic seizures- the congestion of historical traumas a guttural foghorn till it trailed off in a muffled cry, lips purple, accompanied by a twenty-minute whimpering of nonsensical chatter on the floor, having wet herself or bitten her tongue, falling in and out of consciousness and then deep sleep for hours.

The four of us would fall silent, eating together food made sheepishly by my stepfather, showing each other support and affection.

TWENTY-FIVE

An older woman with a fish and chip stomach and red feather boa looked me up and down. "How old are you, luv?"

I lied and told her I was twenty-one.

I was seventeen and had left home to become a stripper and model in Soho, London. My stepfather and I had stopped talking to each other, and subconsciously I knew I was hurting my mother when I took a job in a London back alley. It was a finger up to my mum: This is what you sent me to England for. This is your child that gets abused, beaten, and called names by your husband. This is my rage at your refusal to take medication and causing us to be terrified for you. It was the beginning of creating a persona that would carry me through to the world of rock 'n' roll and all those rock stars later. I knew my mum's Achilles heel: glamor, sexuality, sexual display, so I cultivated it to its sleazy extreme. It wasn't a cultural thing at all, it was personal to my mum, who subscribed religiously to the second-wave feminist sex-negative ideology.

Putting on my Walkman in bed to listen to The Doors, rubbing furiously in my knickers to fall asleep in the giant puddle and getting the coach to London, I made my way to Soho to find myself transfixed by the crackle and fizz of the neon lights. It was the portal to freedom. The building, instead of a ropey knocking shop lost its obscenity. The lurid red of the hallway and the beaded curtains that led to the dressing rooms, seemed not to signal the semen-crusted bowels of Soho but rather became something yawning, like a womb, sheltering me. "Changing room is in there." The woman led me to the small, mirrored room in the back where women of different ages and colors sprawled around smoking. Talk of kids and bad boyfriends, rent money and "extras," swirled in the haze of hair spray, along with the swishing asses and the crackling thighs of the girls walking past.

A virgin teen, mono-browed and chubby, I was scared of sex with a man, but I tried to look fearless as I pulled on a school uniform to go dance on stage.

"The DJ will put on music and call your name. What do you want your name to be?" Linda fixed me with a hard stare as she balanced a fag between her sovereign-studded sausage fingers. Trails of ash mottled her leopard print spandex.

"Roma," I whispered. "My name is Roma."

Stripping in front of dirty old men, I felt like Rita Hayworth.

And it was for wanting to become a Rita Hayworth or a Vivien Leigh that I posed. The money paid for acting school, which I'd auditioned for and been accepted at. I posed for photos with my legs firmly shut and bought vintage negligees to lie on fur spreads and animal prints like a shy crazed Iranian waif. No one asked me for my ID, and I saved enough money to pay for my acting classes.

At drama school, the halls glittered with girls and boys who had been born twirling. Polished kids with million-watt smiles, the shine of wealth stitched into their skin. Stage school brats who had been doing jazz hands since steppity-stepping out of the womb. Everyone's backstory involved a well-off supportive family. Inside me was a Mae West extravaganza bursting to come out, but I felt stupid exteriorizing it and being my true performative self, so I was always mute, the performances I so much wanted to showcase all strapped down and pushed down in my chest. So when I was finally obliged to perform my Steven Berkoff monologues for class there was a fair bit of squirming.

"It's always the quiet ones, isn't it?" Charlotte the It girl with the famous boyfriend sniggered. Things I so wanted to say lodged in my throat like scrabble tiles, but when singing, dancing, or acting, I could be myself. To be honest, I didn't need any classes. Every day I was playing different characters.

Photo by Beki Cowey

TWENTY-SIX

I was sitting with my boy cousin watching *Deep Throat.* That's when I learned about the facts of life. I was eighteen years old. I had thought that sex was when a man rubbed his penis along a woman's vulva. My mother had told me that a woman gets pregnant when she takes a pill, and in sex education class at school, a woman came to our class when we were fifteen to slide a condom on a broomstick

What I saw with horror on the screen looked like a mutilation. A penis repeatedly stabbing a hole in a woman. I felt scared and sick. It was repugnant and so passive on the female's part. If this scene on the screen was what actual sex was supposed to be, I didn't want any of it. It was degrading and I felt disgusted, scared and out of my depth that this was what I was supposed to do now as an adult female. Sex and all its pleasures had betrayed me. It had advertised itself as a heart stopping, bestial, pussy-exploding gushathon that would transcend me into a divine realm, when in reality it was butcher's work, *medical* work. This thing punching in and out of a hole in a woman looked anything but sensual and tingly; it looked like trauma. And I would have to undertake this from now on, if I wanted to have sex? Did I *have* to do that if I wanted sex? Was the vagina really *necessary*? Couldn't I have sex with just rubs on my labia or the naked chests of boys on my body?

By the age of twenty-four I still hadn't properly kissed a boy and was still a virgin. It felt icky and gross, a *violation* to get penetrated by a male. I was terrified and icked-out by having sex with a man, even though I was knocking out orgasms a few times a day by myself and having sex with girls. My virginity was making me an outsider yet again, an alien, and even more isolated than I felt.

It was now 1997, and after a few years in London I'd finally got my own bedsit in Bristol in the same block of flats as my family which my mother had fought tooth and nail for me to get from the council. She wanted me to have my own sacred space away from the abuse and chaos and not have to move back into home and to my stepfather. I had acted in some theater and short films and now back in Bristol I was ready to become a woman.

The Iranian twenty-year-old son of a family friend had come over from Toronto to visit me in my bedsit in England. He managed to rip some of my hymen, but I could not get penetrated. I was like wood down there. The sliver that he managed to tear caused a little bit of blood, but it hadn't done the job properly.

And so my vagina was clenched up tighter than a duck's arse. *Nothing shall butcher me.* I held the blood blotted tissue in confusion. Why couldn't I physically get penetrated? That summer we tried really hard to break my virginity. We went to Alton Towers theme park and went on all the rides so maybe my hymen would soften up a little. We did all sorts of bike riding. I even tried carrots, a cucumber, a rhubarb, and a toy telephone, but nothing would go in. In the evenings my friend made me a plethora of dishes to loosen me up. Lamb with aubergine and chickpeas marinated in fresh tomatoes, garlic, and herbs. Rice with saffron. Ghormeh sabzi: A green multi herb stew with kidney beans, sautéed onions, turmeric-seasoned lamb, and dried lime, served with saffron butter rice. This was his specialty. His mother had passed away a couple of years before and he had taught himself Persian cooking in Vancouver. He even got me my favorite juice: Morello cherry. But nothing ripped or moved.

I started working in a Greek restaurant, where I was surrounded by my obsession: feta cheese. The cacophony of loud Greek families, live music, and late-night dancing made it feel like Iran, and I started to come out of my shell.

There was lamb and tzatziki and baklava whimpering in honey and the owner, Andreas, got me to belly-dance. I subtly merged waitressing into dance, swooping up leftover taramasalata and skordalia plates with twirling arms and circling wrists, dropping my hip and shimming my bum as I walked away from the bewildered middle-aged couple, the plates balanced on my palm.

The constant waft of food satiated my appetite and dulled my hunger pangs. Somehow, I survived on diet coke and tons of cigarettes and occasionally some lamb's liver and a boiled egg. This got me a tiny waist and a banging body, even though my bones jutted out and my leg joints creaked and snapped when I walked up and down the stairs.

"Pink Panther!" Mustafa and the Moroccan workers downstairs had given me the nickname because of my lanky and wiry limbs. But still I ran and ran at a gym every day until all I could only see were wee stars and blackness.

This new persona got me out of my socially frozen self and was the route to getting my hymen bashed in. Enter: Andreas's son, Petros the Town Shagger. Thick black fur covered his body like a forest creature, and piercing blue eyes twinkled beneath a caterpillar monobrow as he chatted up city center slags. He showed an interest in me, as he did any female with a pulse, and because he had the status of being the owner's son, my hymen snapped easily with blood and agony. I recoiled in pain.

"You on yer period, mate?" Petros winced at my blood.

"Erm, yeah," I lied. "Sorry about that."

And so that was it. I had done it! At twenty-four, I had lost my virginity to a Greek furry man who was in the fish and chip business. I was ecstatic. The birds started tweeting, rainbows stained the sky, and everyone on the streets was doing songs from musicals. Petros had left that morning to go get a bacon butty, leaving behind a shroud of black fur on my sheets, and I was in love. I wanted him to be my boyfriend forever and work in a fish and chip shop, saying, "You want salt and vinegar with that, luv?"

But Petros the Greek was trying to get as far away from me as possible because I had told him "I love you" the next day I had lost my virginity to him. This fish and chip guy was used to pissed-up English slags up for a shag on a Saturday night, not a poetic flowery Iranian girl in love with romance and family. I was confused. I thought telling a guy "I love you" would make them love you back. I thought that wanting to be a guy's girlfriend would pique their interest and make them want to be with you.

I was slouching on the bar counter looking like I was about to die from pain.

"He doesn't know you from Adam," Sally the waitress at the restaurant told me in between puffs of a Lambert & Butler. She was my idol. Sally had managed to get preggers from Andreas's other son, Marios. and was now "in wiv the Greeks," as she was fond of dropping into every conversation. "Job for life in 'ere, I 'ave." She smirked triumphantly and flicked her highlighted fringe from her eyes as she proudly scooped up a heap of taramasalata with a thick chunk of bread to shove in her mouth. "One of the fahhmily."

"But we slept together!!" I protested.

"Yeah, that don't mean nuthin', luv."

I was genuinely confused. Why would anyone have sex with someone and not want to intensify the pleasure with love? Not want to spend time with them? To me, sex was about intimacy and love and talking, not this. It seemed that shagging around with no emotion and romance was a normal thing, along with drinking yourself to hospitalization and that was how you were supposed to act at my age.

Petros's favorite music was Celine Dion, which made me even more heartbroken. Mariah Carey and Celine would wail from his car speakers as I'd sit silent with melancholy, wondering why he didn't want to date me and be my boyfriend. I wouldn't mind serving fish and chips for life. Then one morning he flew to Cyprus and brought back a wife he had picked out from a village. A marriage of convenience. I was delirious with pain. Why not me? She stood next to him, a palette of crushed rouge and purple eye shadow, gloss peach lips and dipped in sequin and glitter. Then she read out a list of chores she did not do as wife: washing up, cleaning, dusting, and ironing, as it would ruin her nails.

I considered killing myself. I felt less worthy than when I had been a virgin. This was it. I had no other currency left. My vagina couldn't get me a boyfriend, and I could not even compete with a Greek Cypriot wife from a fishing village and her provincial charm.

Instead, I got a part-time job in a sex shop hoping to learn how to make men want me. I wanted to learn the moves. I started collecting stockings and being a good girl and swallowing, but no one wanted to be my boyfriend. I practiced Feng Shui. I placed love ducks in my southwest corner with peonies and water and a clay pot representing earth. Some romance trickled in in the shape of a Kenyan man who wanted only to worship my feet and a guy called Kemal, who looked like a camel. Then came a beautiful Greek boy called Phedos who could not stop kissing me and touching me and telling me I was a goddess but refused to have sex with me or date me. I could not understand why. I soon realized that like all Greek boys he had an obligation to marry a beige Maria. They all did.

Modelling topless for some twat or other.

TWENTY-SEVEN

Toronto, Canada, 1999

I had set about finding my biological father. Letters and photos to old neighbors and relatives in Iran followed until one day I got a package of his poetry to me. I also found out that his side of the family all lived in Canada. So at twenty-five I left my life in England and moved to Toronto to be amongst the Iranian population. Toronto's immigrant makeup didn't make me feel like "foreigner" or the "other," as ox tongue sandwiches nestled between warm plastic tubs of *asheh reshteh* and saffron rosewater ice cream in the Iranian supermarkets. Every Friday night Toronto's Persian diaspora community steeped itself in vats of eau de cologne and wore their entire sets of gold jewelry and went dancing at *1001 Nights*. White and gold columns and showpiece tasseled chandeliers looked down on vast silver trays of kebab and rice, which we all shoveled down as toupee-d, down-on-their-luck, Iranian lounge singers from the 1970s reduced to the cabaret circuit crooned sad songs about the old country.

I established base at my cousin Shahin's apartment in a Jewish-Russian neighborhood. Our ritual for his post-gig nights—he played percussion for the Persian singers—became smoking skunk and listening to Leonard Cohen or suicidal Persian songs. Sometimes at the cabaret they held Afghani weddings and the leftover food he brought back was congealed in a block of hardened animal fat we had to crack with a spoon to get to the warm gooey stew inside.

I had a student visa to work in Toronto, and after a couple of mind-numbing shop assistant jobs where I had to smother my personality and nullify my brain cells, I saw an ad for lingerie models. I almost hopped and skipped to the interview at a sleazy downtown adult video store, at the rear of which beaded curtains led to a dimly lit sectioned-off reception. Under a tremulous light, a petite mermaid-haired girl hot-panted and platformed-shoed introduced herself as Tattana, the manager, and informed me that the "lingerie model" listing was actually for a stripping job. There were two small rooms at the back equipped with a tiny stage and a CD player. A customer would sit ten feet away from the stage on a single sofa and watch as you danced. Sixty dollars for fifteen minutes of topless dancing, eighty for twenty minutes of fully nude, and a hundred for dancing close to his seat for half hour. There was a box of tissues next to him and he would be allowed to jerk off as he watched, but as Tattana warned, if any customer tried to touch or make lewd propositions, we were to throw them out. (She didn't mention what were we to do if he pulled a knife). There was no security and no cameras and any connection to the outside world dangled by the corroded wires of an eviscerated phone socket. Guys on their lunch could come in with no security checks and be alone in a room with a girl. I took the chance anyway.

There would be two girls on the morning shift from ten to six, and then two different girls would work the far quieter evening shift, the office workers having finished work and gone home. I got the bus and subway from my cousin's at 8 AM, walked to the dingy lair at the back of the adult video store, and swiftly changed to a long floaty silk dress, although my figure was way too gaunt to look sexy. Vacuuming the carpets, I was job-proud. Then Tattana would arrive—it was always me and Tattana during the day—and reposition the dollar-store rug she'd bought to hide the balding middle of the carpet, which had turned a sort of muddy sienna after multiple incidents of beverage spill. Jerk chicken and trashy paperbacks on David Berkowitz, the Son of Sam serial killer, dominated our day as we sat on the black leather sofa beneath the smudgy half-light of the foyer waiting for customers.

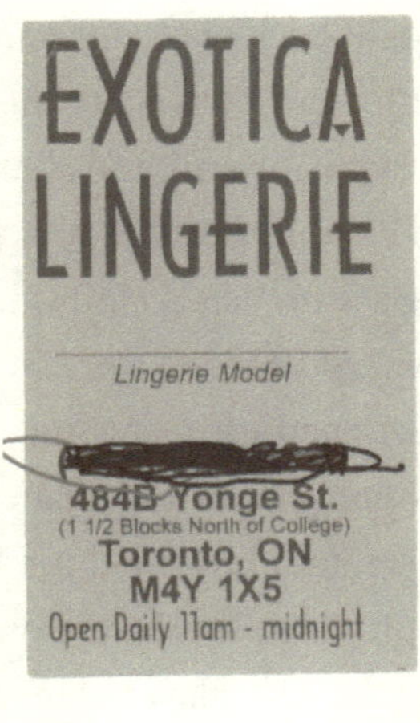

Exotica! Blondes! Redheads! Brunettes! Orientals! Russians! Indians! exclaimed the posters in the store alongside a sequence of arrows pointing to the back. We'd greet each customer, me a skinny fuzzy-haired girl with a demure English accent called Roxy, and Tattana, the spunky teenage street kid. They would appear at the doorway jangling with the shells and feathers curtain and poke their head in.

"Hi, how are you? Would you like a dance? Would you like a show?" Tattana would offer. "Private rooms" and "no one watching" seems now like an invitation for rapists and murderers, but to us it was *the* deal maker.

"Do you have any black girls?" most guys asked.

"Nuh uh, not today."

"Any Koreans?"

"Come back tomorrow," Tattana would answer.

But when I opened my mouth to speak, the guys stopped in their tracks. They were mesmerized by my English accent.

"Actually…can I see *you*?" I was a bag of bones with no hips and tits, but it was my accent got me the most work in that place. I could tell Tattana felt cheated, but loyal and loving, she let me make the money.

She was motherless, with forty years of life etched into her nineteen-year-old eyes. She rented a room from a Portuguese man named Hercules because they could do great volumes of GHB together while wanking off over how great house music was. Sometimes he'd "G out," his great hulk of muscle mass crashing into the floor, and she'd come to work and tell me all about how she had spent the weekend trying to revive him and how the repetitive rhythm culminating in an accelerating crescendo in house music would make her cum in her pants in clubs like *Guvernment*.

A butch lesbian body builder named Alyssa who worked the night shifts was forcing me to date her; I was too scared to say no. She had a buzz cut and a Harley, and her method of saying no to a customer was to hock up and spit loogies on the floor. At work, she'd spoon-feed me homemade Thai soup and try to shove glass dildos up me. Even though she wasn't my usual type of girl, I succumbed to her machismo and aggression. She smelt of lentils and gasoline. Alyssa was ravenous for me the way I was ravenous for guys and would rip into single mothers from Oshawa like Mary, who was always pissed off because customers kept picking me on account of my English accent.

"I am a single mom," she'd yell. "You gotta let me have a chance."

Mary was typical of those white bread white working-class types living in the rural areas of Ontario. What the Italians called *mangiacake.* Hers was a life of desolate highways, Costco, and Canadian Tyre.

Alyssa would protect me from anyone who looked at me the wrong way by growling like a pit bull. Alone, she would take my head and kiss my widow's peak. I didn't talk to the customers except to say hello and proffer the dance menu. Even my close-up dances were silent. Still, it was a turn-on to stand on that small vintage stage and watch the guys love me. My pigeon heart aflutter in my little chest, I'd be elated at this temporary adoration. In downtown Toronto I was a goddess and made money from just being looked at on a stage. Meanwhile, I told my father's side of the family in town and my mother in England that I worked in a PR agency. My mother was still having prolonged epileptic seizures, and I wondered if my stepfather was still beating her but never asked.

Me and Tattana became sisters, hanging out with obese gang bangers that Tattana wanted to fleece money from. I didn't care for dates anymore—they were all nuts—but Tattana had a date with Vladislav, a Serbian porn actor, with a permed, bleached-blond mullet and a seventies porn stache who frequented the video store looking for anal beads. One day they flirted and he asked her out, and she didn't want to go alone so she was dragging me out after our shift. Vladislav would bring a friend so we could be doubles. It was July, but I was flu-y and had already planned a night of ganja and suicidal Persian songs with my cousin, but Tattana wouldn't let it go. So in the end I jumped in their car with my fuzzy nest of black hair and the three of us drove uptown to this Italian neighborhood.

A wiry, chipper man grinning a set of gap teeth came bounding out of a house. He was a truck driver from Iowa and on vacation to see his cousins in Canada. A McDonald's logo T-shirt rebranded as "marijuana" with gray denim shorts hung off his rakish frame. A pure child-like innocent elation radiated from his eyes.

His name was Henry Raccoon.

Modelling shots in Toronto, aged twenty-five

TWENTY-EIGHT

Henry was beaming; it was one of those Christmas-has-come-early-lotto-winner deals when at Henry's cousin's mansion, me and Tattana like the downtown strippers we were, became engaged in obligatory stripper behavior: nudity and 69s, which made Henry color furiously and retreat shyly into the corner of the yard. We were by the poolside, and it was getting dark. Mosquitos had begun to feast on my salty flesh while the four of us in turn noshed on chicken wings and on each other while listening to the house music and techno beloved by Torontonians in the 1990s, occasionally switching to Tupac and Biggie when it was my turn.

Henry was wide-eyed, a lamb caught in a crossfire of degenerates ready to snatch away his innocence. At the age of thirty-one he was still a virgin, and his body couldn't respond to such an onslaught of sleazebags. He had hoped he'd lose his virginity to some nice, homely Maria or Angela in a clean white bed in a God-fearing home , so it was sod's law that when he finally got a chance to lose it at thirty-one it was to a couple of skanky downtown strippers.

Poor boy. He didn't know how to kiss. Imagine!

His sandpaper jawline gave my face razor burn as his tongue darted rapidly in and out of my mouth, slurping my face, scouring my skin with his coarse stubble. As dawn crinkled through, we all hit a roadside Tim Horton's for morning coffee and when he drove me home at 7 AM in his truck, he was still as fresh and chipper as a chipmunk, and even though I felt triumphant that he snogged me, he did it like he was devouring my skull. He'd been starved of girls a whole long time.

Giant livid welts studded my body, an epidemic of hickeys and mosquito bites. Working at the strip joint wasn't gonna be easy as I looked, a) syphilitic, b) like I'd gotten beaten up, c) addicted to drugs, or d) all of the above. I had to explain to each customer as I stripped that I was none of those.

Henry bought me a top and a skirt and an ice cream from the shops on our first date, and when he leaned in to kiss me on the cheek, he beamed at me with such trusting eyes of gratitude that I felt like a dirty old man. Born and bred in Iowa, he smelt like woodchips and hay. He drove trucks and worked on a farm for a living, close to his ma. As a child he had been chained to the radiator by his now imprisoned father, and now his ma was his world and the little money he made he gave to her or spent on buying me milkshakes and taking me to the cinema. In each other we saw reflections of the abused child, the lost innocent soul and bonded that way. In his childlike way, he filled pages and pages of pink paper with poetic words about how I was his precious Persian princess and how he'd found a reason to live when he met me. He was girl-starved and would do anything for me; I was loved-starved and clung onto him like a waif. After just two weeks he quivered: "I think I'm falling for you, Rox." He blanched, trembling at the words he'd uttered to me in his naivete, oblivious to the usual gameplay of "treat 'em mean, keep 'em keen."

Henry had lost his virginity to me, but it was apparent from the start that a blow job would never compare to the ecstasy he experienced from watching car programs on TV. He found dirty talk weird and embarrassing and preferred sensible "nice girl" lingerie to the slutty kind. Strangely, he didn't care that I was a stripper.

A couple of months later, when it was time for me to go back to England and start university, Henry pleaded with me to stay. *But I need you, Rox, I NEED you.* He was the only male who had ever been kind to me. He was my absolute safety and protection, and I was scared to separate from him.

But because I could not give up university, a few months later Henry left his mama and his friends in Iowa and moved to England for me. He had found a job driving trucks all over the UK and my mother thought he was a saint from heaven come to rescue her daughter from the barb wires of the past.

Immediately after his move to the UK, Henry had a "word" with my stepfather. His beaming smile and lamb-innocence had morphed into a spunky Artful Dodger as he squared up to him. "If you touch her again, you'll have me to deal with."

My stepdad was too stunned to retaliate. He was surprisingly afraid of this sweet, innocent, twinkly eyed man, and from that moment forward, the physical and verbal abuse was over.

When I first saw him, it hadn't struck me what use he could be. His looks were not to my taste, nor did I find his truck driver disposition very sexy.

On paper I was destined to couple with an equally nerdy book worm who loved kashk and appreciated Rumi, a deep thinker who could engage in-depthly with me on Foucault and Leonard Cohen's poetry, who was in tune with the time of my menstrual cycle so he could fully appreciate the 'goddess woman' in full bloom. A sensitive but alpha male creative. Russell Crowe machismo; River Phoenix fragility. A poorly managed car that he didn't care about because he wasn't a materialist or a flashy financial success. A fanatical animal lover and rights supporter and not English and emotionally repressed. Cried at my childhood and hailed me an iconic woman, didn't want kids so he'd let me throw back the fish were I ever get too close to his semen. Was saturated in poetry but also fought like a champ. Not necessarily university educated but naturally a political worldly debater. Never perfumed or after-shaved but natural man smell and unassuming.

But along came Henry Racoon, woodchopper truck driver guy from Middle America. Chipped teeth and guffawed at *Family Guy*. Who believed in the American dream with a passion for the ordinary: potato chips, a six-pack of beer, blockbuster films, barbeques, and baseball. Who delighted in hot dogs—not even organic M&S sausages, but the terrifying hooves and anus ones from builders' burger vans. Listened to Bruce Springsteen, the early albums, when he was feeling cultured and nineties techno for when he was feeling wild. Brut aftershave and white towel socks with no brand trainers. Trusting the government, trusting the law. A sensual relationship with car mechanics and Star Wars. Delighted in E numbers and additive-packed candy stores.

But Henry had been a faulty machine with faulty wiring. He swooned when touching car parts but refused to touch any of my meat. We lay side by side like broccoli in the vegetable aisle. He was a meat eater of all kinds except for mine.

"Holy moly, it's like Niagara Falls!" He'd gurgle wide-eyed when my only fuck became from touching myself. He became distressed for the sheets and scared of the wetness. He grabbed all the towels and told me to hold it in.

So I thought about cheating. Rivers of sperm, I dreamt about. Torsos, hair pulling, and the lust of men—I didn't want sensitive, I just wanted a lout. Slowly, it had started to make sense. He would be the one that deleted my life's hard drive, dissolved and sanitized all those rough spikes in my memories. This anodyne celestial creature would be my serene beach, my Valium, my permanent chocolate. Henry's presence would heal my psychology before it morphed into psychosis from all that bloody pain. He didn't know this was his role He just did it because he was kind and meek like a sheep, and he loved me so, so deeply. And I adored the bones off him. He was my entire world. We loved each other like the two broken birds we were. Our love for each other was for safety, for comfort, for nurturing, like mother's milk for baby.

Henry's heart was bursting with sunshine and adoration of me, but his loins were an empty reservoir, devoid of sexual urges. He even deemed French kissing to be a bit unhygienic. After losing his virginity, we had fondled and made love on a few occasions, though my squirting terrified him. Gradually, he became bothered by the wetness, distressed for the sheets, and started nagging at me to hold it in so he could go grab some towels. Then sexual activity started to become a chore for him, with me bribing him with a massage in exchange oral sex, which he timed on his stopwatch, his voice muffled into my crotch as he announced, "Okay, it's been one minute now," before rushing to the bathroom to scrub his mouth with anti-bacterial soap.

And many nights I lay in bed next to him crying, begging him to touch me, to let me fellate him, to engage in sexual intimacy, but he would say, "Noooo, don't want to! Not in the mood! I am watching this car program."

The pain from such intimate rejection was like a dagger in my heart, but I couldn't change Henry. He didn't mean to hurt me or reject me. He just wasn't really interested in sexual things. Lying next to him in bed, I would fantasize about kissing as he read car manuals. I loved him, but I was growing resentful and bitchy from the lack of sexual and sensual intimacy.

"Buy me something original, something romantic," I'd command.

"Something different for you baby," he'd beam lovingly, blue roses in hand. "Thought you might like them."

"Take me to dinner, take me to the cinema," I'd nag when he was being harangued by a migraine. "You're so boring. Your eyes are like a rat. So tiny and your teeth look like someone from *Deliverance*. It's embarrassing."

"Sweetie!" he'd cry in shock, his gentle eyes wounded.

He'd hold onto me because he had a predisposition to habit-behaviors, a coping mechanism from his abused childhood and youth; I'd hold onto him because he was my guardian angel. Complex creative people always need anodyne, uncomplicated happy-go-lucky partners to neutralize the chaos inside.

Still, I thought about cheating. Rivers of sperm, I dreamt about. Torsos, hair pulling. Men who only thought with their cocks. Bad boys.

I tried holidays in the Greek islands.

"The stars are beautiful tonight, Henry. I adore the smell of storms and the sea."

"Yeah, it's nice. Let me just see if I've won this windshield wiper accessory on eBay."

A skilled mechanic, plumber, electrician, and handyman, Henry insisted on explaining the workings of things to me: his eulogy to a broken alternator, his ode to the fuel injector, his salute to the turbo charger. And I would zone out, just loving him for who he was: a pure-hearted soul. I would try to induce romance on those blue moon nights when our hotel room occupied by us, yet another holidaying couple, braced itself for the inevitable sex that would take place. It was torture not being kissed because of the car section on eBay. The crispy white sheets went to waste. My vagina went into depression. My womb ran black from the utter denial of being made love to. Even in paradisiacal settings, Henry found it hard to feel amorous.

"I might as well touch myself then."

"But the sheets, the sheets!" Henry would exclaim. "You gush like Niagara. I'm DISTRESSED. FOR. THE SHEETS."

I had reached the end of my studies and my brain was full of Derrida and deconstruction and Plath and Poe, but my sex holes were empty. I was quivering for pink meat. I was also quivering to engage intellectually with my beloved, but there was only air. My social and political commentary hung in the air, and he would *hmmm* and *ummm* without any clue what to say, which made him feel inadequate, I guess.

I eventually started having sex with myself. Fantasizing. There were boys at university who aroused me intellectually and sexually and stared at me constantly but who didn't want to date or fuck. Sadly, being English meant they were emotionally constipated and physically unable to express desire, and those flirtations and gazes were all they could do. English men never wanted to go further than a nudge and a wink. They were either affable soft-spoken stiff upper lip types or Jack-the-lad chavs. Nevertheless, neither type wanted to fuck me however sweet, meek, sexual, happy-go-lucky, aloof, girl-next-door, or vampish I played it.

I could not even imagine breathing without Henry. To be without Henry would be to be lobotomized, to be without oxygen. But I needed more, and so I ventured further in search of sexual excitement. I sought intimacy and creative entanglement from members of Guns n' Roses and Mötley Crüe, and a sense of intellectual stimulation from a politician who turned out to be scummier than any knucklehead rock cliché. Touring with bands and having rock star sex all over the world, backstage, and on tour buses was a continuous IV drip of dopamine and serotonin, but when it developed into feelings and wanting to bond with rock stars, well, love had no place in rock 'n' roll.

It was mostly abortion and heartbreak.

While I went on tour with rock bands and told him about it all, Henry waited patiently and lovingly. His heart splintered a thousand times over, but his love was so pure and always there as he sat on his terracotta leather sofa in Scotland, steadfastly fixing my parents' things, still loving me and waiting for me with undying devotion. It was strange times when I would see him and go cry silently in his bathroom, wracked with the torturous pain of some piece of utter garbage having broken my heart, my puffy eyes hidden from his gaze.

I took him for granted, thinking he'd always be there no matter what. I thought he'd always be there for me because he loved me, and I loved him so much even though he wasn't interested in sexual intimacy—because he was the only one who loved me for the real me: Negar. With everyone else, I felt I had to constantly perform my "Roxana persona" in order to be accepted.

So I tried to live without fever and passion. I chose Henry. Romance and lust had always vandalized my insides anyway, so I anaesthetized myself to them, choosing instead to plug up my sexuality for a serene river of calm with someone who loved me unconditionally, respected the real me and liked to do normal things like me. I would just have to live without sex.

"Boundless reserves of that stuff you have, stored in you like in a camel's hump, my mother had chortled whenever I complained about Henry's dislike for sexual intimacy." "You have had enough of that stuff [sex] to last you a lifetime." She adored Henry's pure heart. It was one small sacrifice to make after all the wrong "uns.

But somewhere in the deep salty fug of my psyche, I must have craved psychological bedlam. When all was good and calm, when all was respectful and healthy, I lavished all my vitality onto the dark, and when Tommy came along in 2010 like a virus, I celebrated the arrival of this snake oil salesman who was pitching a guaranteed program of abuse and pain to my mental and physical health, destruction of my new amazing career as author and total carnage for my serene love with Henry. I said "Yes, please! I will take up your kind offer of physical and mental, because shit, everything is going too well for me. I have a new book out, my life is complete, my relationship with this saint who adores the ground I walk on is better than ever, so yeah, if you are a harm guarantor, just tell me where to sign up."

Publicity shoot in New York, 2011, by Andrew Walker of Wire Image

TWENTY-NINE

Cairo, 2016

In Cairo I was to go to the *Khan El Khalili* district in the old part of the city to meet with a man named Ali and his family so I could accompany them to Istanbul. Draped in a niqab—less a garment than a fabric-based apology—I felt absurdly more secure than in the airy scarves and billowing robes I'd braved in Jordan, though the choice quickly revealed its twisted ironies.

The city shimmered with heat and the constant honks of battered sedans—a rolling museum of seventies automotive junkers, their roofs piled ridiculously high with threadbare rugs and battered furniture. Women in identical niqabs navigated traffic with grocery bags balanced atop their heads like reluctant carnival performers, dodging through narrow gaps, between grinding bumpers, past motorbikes belching smoke and farm animals—the roadside aflap with chickens, herds of goats and russet rams with corkscrew horns. Men swaggered by in pale *galabeyas*, crowned by baseball caps and swathed in ragged cotton to combat sunstroke.

I quickly learned that harassment was more glutinous, as if the male harasser had suddenly became possessed by some crazed lust when a lone woman wore the full-on niqab rather than when she walked around without one. My anonymity—just two mascara-framed eyes peeking through—invited hands and lewdness. One bus journey turned nightmarish as a leering man gesticulated obscenely toward his groin and made a hand to mouth see-sawing motion. Having a man want you to perform fellatio whilst you're sitting in front of him swathed in a niqab makes you feel more vulnerable and frightened than being naked in public.

The next day from my hotel in Khan-el Khalili, a tenth-century district, which was originally a mausoleum known as the Saffron Tomb built as a burial site for the Fatimid caliphs, I walked to the bazaar to find Ali. The onslaught of scorching desert heat engulfed me, settling inside my tent-like cover like a fully functioning heater. My cream plastic slippers were soon filled with sweat, making my feet slip and slide past the twelfth-century mosque and the mud-baked brick huts as I entered a labyrinth of alleyways and souks. The grand archway, a beehive-dimpled arc split open like a pomegranate, led to a scene buzzing with merchants hawking spices, perfumed oils, and synthetic trinkets—all infused with exhaust fumes, sizzling meat, and incense. Alleyways darkened under hanging textiles as loud scooters zoomed through the congested narrow paths amongst piles of rubble and garbage. I walked past hessian sacks full of spices, dried fruit and poppy seeds, tin containers full of brine-soaked white cheese, with burqa-ed women behind wagons selling enormous bath loofahs and pencils.

Ali's lantern shop would be lodged within the labyrinthine maze of souks, like finding a tiny gem within a cluster of ornaments. Through my peephole, I saw men come up close, grinning and then grabbing my breast or behind, whispering words in Arabic and making kissing sounds. Maybe it was the small area of bare skin around my eyes peeking out from behind the velour of black. I don't know, because my body was covered as was my hair. Can peeping eyes be the object of such febrile lust? Such filthy "sucking," "fucking" motions and hot whispers trembling past lips? Maybe it was because I was walking alone. I focused my gaze on the jade and the turquoise embellishing the exterior of a dilapidated Ottoman building with its colossal solid oak door. Baroque scripture and Arabic verses written above recited a poem or verses from the Qur'an. In this lattice-work of dark chasms and hidden chambers there was no sky, the cluttered arteries of passageways darkened by traders' hanging blankets, silks and sheets, as well as tenants' rows of washing hanging from metal balconies of buildings. Centuries ago, city gates had guarded this district, locked at nights. I could envision the scenes from history: of snake charmers, hammams, madrasas and merchants; a real Arabian *One Thousand and One Nights.* I re-examined my features: liquid liner extended out on the corners of my eyes, blue powder and arched brows, peeking through my niqab. It probably screamed "whore." Quickly, I rubbed off my eye make-up.

Not too far away the sound of a Qur'an recital was cracking out from an old radio, lulling all into an intoxicating haze. Like Amman, young boys scurried through the narrow passageways carrying a chain of trays of hot tea to the vendors, who chattered away as they pitched and forced their sell onto the crowds, simultaneously smoking a shisha and drinking tea. Underneath the overhanging quilts and billowing laundry pieces, barber shops were the heart of social activity. Unintentionally sixties kitsch, their interior displayed loud pastels and blaring pinks, teamed with Christmas tinsel.

Cats lounged regally on precariously stacked fridges, impervious to the cacophony of flapping hens caged above, while packs of dogs gazed mournfully upward, optimistically scavenging scraps. Why didn't they devour the kittens? Maybe Cairo's animals, pampered by sentimental butchers tossing off-cuts, were too sophisticated or too spoiled.

A woman with a cart heaped with bath loofahs and plump peaches gestured toward Ali's lantern stall across the bazaar. Just as I set off in that direction, a leather-skinned, toothless relic lurched from a shadowed alcove by the girls' madrasa and began trailing me, his eyes glittering with malice and amusement.

"Fuck off," I snarled sharply, choosing English deliberately.

Undeterred, he crooked a gnarled finger, beckoning me closer with a rancid grin, whispering Arabic obscenities. I shoved him back roughly, but my rebuff only sharpened his persistence until I reached an onion vendor who inexplicably sold pencils and erasers alongside his pungent produce.

At that very moment, a burst of high-pitched giggling erupted from the madrasa. The niqab-shrouded girls spilled out chaotically, eager for ice lollies, clustering noisily around a makeshift lemonade stand, their chatter a welcome distraction. The leathery harasser finally drifted away.

I stood momentarily in bitter contemplation. Did Egyptian women ever tire of this ceaseless humiliation—the cat-calling, the serpentine hissing, the crude clicks of tongues, the relentless jeers from hawkers and passers-by? Meanwhile, oblivious foreign tourists in shorts strode confidently past, ignored entirely, immune to the indignities casually reserved for those who blended into the scenery.

Rows and rows of metal sheet workers packed the backstreets. Freshly spun industrial-sized cookware sat gleaming on the powdery yellow sand. The tradesmen yelled through the racket and the clink clonk hammering of the traders in their chambers as families sat outside the stone steps of shacks, their lives spilling out the front doors as herds of dirty sheep huddled in corners waiting for the beeping scooters to pass.

I patted and cuddled more cinnamon rams, their waxy wool, clotted with muddy leaves. Men and women with barefoot dirt-faced children yelled and shrieked as they scampered through the pandemonium of metal sheets, all the while eating from dishes of chicken and rice they balanced with one hand. All these animals, from goat to rams and sheep to the scatterings of abode-less chickens and stray cat families and dogs were a fixture on the streets, mingling in the daily hustle and bustle of residents' activities, watching from the corner, waiting to spot food.

Relying on a mix of sheer luck, street smarts, and charisma, hundreds of stray dogs and cats survived on the streets, lounging around the alleyways, sleeping on motorbike seats, curling up in the basin of a cement mixer, lazing on pages of torn fashion magazines. A patchwork of ginger and tabby, smudges of black and white, charcoal and sienna mottled with soot and tormented with babies and infested with conjunctivitis. Swarms of cats patrolled the lanes on the guard for food, never neutered, perpetually bringing babies into this world. Tiny mama cats, themselves babies, white fur blotted with patches of dirt, rows of nipples drooling milk, slid out stealthily from under the shutters of locked up vaults, their kittens housed safely behind the metal shutter and meowing hungrily. They existed side by side with the stray dogs of the city, slumped down outside locked up shutters, sniffing around the bazaar shops and debris, emotionally derelict, looking up with a glimmer of hope in their eyes as I approached, tails wagging at the slightest smell of edible garbage.

In an alleyway, a handful of plump white rabbits stood on hind legs on a stack of plastic crates, noses twitching.

"What're they for? To play with?" I asked the man standing by the crates, glossing over the reality of their dinner plate fate. I comforted the rabbits, stroking them, kissing them. A gang of gangsta cats stood salivating at the foot of the crates, waiting to pounce on the rabbit the moment it was butchered.

The man guffawed at my cossetted Western-ness.

"For eating?" I made a chewing and knife and fork motion.

The butcher grinned wildly.

"Vahsh!" I shrieked the first Arabic word I had ever taught myself. *Cruel.* Whenever I went to a new country, I learned how to say *cruel* in its language so when I went past shops selling fur or caging cats and dogs, or hunting stores or donkey or horse rides, I could shout *cruel* to the perpetrators in any language.

And still I ate chicken and lamb and dairy.

I realized the street food vendors were the stray cats and dogs' lifeline. A chunk of cow here, a sliver of gristle there. I walked up to a butcher and made small talk and managed to hustle out of him a few chunks of meat for the puppies staring hungrily by the door. I put the chunks of meat down in front of the hungry stray puppies who took one sniff and walked away. Elite homeless puppies.

Farid had given me Ali's address in both Arabic and English, but the back alleys had no signs. Darkened vaults, derelict shops, and still not a rat in sight—just a mad girl walking under the shadow of drying rugs and carpets, under tiger and zebra print quilts, Barbie and Disney bed-spreads swinging down from homes' balconies where mothers looked over kids playing football on the engine-oiled earth below.

At the corner of one lane I saw what looked like a café, a dark snack den carved into the passageway wall, its few outside steps dotted with men smoking shisha pipes and drinking tea or dozing off. It was a male only café. Legally, I may have been be allowed in, but it was a cultural faux pas. I was exhausted and didn't really care anymore. A plastic chair was quickly pulled out and a sugar-packed fizzy drink immediately placed in front of me. Sitting down to rest my feet, I fixed my gaze onto the plastic oilcloth not wanting to meet the stares of men. I was still detached from what I was about to do: meet strangers to cross the border into Iran.

Everybody in Cairo wants a tip from you. If you ask directions, and someone tells you to turn left at the corner, you are then immediately asked, palm held out, for a payment or *bakhsheesh*. If you go to the mosque and someone there says hello to you at the door, they'll hold their hand out for bakhsheesh. If you take a photo of a camel and you accidentally capture someone who happened to be in the background, they will come up to you and hold their hand out for an obligatory tip. As you ponder the marvels of ancient monuments, children will lurk in corners then casually stumble into your space and throw in some mind-blowing bit of historical trivia that they may or may not have completely made up on the spot and then immediately hold out their hand for a bakhsheesh. If you protest this, deny them their reward, a guilt trip of such a Greek tragedy scale will be meted out to you that you may start to wonder if this is some street theatre performance. *Oh woe is me and my sixteen children! All starving! You have taken the bread out of their mouths. You with your own hand have taken the food out of their mouths. They will surely die! I gave my time and energy for you. It's blood money*. If that doesn't work, they get angry; and if that doesn't work, they start making threats.

A man who had ignored my protestations and forcefully grabbed my suitcase to carry it to my hotel from only the end of the street was so enraged when I wouldn't give him ten dollars as a tip that he threatened me physically and I had to summon the police over. So you end up not making eye contact with anyone for fear of having to give a tip.

Sitting in this café/clinic/vault, a congregation of Egyptian men pointing and staring at me and whispering to each other, seemed for some strange reason like sanctuary from the exasperation that was bringing me to tears from the outside sexual and financial harassment. I paid an extra tip for the directions I was given and walked back out into the catacomb of passageways.

Eventually, I reached what appeared to be Ali's lantern shop—a miserable storefront beside a decrepit man inhaling gas fumes from a butane gas canister, eyes clouded by cataracts. The door was padlocked and no one else was around. Panic set in. Was this skeletal figure my smuggling contact? Had I deluded myself into viewing this hazardous jaunt as merely adventurous tourism?

My mother could lose her daughter. I was so selfish. These were random men I had met in the Middle East, not holiday reps. I walked to the back of the shop. In a bare room a boy in his twenties sat at a worktable mending men's suits with a sewing machine. He caught my gaze, beamed, and got up. He was walking toward me, oh no. Another tip.

"Hello, madam!" His fingers were punctured and bleeding. His jeans flecked with loose bits of thread and fabric.

"I think you are Rosanna?" Matchstick teeth wrecked by sugar. I nodded as "Rosanna".

"I am very happy to see you. Please go to see Ali. He wait for you in his house. He say to me to say to you when you come to give address. Go with taxi please."

I took a piece of paper with Ali's address written on it.

"El'arafa? Is it far?" I asked.

"It is the City of Dead," he said bashfully.

"What's the City of Dead?" I tried to think of it as some sort of Disneyfied theme park.

"It is one place where poor people sleep on graves. Families, children live on the tombstone and are collecting garbage for selling."

I called Farid from an old Nokia phone.

"Ali isn't here. I have to go to this place called City of Dead. I don't know where to go. I'm scared."

"Why do you always worry?" Farid laughed. "Okay. The City of Dead is a just a place like a necropolis. Full of graves and tombs and people who are poor live on them. It's like the slum settlement of Cairo. But very interesting."

"Well it sounds fucking horrible. You didn't tell me I would have to go there."

"Just get a taxi but make the driver wait for you. You cannot be alone in the City of Dead. Things happen if you are alone. But Ali is a good man. He will look after you. Don't wooorrrreee, my dear Roxana!"

The phone clicked off.

Things *happen* in the City of Dead if you are alone? No shit.

I'll make the taxi driver go to Ali's door and wait there. I'll make Ali come to the taxi. I don't need to even get out. I reassured myself. But what if the driver and Ali were in cahoots together? What if Farid was in cahoots with Ali for some sinister plan? In the City of Dead of all places? It was like the script of a bad 1970s horror film, just waiting for me to jumpstart it.

Somewhere in the deep recesses of my subconscious, I had a death wish. It was like a demonic energy had latched onto my soul and *compelled* me to walk toward doom. I felt a sense of serenity and beauty as I ventured out of the catacomb of the bazaar to find a cab. The boy waved. "Bye bye, dear Rosanna. Good luck, my friend."

How lovely it would be to have a job mending suits. Be a tailor at a work-table. I had always harbored a perverse fantasy about being someone's wife, a homemaker at a sewing machine, cleaning, cooking, and dusting, and waiting for my husband to come home.

THIRTY

City of Dead, Cairo, 2016

The taxi driver was kind, an unlikely mathematics professor who'd once lived in Berlin.

"But why go to the City of the Dead? Dangerous people there!" he protested, his Egyptian accent shredded with German. "You must stay in the car. I will show you."

"It's okay, I have to meet someone important." (The demon that had latched onto my soul would now be cackling raucously). The afternoon sun was sinking as we sped from Cairo's hectic heart, the city thinning into ragged outskirts. I nestled deeper into the luxurious comfort of the shag-covered seat, feeling nostalgia rise. The sensation carried me straight back to Tehran—those nights in a speeding car, my stepfather's tense grip on the wheel, my mother silent, Tehran's gloom broken only by street-corner shrines glowing luridly, shrines dedicated to boys, thirteen-year-olds declared martyrs, their families comforted by the guarantee that their son had gained automatic entry to paradise by Allah for his martyrdom.

I rolled down the window and breathed in the gasoline of the city. I didn't give a fuck about danger. Each second was bringing me closer to Iran. As we approached the City of Dead, where half a million souls lived, I saw miles of densely packed grids of tombs and mausoleums, the plain only punctuated by the mosque spires scratching the sky. It was late in the day and a jaundiced haze of amber seethed over the necropolis with inhabitants nesting amidst endless grids of tombs and crypts. Some had fashioned rags to sleep on the dirt ground and some made rooms inside mausoleums. Make-shift homes inside crypts formed communes, and the inhabitants collected garbage to make souvenirs and trinkets for tourists. This was their livelihood.

My driver came to a slow halt on top of a hill and pointed down to a colony of slums.

"Down there, it is called Garbage City. I think your friend is living there," he said, examining the piece of paper with the address.

We drove past a squatter settlement where patches of dirt were segregated by ornate green fencing to accommodate rough sleepers and groups of families whose accommodation was a dirt plot. In the slum network women wrapped in layers of rainbow prints balanced giant white bundles on their head as they threaded their way through the web of squalor. Children picked at scraps of tuna from a can as stray dogs watched impassively, and grimy-faced boys sporting *Teenage Mutant Ninja Turtles* shirts or *Knight Rider* tank tops engaged enthusiastically in a vigorous match with a deflated ball. Their delight at each corner or off-side rendered the dusty street a surrogate World Cup arena. Better, perhaps, than their Western counterparts, faces endlessly illuminated by the glow of screens, imprisoned in virtual worlds.

This was Garbage City, *Manshiyat Nasser*, apparently, with no running water or electricity, and it seemed, no infrastructure.

I got out of the taxi to look for Ali's house and the driver walked by me through the neighborhood, to make sure I was safe. Such a kind man. He didn't even want bakhsheesh. Stacks of garbage outside doorways were each family's bread and butter all brought here to be dumped for families to retrieve and sift through, then sort, recreate and trade. Children expertly sorted glass from metal, paper from plastic, transforming waste into vivid lanterns and glittering baubles. Teenage boys guided weary donkeys burdened with mountains of refuse and I wondered what category of garbage Ali's family specialized in.

"In there, in there." My driver, the professor, pointed to a narrow winding mud road strewn with hay. Those fuckers, Farid and Ali, expecting me to come here on my own to formulate the plan for escaping to Iran. What shoddy amateurs. Walking through the restricted back street I noticed a makeshift stall piled with beautiful vintage film cameras, ravishing 1940s/50s radios and telephones, and cans of film, all haphazardly balanced on top of each other. It was as if the museum of vintage gorgeousness had been raided and brought to this mud alley. How I wanted to grab these treasures, all stunning pieces of vintage glamor, and take them home. The old man selling them was asleep on a crate, not knowing their real value. I wanted to shake him awake and find out why on earth these precious items were here and why he wasn't selling them in a shop elsewhere, but I had no time, and I was afraid. Afraid of causing a scene or raising suspicion in the neighborhood.

I opened a heavy iron door. In front of me was a tight cubby hole interior where immediately a set of steep (almost vertical) stairs led up to a naked light bulb dangling from the ceiling. I could hear children laughing, and smell cooking.

"Hey!" the man who opened the door at the top must have heard us. "Come in, come in! Roxana!"

His two screaming kids and a woman all rushed to the door.

I just had to trust *everyone*. The driver and the family and all those who would follow in the coming days. I eschewed any fears of entrapment, murder and theft in this slum and walked up the bunker-tight stairway as the driver waited. Ali's wife had made food with meat, an expensive ingredient for a poor family. I was handed an icy yogurt drink loaded with garlic.

"Ali, I was supposed to meet you in your shop. I had to come here by taxi, and I can't stay for too long," I said. "The driver is waiting for me. I just came to talk about the plans for tomorrow."

"It is better here in my house. You can eat. My wife, she make very good *baba ghanoush*." The pureed smoked aubergine dip was my favorite. I walked back outside and asked the driver to wait for a bit longer and insisted he take a bakhsheesh from me. It would be rude to go to someone's house and leave after all the effort they had made.

Inside, deteriorating walls held court to a dirt floor strewn with slabs of tomb stone decorated with Christmas tinsel. The chunks of stone were used as seating for the family as well as headrests for sleeping on and polyester sheets and bedding were strewn all over the floor. Sleeping next to broken chunks of tombstone couldn't be very good energy, I thought. The condensed residue of all those human lives and histories oozing through into the very zone you were sleeping in.

Two adorable little girls clutching dolls peeped at me, matted ringlets bleached gold by the sun which burnished their skin a blistering copper. The absence of shoes had split their little feet and they had been given bricks to play with indoors to distract them from going outside again. I felt humbled by their kindness and warm welcome despite living in such squalor. They needed to escape Egypt and find a new life in Turkey. They needed me.

"So plan is we meet tomorrow in airport and we go together to Istanbul. You have to say you are our friend from England, okay?" Ali clasped his hands.

"So you all have passports, right?" I asked.

"Yes." Ali got up to bring me their passports. "I will show you the contact in Istanbul. He is very nice. Young. Strong. You will like him." He flexed his bicep muscle and chuckled.

"Ali, do you know why they made me come with you to Istanbul?"

"It's okay, Roxana. We need you to come with us with your British passport to Istanbul and we introduce you to contact. Don't worreeeee!"

Everyone kept telling me not to fucking worreeeee, like it was a bloody holiday.

"Whatever. But I want to check your luggage at airport," I added. For all I knew they were smuggling dark shit and wanted to use me as a mule.

All this hassle and stress to get to my country. Wouldn't it have been less grief to just go via the normal route, get interrogated and imprisoned for a few years?

"Yes, yes," Ali reassured me which made me even more paranoid about choking down the meat and downing the garlic yogurt drink, in case it was drugged. I thanked Sharifa and kissed the children goodbye. I hoped my driver was still waiting for me. I would meet the family at 2:00 p.m. tomorrow at the airport.

"Wait, Roxana!" Ali ran after me as I walked down the cramped stairway. "I have a present for you to say thank you." He brought out a small bottle of liquid and opened the lid.

"It is rose oil perfume for you," he whispered. "You will like very much." He poured the rose oil on the palm of his hand. "Massage?"

"No, no, I don't need a massage." I said politely, but before I could leave, his hands were on my feet rubbing oil in, right up to my knees massaging my thighs. I pulled away.. The lone orange lamp up the stairs was fizzling in and out making the steep stone steps more eerie. I wriggled out of Ali's grip and mumbled a *see you tomorrow*.

"But it's *rose* oil," he shouted, as if *rose* were something you should never turn your back on. It had been a long day in Cairo. It was dark outside. Thieves and robbers and wolf men crept from corners of the tombs. The professor cab driver was still there, bless him. I got in the cab and went back to the hotel. My journey through the mountains would require a steelier resolve than this.

Top: Vintage cameras in Cairo. Bottom: City of Dead.

THIRTY-ONE

It was interesting that the Rock Star's fetish was me wearing the Islamic hejab—a full on burka—with sexy lingerie and stockings peeping from underneath. He seemed to get off on that. We had met a few times backstage, including once at a rock festival in 2010, when he was with a particularly despotic partner. I had watched Billy Idol's set from side stage and walked to the porta cabined area of the dressing rooms when I had heard him calling my name. I was wearing white lace and satin, head full of unicorns and rainbows when he asked me to go to his dressing room, and internally I had gone full on Beatle-mania ready to hyperventilate.

"There's not much rock 'n' roll here except you, Roxana," he drawled in that cool Californian beat. We had sat down sprawled on his sofa and I had just kept thinking: these porta cabins are like something out of a construction site. A lick of paint and a Moroccan lamp wouldn't go amiss. But they are all just a gray square space with a sad little mirror placed in the corner with packets of crisps and orange squash.

He had pursued me before, but being under lock and key of his big, loud overbearing partner who policed his every move, meant that he was shut in his hotel rooms on tour being monitored. So here, in his dressing room, with his body guards outside, we talked and made out. I gave him my book which had just come out.

When not long after that, he slid into my social media DMs and asked me to go to the cinema with him, I had frozen with terror. He was Coca-Cola-famous. We had never met one-on one alone. How would I act? How would I be? I had to be something otherworldly in front of him to keep him interested. A goddess. A siren. I pretended I had a hideous cold and didn't go. It wasn't just out of my depth to do a normal date with the Rock Star, I didn't know if I had the stamina to put on a durable performance of my sexy Roxana Persona for so many hours.

The ingredient of fame is an instant "Superior Human" maker in the human social hierarchy. We have been sold the idea of fame as a device with which to evaluate one's human worth and the obsessive pursuit of fame has been equated with making one a superior human being. The power dynamics between a male of that level of fame and a non-entity female are very unbalanced and hugely in the man's favor.

Famous rock stars were pretty much the only sexual partners I had ever had, temporarily filling some void like Pollyfilla, me having bought into this mythology of superiority. I realized later how their misogyny of demonizing women for their sexuality and lionizing men for theirs, and only having female partners who were meek and subservient to them actually made them very *un* rock 'n' roll. So it was with trepidation that I started messaging him back knowing his legendary status and the fact that I had loved his band from a young age, would always tip the balance of power in his favor.

My immediate gut reaction had been of confusion; why did such a rock legend want me? I didn't understand why he texted me so much or why he was so attracted to me—he could have any woman he wanted, more beautiful, famous, sexy and successful. At least I had a great bulk of education and academic success on my side. Maybe this was my appeal, a novelty for him, a new strange toy from all the porn stars and models he had fucked and dated.

"I don't believe in monogamy," he had messaged me. "But don't tell anyone. In fact, let's get off social media and I'll call you."

Sexual flirtation soon turned into conversation about politics and life. And so it began. He wanted to see me, take me on dates, and take me away. And it timed exactly with him leaving his partner and embarking on a new relationship with a simple beige girlfriend, the polar opposite to his previous partner. And I wondered if she knew his views on monogamy.

As our involvement became more frequent and intense and he hid me from the world, I thought, *It is not your fault, not your fault.* I was the only dark thrill he had now in his sanitized vitamin-popping, granola-munching life with his simple girlfriend. I replaced the thrill of the booze and narcotics he'd been addicted to for so many years. I was the wild tiger, the temptress, the surge of seething febrile carnality he devoured in hotel rooms. I became his secret, lurking side stage, his band nodding their all-knowing smirks at me, sneaking into his hotel rooms after midnight, avoiding photographers, eating separately, stopping my heart. For my heart is a hemophiliac, too late to stop the seeping of the fucking adoration I started to develop for him.

THIRTY-TWO

USA, Ku Klux Klan Compound, 2015

I had been saving up to fly to the southern states of the USA to interview the Ku Klux Klan (or the White Knights of the Klan) in 2015 to add to my journalism portfolio. The Rock Star was playing a show and we arranged to meet. I was determined to be myself and let go of the sexy persona armor. He had told me it was '"safe" territory as his new partner wouldn't be there.

"I am so proud of you and this assignment. I cannot wait to see you," he had messaged.

I could not tell him that I had to work manual jobs so that I could save and fund these assignments. I couldn't tell him that I was seen as an abomination to the world of employers. I was embarrassed, but at the same time, having so much attention and adoration from a rock legend was an antidote to the daily rage and degradation I felt. The texts to my phone that streamed through from a rock legend were little sugar flower love explosions into an otherwise feckless existence.

There were quotidian exchanges and shit Ab-Fab jokes.

"I am so flattered that you like *me* when you could have your pick of rock stars," he said in a text, and I recoiled, the stagnant state of unemployment and *un*-employability jolted by the wanton adoration from a person who was worshipped and at top of the social food chain.

"I just want you to know that I am there with you on that plane when you get scared," he said, knowing my fear of flying, so my usual distress as we hit turbulence morphed into a strange glowing high.

I flew to New Orleans first, to smear myself all over the city. The murky, funereal heavens enveloped me. I was smudged with jazz and French and Spanish colonialism, and prickly little voodoo shops all festering with the city's heritage of slavery markets, ships bursting with human cargo, shackled and muzzled and paraded for auction, the silent heaving of drowned souls and powdered bones retching from the haunted Mississippi river.

I ate my feelings with crawfish and jambalaya because I wasn't quite ready to hop over to the Rock Star's hotel in New Orleans as he had suggested. I would just wait till Nashville. I had to mentally build myself up. It wasn't a concert day, so he was relaxed and happy, waiting to see me. It would still be too "normal" of a date for me, and it terrified me that the real me might break through from behind the satin corset and pillow lips: It would be icky. I felt more *in flagrante* backstage or in post-concert groupie mode. I could not get comfortable that such a rock legend liked me for me. Instead, I left his texts unanswered and lavished all my energy on the voodoo woman I had made an appointment to see.

A few days later, in a city to meet the Ku Klux Klan, an old marm cab driver, silver-bunned and moist with chicken grease, told me that she could feel that I had a special place in hell. I was in her taxi and she was driving me to where the White Knights of the Klan were waiting for me to join them in their compound. On the long drive, during which she put on wailing evangelical music CDs and praised Jesus, I had somehow ended up telling her that I was seeing a legendary rock star who already had a girlfriend and that I had spent the previous night with him.

"Rock 'n' roll is the devil's music and fornication with the man whose demonic body is possessed to bring in Satan's music is fornication with Satan himself!"

Last night, "Satan" had been shy and weirdly flattered that I would be interested in him. Alone in his hotel room after his concert, this was our first pre-planned one-on-one alone. Having finally left his controlling partner for a new girlfriend, he was suddenly catapulted into the outside world, blinking into the sun after years of darkness. He had found himself a total opposite girl but still wanted to start things with me to add fire and spice to his life.

He was so charismatic on stage, his aura and energy hypnotic. With me, he was like a different person; the bloke from down the pub. But still, the power structure was massively unequal. He was worshipped and adored, and unless he was with someone equally famous, the power dynamics always worked in his favor. He'd had celebrity girlfriends- beautiful models, actresses—in the 1980s, when he was pickled in booze and fried with narcotics. But now that he was sober and clean and could make clear judgements, he still wanted me.

"The devil's music," the cab driver repeated, turning to look at me. Thick cola bottle glasses magnified her eyes into giant owl peepers, and she fixed me with a hard stare, her grin a set of blackened jagged teeth. "You are cursed," she drawled, the slick of lard a-shimmer on her fleshy pudding face.

Bon Jovi came on the radio.

She shrieked.

When I told her I was from Iran, she stopped the car and told me to get out. I got off on the dirt road somewhere near this town and hitchhiked to the place where I was going to meet the KKK.

Photos by Anthony Karen

THIRTY-THREE

A girl named Clarice who was a fan of my book had put me in touch with the exalted cyclops of one of the chapters, and through a series of anonymous skype calls and messages I made plans to meet with a couple of ghouls—probationary members—for a cross illumination ceremony.

When I got to the meeting point, Dwayne, a local Klansman, was waiting in his truck to take me to the compound, and I was driven into the woods by two Klansmen as Dwayne sang *The White Man Marches on* in his whiskey-soused baritone.

My eyes have seen the glory of the tramplin at the zoo, We washed ourselves in n***rs blood and all the mongrels too, We're taking down the zog machine jew by jew by jew, The white man marches on…

As we chugged along sluggishly in an old truck toward a cross illumination ceremony, Larry talked about AIDS.

"Hey, you listen to me now," he slurred, the luscious pulp of his nose sprinkled with blood vessels. The black cloth of his uniform stamped with patches of the KKK insignia. "We're jes tryin" ta educate you. You from England, you need to learn a lot about our history. All the lies that our government has told you. AIDS is a black disease. It has scientifically been proven that the white race—even white homosexuals—have a natural immunity to AIDS because of their race."

The Rock Star had begged me not to tell them of my Iranian-ess even though I had been dying to, just to see their reactions. He had made me text him the exact location of where I would be and at what times, and it occurred to me that he was the only one who knew my exact location and who I was with—not my family or friends.

I had done my homework on the Klan—their roots, their rise, and what their now-dwindling numbers might still represent, if anything at all. From the confederates in the aftermath of the civil war thwarting the newly freed slaves' rights by returning them to a state of captivity, to hooded Klansmen posing as ghosts of confederates to frighten newly freed superstitious slaves, to the surge in membership during the 1920s when fear of immigrants fuelled their expansion into the millions, and their members quietly claimed positions of power in small-town governments—it was a long, disturbing lineage. If I could link all that history to my own experience at a cross lighting ceremony, I figured it would make for a deep, complicated piece—too compelling not to publish on my blog.

I was searched when we reached the compound. They checked my bag, body, and shoes before we drove through to the sanctuary of the Klan. Babies were bouncing on laps, wooden benches spilled with happy, animated folk, their apple-cheeks a-flush. A band was playing on a makeshift stage. There was a bake sale and a sizzling barbeque and gurgling rings of children. From a distance it all seemed like a typical suburban family gathering, except the little children running around were occasionally cooing "white power" as they waddled around, and their proud mommies and daddies all wore robes with squiggly insignias. And the snacks were displayed under swathes of swastika and confederate flags. And the band was not drawling bloated country love songs but screeching lyrics about how "niggers must die" and "kikes and mongrels belong in the jungle."

A couple, senior Klan members, took me aside for a little tete a tete: "Our teenage boys have been Klan members since birth," Linda told me, her eyes peeking from the slits of the conical white hat. The rest of the family, their heads hidden under white pointy hats, nodded in unison.

"Do you like being in the Klan?" I asked one teenage son.

"I do, because I hate disgusting people," he told me. "Minorities are only concerned with selling drugs at schools."

When I proffered that white people sell drugs too, Linda gawked at me incredulously.

"Only because the Mexicans, the muds have been forcing it onto them as kids. They have ruined our race, our white nation."

Elsewhere on the craft sale stands were black wooden dolls with knives stabbed through them and a noose around the neck.

"Ornaments for the home, dear. Twenty dollars. Would you like one?" An old lady was selling cakes and cookies next to the dolls, her voice warm and churchy toned. "They make good kids' gifts. One to take back home?"

I was not so naïve to have imagined educating these people, nor did I for once second believe that by challenging them in any way I would be reciprocated with enlightening discussions.

"Do you think these dolls with knives in them are healthy for children to play with? Teaching them violence from an early age is good?" I asked Linda.

"Hell, we played with toy guns pretending to shoot Indians when I was a kid and that teached us from early on who the bad guys were," her husband replied from underneath his hood.

The dolls had exaggerated features like bulging eyes and big lips, but the way they had been carved, was to have miniature knives stabbed through them and nooses around their necks. Disassociation, developed by me as a child as coping mechanism, was a superb skill to have as an investigative journalist, and I was lucky I didn't have to feel anything in situations like this.

Before interviewing the Imperial Wizard and the Grand Cyclops, there were speeches on the podium, and Joel the Grand Dragon was whipping the crowd into a frenzy.

Apparently, the Bible was all about the hate.

"The Bible says don't mix races, the Bible says sodomy is evil, the Bible says the Jews are the enemy. It is against the law of Jesus to produce mongrels and under-breeds." Despite these proclamations, Ron, Joel, Justin, and Wayne, a couple of grand titans, and an exalted cyclops were adamant that they were spreading a message of love and that the Klan's history of murder and violence was due to "Our forefathers had to do what they did because savages were raping their women and children, stealing, being like wild animals. For the Klan, it was the only way to protect their families."

There was phrenology drivel and musings of the Antebellum South and a palpable inanity I couldn't wait to regale my rock star with. He was proud of my assignment and had been worried about my safety, but he'd have a chuckle.

"There's a war against white people. We have no rights in this country," Wayne, a Ghoul, looked at me, a blurry alco-gaze and a patina of self-harm scars on his arms. "My brother was killed by a black gang in an initiation ceremony. Not one fucking person was convicted of the crime. I went into depression for one year. I decided to join up when I saw how the White Knights wanted to change the law to stand up for white people. All the black and spics get all the jobs. The kikes are running this country. Niggers have brought AIDS and disease from Africa and our communist government is letting the faggots make a mockery of Christian values. We the whites don't get any jobs. We don't got nothing, just a kick in the teeth since we was kids."

The cross illumination ceremony was about to start, and Ron and the others walked to the middle of the wooded area. A huge cross was steeped in kerosene and set aflame; a circle of Klansmen lit their own crosses from it.

"Klansman, do you accept the light?" asked Ron.

I asked about the burning of the cross, which had been a sacred Klan ceremony since 1915.

"We are lighting the cross to glorify the light of Jesus Christ; to bring him back from the dark," Joel said.

Several gay pride rainbow flag were also set ablaze, and I noticed that the compound, itself ringed in barbed wire, was a training ground. New recruits were going to be taught armed and physical combat and indoctrinated into white supremacist ideology here.

After my interviews under the pewter sky burnished crimson by burning crosses, I savored my last lungful of sweetly toxic cigarette smoke before hopping in a van with a couple of monosyllabic inbreds, their pamphlets stacked in the backseat for a night of leafleting, and I was driven back by my hotel, where I'd sit all night to write the article. I fell asleep on the floor curled up beside the bed, lulled into euphoria by the honeyed words of pride, support, and admiration dribbling into my ear from the rock star.

THIRTY-FOUR

Back in England I continued with my full-time job applying for jobs and being told the same thing, my affair with the Rock Star still the only thing holding me together.

"A whore she is," my stepdad said, loving as always.

I had worn a long, high-necked conservative dress to some Iranian celebration I had attended with my family and seen him snigger from across the room.

"Everybody, and I mean everyone, was laughing at you behind your back," he'd hissed at me later that night.

"Why?"

"You looked like one of those working-class tacky old women," he spat back.

"No, I didn't." I stood my ground. "I think I looked really nice."

"In your dreams! You haven't got a job, you don't even have a PhD…you don't have a life." He said the last bit with a cockney accent for effect.

My mother interjected and told him to hush up and my phone chimed with texts from the Rock Star.

"I am more than flattered that you have any interest in me," he said.

"Are you crazy?!!" I replied. "You have been with super models and porn stars. It should be me that is flattered."

"Don't be crazy! You're not just a pretty face. You are intelligent, courageous, academic, and beautiful."

I laughed out loud at the absurdity of my life.

We met in Europe a couple of weeks later. He had been bombarding my phone from the tour bus on the way to the hotel.

"Are you in your room? What are you doing?"

"Alas, yes. I am having one drink and listening to The Doors," I replied.

"Do you need me to bring you anything? I can't drink anymore, so I can't join you."

"I know that," I said. "And you should never smoke either. Just keep eating healthy and look after that punctured heart. You have damaged it enough over the years."

"Fuck yeah, I gave up cigarettes, too," he said. "I love how you don't want me to drink or smoke. My ex got high all the time in front of me."

The fact that he was so sober and normal made me more jittery. No chemical smog distorting his gaze. Just raw, alert presence. Although it was such a turn on that he wasn't a slave to substances, his composure left me exposed. With him sharp and unblurred, it would be harder for me to keep up my larger than life sexually confident persona, to smother the pedestrian truth: that I was, in fact, the sort of woman who genuinely liked reading academic books for fun, doing laundry, and wearing socks to bed.

Walking—*floating*—through the warm velvety corridors of midnight silence as I inched closer to his room, I was petrified, and any sexual arousal was choked and suffocated. He opened the door, and it was like a film had come to life. I was shaking as

We laid on his bed cuddling and kissing all night. I gave him a massage, and we talked about his life and his girlfriend. He loved her so much…yet he wanted to spend time with me. I tried to decouple my body from feelings of affection—an unnatural exercise—whilst making out heavily, but one necessitated by the fact that I couldn't let feelings get in.

We talked about my book.

"I don't want to know your sexual history," he stopped me. "I don't want to think about it."

"Really?" I said, "Why? Your sexual history makes me look like Mother Teresa!"

He bristled—his shyness laced with a vintage sexism. This was a man who could casually mention a night out with a supermodel, then cringe at her "looseness."

"Loose?" I repeated. "As in, sexually?"

"Yeah. She's loose."

"And what does that make you?" I shot back. Smile, but not joking.

The next day, he messaged: "Why didn't you make the first move? I wanted you to. I was so turned on but didn't know what to do."

"You *are*..." I began, unable to finish. I still couldn't call him by his stage name—it felt like invoking a cartoon. I used his birth name. It suited this iteration better.

Outside the hotels the band stayed in was always swarming with fans, waiting outside for photos and autographs and security that made Fort Knox's look lax. It made our meets exciting at first, and then extremely upsetting and stressful for me. His bodyguards helped, meeting me and taking me through the throng of hysterical crowds. But more than once, I found myself subjected to gestapo-style questioning by hotel personnel to the point that I was in tears and forced to furnish proof of my legitimacy in the form of text messages—"See, he invited me"—as though I were bluffing my way into the presence of the pope, until he sent his bodyguards to confront the hotel staff and to get me.

We bonded fast and I realized that the same way I was nothing like my persona, he was nothing like his. He became a man I adored rather than a mythical creature. Less a legend, more a contradiction. It was jarring. As if the man I'd idolized since I was thirteen had died mid drug overdose in the eighties and been replaced by a clone—a laidback, soft-spoken imposter who liked me to take charge in life and in sex, to initiate and formulate our plans.

Maybe his crazy debauched iconic reputation had been manufactured in the rock star factory by little Oompa-Loompas. Maybe the "crazy" version had been a PR construct, the kind churned out by record labels and cocaine.

Nevertheless, now sober and clean, he chased me unobtrusively and I was astonished all the time. What was his agenda? For there is always a warped agenda for a rock legend to chase a council estate loser like me. I was probably just a novelty, a palate cleanser between porn stars and his sweet girlfriend.

And when I saw him next and he listened to me talk about Henry, his face darkened, and he snatched my phone. "I'm gonna call him and tell him you're here with me," he giggled.

"Please don't do that," I took the phone off his hands. I didn't know whether he was jealous or just messing around.

"I am not so naïve to think that I am the only rock star you are seeing," he said as he gave me phone back. "I am just flattered you like me."

"Are you still on the gear?" I fixed him with a loopy grin.

This boy—because he *was* a boy, curled inside a man's mythology—was leonine one moment and bashful the next. I'd read books about him: stadiums, hookers, OD comas, the inevitable groupies. But global wealth brought pat-a-cake friends and yes-men which insulated him from the real world. When I told him about a violent ex, he considered it earth-shattering, like these things actually happen to people? Or when I told him about the human rights abuses in Iran, he gawked at me incredulously, as if I were talking about an alien race. It was like he lived his life in a Disney bubble now. That, or the drugs had really taken their toll and his rational thinking was all out of whack.

We talked almost daily, and I would kick my phone away every time he texted me as it was too overwhelming, and for the fear of the heart's first leak that inevitably becomes the tsunami of adoration. I had trained my heart well into extracting that blood red mojo of adoration and pouring it into a capsule for storage.

As time went by, I had started to realize that he liked to be told what to do, that he wasn't just submissive in bed. He wanted me to take the lead, to tell him where to meet, what to do and how to do it. That summer in Spain, when the incandescent Mediterranean heat grilled me charcoal and the dusty scorched concrete burned my feet as I walked the city's streets, most vexing of all was that once again I had to go to the show and pretend to be a fucking fan. I understood that I had to be a secret so his sweet girlfriend wouldn't find out, but at the same time I wanted him to be proud that he knew me. Being kept a secret sometimes made me feel like some criminal.

The night before, on my way to get food, I avoided his bandmates and scurried back to my room, which was practically next to his. I waited till he finished with interviews and had gone to his room, where we fell into each other's arms as soon as he opened the door, and despite my anxiety that my gooey emotions were starting to drool over from their solidly sealed vial, I felt so happy to see him. I laughed at his downtime attire of white towel bathrobe and scolded him for wearing jeans that were too tight—he liked me being bossy and telling him off .

His room was bare as was his bathroom, and he was divinely devoid of all I found repugnant in men: aftershave, perfumes, artificial smells, blindingly white cosmetic dentistry and manicures. His skin was velveteen, typical of those with extreme wealth and a good life, his mouth a plump perfect cupid's bow. His breathing was shallow, his lungs and heart rusty from years of wear and tear, his voice a warm velvet whisky drawl as he leaned over me.

"Baby, why are you so nervous?"

I squirmed beneath him.

He brought his face down close to mine and sucked my mouth and lips. My body remembered how other rock stars had also love-bombed me: needing me, being romantic and adoring, and then suddenly flipping the switch to cold or abusive. I couldn't let go. He was on top of me and even though he was so shy and sweet and down to earth, my body was not falling for this shtick again.

"Why are you so nervous?" he asked again shyly.

Images of his famous past girlfriends were flashing in my head. I looked like a potato. A dumpy council state potato. He was so beautiful and naturally sensual that I felt tiny. Exploring his body, touching his hair, kissing him, letting him make love to me, I did it all with such fear and nervousness that he must have thought I was such a shit lay. But also…I did not want to feel a thing; like being at the dentist. If I let myself feel, the sutures of my heart would gently loosen, commencing a bloody lovely adoration that would metamorphose into a volcano of love that would be the death of me—because I could never be with him. and I did not want to be his girlfriend or partner. I wanted him to be with his Mini-Mouse girl and for us to be lovers and friends.

But it doesn't always work like that; feelings get in the way. So when he kissed me, I was a mannequin, so much so that when he went down on me my orgasm felt like stifling a sneeze.

I was on my period. Still, he was happy to give me oral sex.

"Are you bleeding?" he drawled.

"Yes," I froze, even though I had always liked blood-sports. He devoured all of my bleeding pussy, but I just couldn't fully let go, because my vagina recognized that this was a rock star and all arousal would serve as an appetizer to the main entrée of hell that would follow.

He was quiet and meek even when he was performing anilingus. Maybe he felt *obliged, coerced*. Maybe he felt he ought to live up to his image. He wasn't nervous or awkward or even alpha-male sexually aggressive but little boy shy and cute. How had he fucked so many porn queens and models? It must have been the colossal number of stimulants and opiates he was eyeballs deep in that had made him a different kind of creature back in the 1980s.

"Was I okay? Did I live up to your expectations?" he asked.

"You know how much I like you." I stroked his face. "You are beautiful."

"Oh God, stop, I am not." He put a pillow over his face and squeezed hard.

" I do adore you, Roxana," he said. "It is torture. I can't break her heart."

"You're naturally polyamorous," I sighed. "You need to be true to yourself."

I would have loved him to fool around in bed with other women; it would have been a real turn-on had I been his girlfriend.

I gave him a massage and kissed his back and his legs full of history, full of stadiums, booze and over-doses, full of the gods' magic sprinkle. The room went all liquid and wobbly and I swooned. How many women would give their life to be with him?

"I don't know how I am still alive," he said. "I should be dead by now."

"Do you ever miss alcohol?" I leaned over him exploring his tattoos, faded and crude from the eighties.

He looked up at me. "No. I miss the *other* thing." Then he kissed me. Took my head in his hands and kissed my lips, neck, face, and hair. "Let's go to Edinburgh for a week."

I had been going on about its underground city and its history and he wanted to go away with me. It would be good to get way with him, to be make-up free, to be me, to be normal. We both had a fetish for the haunted, for the gothic, and I was an expert of haunted places in the UK, having spent time exploring Edinburgh's underground city and its history. Macabre curiosities we had in common, except he had lived in a Disney chimera of wealth and cossettedness, and I had lived the real horror of things.

Beehive houses in Harran.

THIRTY-FIVE

Turkey, 2016

The authorities had said nothing of the raggedy family and their British "friend" at the Istanbul customs, and I wondered if I had been used as some sort of bait for whatever it was they were doing. That they were utilizing me as some sort of mule, had crossed my mind at the airport in Cairo. I had checked their luggage as well as mine, but that still wouldn't stop everything becoming a bit Midnight Express-y. I was yet to pay my first installment of the smuggling fee to the contact in Turkey, so between this favor and my non-payment, I wondered if any plans would actually materialize or whether this was just a ploy to get me to come to Turkey with an asylum-seeking family for whatever reason. I helped Sharifa with the children. I was sure they preferred to live here in Turkey than the City of Dead, on the corner of Trash Avenue and Death Boulevard.

I got a room in a bed and breakfast in Sultanahmet, the old part of Istanbul, and bid goodbye to the family, who were off to stay with friends. Ali gave me the main contact's number and arranged with Elijah to meet me at a hotel in Sirkeci, a district on the tourist strip crammed with hostels and souvenir shops. In my rucksack for the Middle Eastern leg of the journey before the smuggling, I had brought some change of clothes and a couple of chadors and head scarves, my cosmetics and my epilepsy medication, and now I bought a knife, which was probably about as effective as a field mouse preparing for a showdown with a gang of alley cats. But, hey, it made me feel safe.

I felt safe as soon as I met Elijah. He was young, intelligent, a devotee of Persian history and a piquancy for my travails. He had a wealth of contacts in the Turkish Kurdistan region and had been an accomplished human smuggler since he was in his teens, when he began helping people escape Kurdistan or Iran on foot. The Egypt segment of my journey thankfully over, I gladly let myself be wrapped into the fold of Elijah and his tourist group. I transferred the money—in hindsight, given his alpha vibe and over-zealous seduction, he could have easily been a scammer—and instructed my friend in the UK to take over my social media. I had to trust him, for there was nothing else left. The plan was that we would fly to Kars, on the border of Armenia, and then drive with the group to the city of Van on the border of Iran, where I would meet the smugglers and stay on. But I had to meet "the Sheikh" first. Elijah said he had "backup plans" in case the Van deal fell through and I had to go through Iraq. So first we were to fly to the border of Syria to a small town called Sanli Urfa.

That night I went to a Hammam a relic of a bathhouse still inexplicably open long after midnight. From the darkness of the street, I slipped into a warm hum of steam and the peach fuzz of lamplight. Heat-diffused rose oil and foam hissed into a sweltering dense fog and visibility became non-existent. Just like the twilight in Tehran, when my grandmother and I would click shut the door of our home in the alley to venture for a trip to the local bathhouse, my plastic doll in tow.

I lay down on a marble slab alongside the others as groups of women staff walked in a sequence of circles to tend to customers. First it was a rub and lather with some soapy liquid which rose up to castles of foam till your body became just a limp giggling cloud with flailing arms. Then the head and hair was lathered and shampooed, and a succession of metal bowls full of lukewarm water from the fountains were used to wash away the dead skin cells. Soft laughter and the ping of glass and steel echoed against the high frescoed ceiling. Then there was a dark room where a woman gave oil massages on a large tea cloth. The night prayer from the mosque made me feel so lonely. The matronly masseuse, head-scarfed and wobbly, was giddy about going home: brothers and sisters, cousins and neighbors were all at her house—dining, dancing, gossip.

I had lived in England for thirty years and was still considered a foreigner.

"Where are you from?"

"No, I mean originally."

"You look foreign. What's your background?"

From taxi drivers and tipsy pub-goers, from the teenagers I taught to the neighbors who never quite got past polite—some variant of this inquiry always arrived within the first five minutes. They needed a pin on the map. I was someone from *elsewhere*, and the fact I hadn't returned to *elsewhere* just made me peculiar.

From Istanbul we flew to Sanli Urfa, a town near the border of Syria so, Elijah could let his group explore the cave where Abraham was born before hastily driving me to the 5,000-year-old village of Harran to meet the Sheikh. Clusters of beehive-domed houses made of mud and clay bricks—a 3,000-year-old architectural tradition—dotted the ruins like kilns, the domed design designed to fence off the scalding heat and retain cool air inside. The beehive shape of these homes allowed them to endure earthquakes, heavy rain, and violent windstorms, making them a comfortable home, and still in use thousands of years on. They were interconnected by arched passageways to form one big, curved home surrounding a mud courtyard strewn with straw, clay pots, and wagon wheels.

A pair of Bedouin shoes dangled in the arc of the entryway. A snug carpeted with Turkish rugs and kilims layering the walls. It was a culture house for tourists, full of ancient Bedouin culture, kept cold by the stone-built structure and conical stone ceiling, although no one had lived in these particular houses since the eighties. Bedouin costumes and mosaic tiles hung from a sequence of low arches so low we had to crouch down to get into the rooms. Tiny square peepholes chiseled through the lower half of walls let in powerful spotlights of sun-beam into the cool shadowy vaults.

Elijah picked out a Bedouin dress from the overflowing sacks nestled amongst piles of cushions which were stacked against the wall for sleep gatherings.

"Put this on."

I held up the canary yellow robe to the light. The velvet-heavy cloth dragged on the floor.

"You need this," Elijah said as he wrapped layers of turquoise silk around my head to cover my mouth and nose, with only my eyes slitting through.

"And now, for the dress." Elijah put the heavy velvet over my head which shrouded my body tight, falling down to my feet to gently sweep the ground. He then placed a crimson gown over my shoulders, slowly clasping each eyelet, hook, clip and button, to cinch and pull everything into place. My body was bandaged up a rainbow of colors like a traditional Bedouin woman.

We walked out to a waiting white 1970s Mercedes spluttering in the courtyard. Two men with long white *dishdashas* (full robes) and *ghatras* (red and white checkered head covers) and black sunglasses swung out of the front to open the rear door. That's when a bony old man with a shabby houndstooth jacket over traditional robes sluggishly stepped out. His white headdress was secured with the *agal* (the black band fastened to the top of the head to hold the headdress in place) over a weathered face with wire rimmed spectacles. The crowd parted for him as he sauntered to the dais area of the courtyard where kilim-covered canopy beds stacked with Ottoman cushions hosted the shisha smoking and tea drinking area. He beckoned Elijah over and I heard them muttering about the plan while I waited back with an orange Fanta.

"He wants you as his fourth wife," Elijah announced, as if the arrangement were already in place. "He already has the village's most beautiful ones, and he treats them well. The third one he is bored of. She is a teenager." The Sheikh's gaze bore through my shrouded face, his salt and pepper imperial moustache reminding me of old Qajar kings. He fully expected me to break into an ululating, ground-kissing, Allah-thanking exultation at having been given such a coveted golden opportunity—after all, as a female over the age of twenty-five, I was already considered an old spinster.

"Is this part of the deal? Do I have to?"

"No, not if you don't want to, but it would help the situation. No one would mess with you if something happened during the smuggling."

I looked over at my potential husband sprawled back on the canopy bed, smoking a shisha, scratching his balls.

"He says he will shower you with gems."

I imagined a hailstorm of amethyst, jade, rubies, emerald, and sapphire raining down on me. "This is crazy, El. Just sort out the plan and let's get out of here." I was worried that my marriage refusal would anger the Sheikh.

"You need to tell him gently that you will think upon it. Don't just say a flat no. it would be an insult," Elijah muttered as I approached the Sheikh, thanking him for bestowing such an honor upon me by asking me to be his fourth wife. The sheikh gave me his business card just in case I changed my mind or anything happened on my journey.

I snuggled up to Elijah on the way back. I had been so lonely. We laughed about the Sheikh and drove up a mountain to smoke. His tourists could have an evening to themselves. I had to trust everyone I met because otherwise I'd be a paranoid slobbering mess.

I kissed him so he wouldn't hurt me, if hurting was his business.

When we got into Mardin a town near the border of Iraq, I stuck into his hotel room and stayed the night. The illegality in eastern Turkey of an unmarried couple sharing a room and the fact that he would get fired from his job made it more delicious. But the next day in Mardin Elijah was told that one Canadian male in the group had complained to the hotel and made them check their security cameras to see if I had gone into his room. Elijah was going to get arrested. We quickly drove to the city of Van and that night again in his hotel room, Elijah introduced me to Hassan the main smuggler. I was about to embark on my journey to my home. Finally to Iran.

THIRTY-SIX

After my time with the Rock Star in Spain I started to get scared that I was getting in too deep. He had messaged me as soon as he stepped off the plane in LA.

"I want to see you very soon. I miss you profoundly," he said.

I had to be honest with him: "This is an emotional rollercoaster. It's really hard because I like you and you have a girlfriend."

"I feel the same. It is really hard. I don't know what to do. It would break her heart. I adore you, and it's really hard," he kept saying.

I thought about all the famous men I had hung out with, some more iconic than him. I had felt nothing, sometimes even queasy by their energy. I had not wanted to connect with them or be intimate. I had not wanted to be in their life.

It wasn't his fame. He could have been the bloke down the pub.

I didn't know what I was. What do you feel when a man is sexually intimate with you, tells you he adores you and misses you, and messages you all the time to talk about life?

"Why haven't you been messaging me? I never hear from you," he said one night as we had dinner. I had probably not responded to his texts as much as he had, but that was to protect my heart. I kept having to wait until he found out which cities his girlfriend wouldn't be coming to on tour so I could see him. Sometimes she'd change her mind and decide to go to a city we had arranged to meet in, and plans would suddenly change.

An emotional rollercoaster.

"Tell her not to come!" I'd started to grow impatient at this ditzy giggly girl who followed him around 24/7. He wanted basic but he also wanted complex, academic, independent, and sexual. He didn't quite grasp that a woman can be both girl next door housewifey *and* complex.

His constant messaging/love-bombing made me uncomfortable because he was pulling me in, and I knew I would fall for him—and there was no way of recovering from that kind of pain because it was inevitable that one day he would get bored and move on to the next novelty. I tried to stem my heart; to freeze it, to compartmentalize feelings (such nasty little critters) but as legendary rock stars go, this one had subjugated me, the warm hum of his desire for me, (his addiction?) his confusion as to what I am; his mistress? His other girlfriend? Even he didn't know. She would never know of us. She, the doe eyed Bambi, the girl next door, the simple uncomplicated beige love.

I had reached a point where I could not bear another man touching me, and even on my own I could only orgasm if I thought about him. This shocked him, of course.

"Why don't you talk to her honestly? Tell her that you are a wild free spirit and want to be open to being with other partners. She adores you and you her. Be real with her," I told him.

And then, maddeningly, came the music festival. My own laminated access-all-areas badge felt absurdly juvenile as I messaged him from the portable toilets—only to bump into her, that sweet, oblivious Bambi with her blue jeans and innocence. She smiled warmly, utterly unaware of my existence in his darker corners. I felt bad, but I got it. He *wanted* an oblivious girl, a quiet giggly girl who didn't challenge him. I would always be the girl he kept hidden from the world. He loved subterfuge—complications neatly managed. He enjoyed the thrill, the secret tension. I felt reduced to a shameful fascination, like a narcotic.

He had his own Henry Raccoon.

I have never understood music festival goers. Hundreds of thousands of sheep herded into a urine-soaked field having actually *fought* to pay to be in a tent pitched on feces-encrusted mud, eating burger-van meat at arse-fucking prices as the heat or pissing rain scalds or drenchs their drug-addled brains. And apart from the times when Rammstein were there with designated champagne-filled porta cabins in the backstage area to host a collection of girls their roadies had cherry-picked from the crowd, backstage consisted of a bunch of male groupies (also known as male rock journalists) who basically wish they had vaginas to get fucked by a James Hetfield or Rob Flynn. Backstage at Download had become a hive of metrosexuals munching quinoa and guzzling organic chamomile tea, everyone staring into their phone and talking in hushed tones. His apathy extended to the trailer trash trolls who ran his many international fan sites and constantly fed him the most toxic lies about people around him in an effort to curry favor. I kept asking him why he clung on to such vile racist, body-shaming, woman-bashing thugs, and I kept exposing their lies to him, but I realized that their sycophancy was a weird validation he needed all the time.

I nagged him for his utterly bizarre choice of hangers-on whose abusive messages to me had escalated as he had started following me on social media. These associates and fan site runners' entire woeful existence consisted of waiting for him to "like" one of their photos or posts on social media and in a way he fed off it, addicted to these parasites and sycophants who fed his ego. A festering cesspit of subhuman orcs who creamed their pants whenever he so much as tweeted a thank you to the fan club website they had set up in some small-town shithole America.

Yet still he messaged—Christmas mornings, birthdays, Valentine's—he always remembered. But publicly, he recoiled.

THIRTY-SEVEN

Leading up to 2016 the abusive messages on my social media started to come in the form of a middle aged man and woman from the UK whose sole purpose in life was his existence, engaging in any social media posts related to him, his movements, food and beverage consumption.

You skin is shit

You are fat

You are a monster, you deserve to die, kill yourself...

These two had decided to make it their job to send me body-shaming, skin shaming, ethnicity-shaming messages as if a female's body shape and skin, defines her humanity or affects their lives. I would tell him and even though he berated them, he continued his friendship with them which gave them more fuel to send me more and more abusive misogynist messages. He was like the lion in wizard of Oz who has no courage; no backbone to defend me.

I had spoken only to a couple of close friends and my mother about him, so no one knew of the sexual and emotionally intimate nature of our liaison. Perhaps I had been seen at a concert, or at his hotel. Maybe a crew member or band mate had said something to someone. Or maybe it was his bodyguard. I found my social media scrutinized by his fan base and bombarded with personal questions.

These neanderthals berated him for knowing me, because I was of the female gender and had written a book, whereas he, who had also written a book about his life including his many sexual escapades was a hero for it. His followers' attitude was that women should be demonized for their sexuality whilst rock stars such as their beloved who had also written a book should be idolized and celebrated for the very same thing. And although he defended me at times, he was nevertheless very insistent on keeping our association, even as friends a cloak and dagger operation. Sadly he had no balls, no ethics to defend a woman he adored and held in such high esteem like me.

One day he messaged me and said that he wanted to see me in Boston. "It's safe as *she* won't be there," he said as usual. We had missed each other, and I knew how intensive his touring schedule was and how much she was always present. I made plans and got excited and even though I was tired of this secretive business, I was looking forward to just kissing him. I didn't tell anyone but wrote a comment on his band's social media about how much I was looking forward to seeing the band when about two hours later I got a barrage of angry texts from him that fans were messaging his girlfriend to say that I would be present at his show. He was panicked. Why was I telling the world about us? Why couldn't I keep things private?

"Yes, I know a lot of people have a fucked-up mentality, but if any association with you becomes public, it causes me issues."

"You need to change your friends then. Why be friends with misogynists and internet trolls who body-shame women?"

"You don't get it, I don't want the hassle. You are being immature and throwing a tantrum."

He would not defend me to them, the person who he said all those adoring words to because he didn't want the hassle. Whether it was because he didn't want it to get back to his girlfriend, or whether he didn't want public association with a strong intelligent woman, was not relevant. All those rock stars buddies of his who had written boastfully of their graphic sexual encounters and in some cases abuses of women were glorified by him; his best friends. I was hidden, tucked away, invisible. He'd rather not defend me or be proud of being my friend because of the hassle those trolls gave him. And just like that, he lost an amazing woman, a great friend and lover in me. Even though he'd turned out to be another rock star cliché, even now, when I miss him every day, I wonder if he has found another dark thrill to make the beige more manageable.

THIRTY-EIGHT

After all the rock stars, after the mafia boss in LA and after Tommy the psychopath and now a rock legend, Henry had finally had enough. I could not be fixed. This feral rabid creature was still thrashing about, foaming at the mouth, trying to find an outlet for her mixed insides.

So he left. I had damaged him. Taken any form of humanity he had and mangled it. I was the monster, the malignance and had contaminated him with my baggage and rage.

The day after his mother died in Iowa- the mother he had left all on her own to move to England for *me*, for this fucked up unhinged entity- he took me hands in his and looked into my eyes calmly.

"We are no longer together." And just like that he walked off. Off to anywhere. Off to find actual happiness.

I was terrified of what I would do to myself. My grief and pain such that I wanted to be obliterated, exterminated. It was 2016 and I had no one. No friends, no family, no employment.

Since my book had come out in 2010, the ache and longing for Iran had intensified as I felt more and more rejected by the UK media and told that I was unemployable because of my book, my selfhood. The feeling of having this void since the age of ten that was never fulfilled by anything and to remedy this state of being lost, fragmented and isolated, I searched more and more for a way to go to Iran, albeit illegally.

It was after sitting in front of a so-called diversity panel, being told that I did not fit the "correct" diversity category and would probably never get a platform or job in the UK because I wasn't a stereotype, I looked at ways to make contact with human smugglers. A lot of my family had escaped Iran after the revolution on horseback through the Turkish mountains. Why couldn't it be done in reverse?

It wasn't to see my biological father. It wasn't to escape my unfulfilled, chaotic experiences in the West. It was to find silence. It was to suck on the nectar of myths, to seep into villages etched into the mountains like forgotten verses of the Shahnameh, to get sozzled on the air dense with the whispers of spirits and gods, the murmurs of Zoroastrian fire temples. I probably could never live there and always be enraged by the lack of freedom of speech and human rights, economic and societal chaos, but for now, I just needed an infusion of its nectar to pump life into me.

It had been easy to make the contacts in London in the Kurdish communities. Piss-easy. After all everyone wanted to come *to* the UK. For a few thousand US dollars I could easily go back. I wanted to and needed to start my journey in the Middle East first though, to meet with some contacts before I went to Turkey. I also had to get the money and make sure I had enough supply of my epilepsy medication with me. Money was the main issue. I was going to turn to Frank, the mafia boss whose mistress I had been and who had taken me to the Golden Globes back in 2007.

THIRTY-NINE

Los Angeles, 2007

It was the post-abortion trauma and the post brutality that came from the source of that pregnancy that made me leave for LA in 2006. Rock 'n' roll had become my adopted home, so it was inevitable that when I lived on and off in West Hollywood mainly in roach motels, the Rainbow Bar and Grill on the sunset strip became my refuge. Decades-old funk of booze and sweaty balls, underage groupies, runaways and outcasts, hair metal dudes in spandex and unprotected sexual intercourse permeated the décor, never wavering as *the* rock 'n' roll bastion in all its legendary overdose glory. For those wanting to dip in for a bit of 1980s hair metal bubble, it was the best time-capsule.

In 2006 all my acquaintances were sunset strip fixtures: broke and obsessed with resuscitating the corpse of eighties hair metal; boys with washboard torsos not from a gleaming LA gym but from hunger, and strawberry-sweet females that were still box-fresh and un-plagued from the contagion of LA.

On Hollywood boulevard I was eating from taco stands that spewed salmonella and bought my outfits from neon–lit stripper outlets. I hopped from the Rainbow to the Whiskey to the Viper room trying to forget my reality by dressing up in stockings and corsets, stained with roach motels, fags and street food. I was a cliché: bruised heart-fucked female on the strip, post-abortion by a Guns n' Roses member, lonely, swathed in lace and satin, looking for love even though I had a perfectly safe and loving but incompatible Henry back in England.

I had been sitting on my own at the back on a quiet night at the Rainbow, writing a dissertation on "Foucault vs. Freud: the manufacturing of truths" for a rich college student who was paying me when a bovine woman in a dove-gray uniform approached my table. A severe ponytail bungeed her face back, thin pencil brows drawn on.

"Mr. Russo would like to meet you," she said, nudging her head toward the table near the door. At it sat a sallow man with a beak nose hooked over a squiggly mouth. Puddles of eye bags dangled from under his cow-brown eyes and his tuxedo was stuffed with a paunch that spilled onto his lap. He was of penguin man proportions. The napkin tucked into the neck of his shirt had splattered spaghetti sauce on it and he gazed coldly into the distance. His enormous girth no doubt signaled a history of restaurant dinners…Beverly Hills, New York, ravioli, lobster, veal parmigiana, aged whiskey.

I glimpsed at the pile of theory books stained with cockroach matter from where I had whacked them in my motel room. The residue of pureed garlic masked my hair extensions, and my corset was soiled with a film of poverty and upsets. I wondered why this guy had any interest in me, and out of curiosity for the peculiar, I acquiesced. And it wasn't just the men who looked like snitches from *Miami Vice* who scurried to the table that gave me the impression he was some shady wise guy, it was how everyone at the Rainbow blanched when they clocked him. He introduced himself and asked outright if I wanted to go to the Golden Globes with him in January. A girl in a corset poring over academic books had piqued his interest and he wanted to spend time with me. Marsha would take me shopping so I could pick out a dress and jewelry, and we would stay at a hotel together the night before and after the event.

Ahhh…so my carcass and its orifices would have to be available for his use if I were to say yes to the awards and the material goods. I recoiled, I cringed, I felt frightened, but I was dying to meet Harvey Weinstein. I had always harbored a fantasy that meeting the universal gargoyle would be the answer to all my acting dreams. Plus, I was weirdly attracted to his terrifying Goliath thuggery and general sleazy scummyness.

"Marsha will pick you up tomorrow and we'll go for dinner in Beverley Hills," he stated. But I was already meeting up with yet another loser musician who wanted to spend all my money and use me as a cum rag before hurting my feelings, so this was a very difficult choice for me. A limousine and dinner in Beverley hills would totally disrupt my identity and my sense of low self-worth. I was not attracted to Frank and his enormous girth or aardvark face. I was not attracted to luxury Beverly Hills things but to life itself, to a life that I had always known: full of lepers, pariahs, and empty bellies.

The next evening, as Marsha arrived in white leather gloves and driving a limo, a gift was waiting for me on the limo seat: a jeweled bracelet from Frank.

All I kept thinking was how much free nachos were next to my seat and not what shady characters might be waiting for me at our destination.

When I got there, the restaurant was deserted. Frank sat in back with two men who instantly got up and stood by the door as I arrived. Everything on the menu had already been ordered.

He stood up, spangled with martinis. "Hey, baby cat, you know how glad I am to see you? You know how glad I am to have met you? It was fate kid."

His eagerness was rube-ish and elementary. Holding me in high esteem because I had a cut-glass English accent and was cultured and educated would have been flattering through the lens of an erudite man, but from a boorish Mafioso whose palate was desensitized by a life-long conveyor belt of Vegas strippers and hookers, it didn't hold the same weight. He just didn't understand why I liked hanging out with musicians—sleazy, broke knuckleheads who were clearly so "beneath me"—when there were guys like him proposing fur, Bev Hills dinners, gold chains, and limos. I don't think he'd quite grasped the concept of "Gotti" and nouveau riche or that he was the epitome of it. I tried to imagine what rank he was as he sang me Dean Martin songs. Definitely not a foot soldier but probably a caporegime or an underboss. I didn't really care to find out. His bodyguards planted by the door in an empty restaurant intrigued me, though.

"I'll get you what you want, kid," Frank beamed. "Let Marsha take you shopping tomorrow. You get whatever you want. Any dress, any shoes, anything."

A man taking me shopping was so strange to me. Too saccharine, really. It signalled a get out of jail free card; giving him carte blanche to do what he wanted with me, to own me.

"You don't realize how beautiful you are," Frank simpered, gooey with Glenfiddich. "That's why I like you so much. Natural, educated, and not LA and fake."

I cringed as I shoveled gnocchi, pasta, lobster, clams, ice cream, cake, and champagne into my gob like a stray dog. Food, clothes, Golden Globes. Christ, I was really selling my body, wasn't I?

In the back of the limo, I watched him ugly-cry as he crapped on about someone he had killed.

"I killed my father, I killed my brother..."

He wept to himself, eventually trailing off incoherently, slack mouth drooling. I rolled my eyes; probably just some lines from *The Sopranos* or *The Godfather* he'd wished were true, so he was the Don or Capo di Tutti. Rolls of notes tied in elastic tumbled out of his pockets like a bundle of skittles on the limo floor. I gathered them haphazardly and stuffed them back into his pockets, Marsha stealing glances in the mirror. It was probably a test of trust for them. Then I kissed his sticky cheeks and went back to my cockroaches.

That night I called Henry and regaled him with the night's stories. He chuckled and mimicked lines from the mob movies we both loved. He was missing me so much and as with the rock stars I hung out with he didn't ask details of what I was doing with them because his sweet innocent Robin heart would be lacerated if he acknowledge what he suspected deep down. Ignorance was bliss to him. I really missed him too and deep down, I wished I didn't have such a gamut of issues, demons, and ambitions that needed feeding and facilitating. But then I wouldn't have suctioned onto Henry as safety if I didn't have those issues.

There is no fashion in LA. London, Paris, and New York spawn art, the avant-garde, punk, and kitsch. LA is generic mall fashion: imitations of conceptualization. Even the so-called rock 'n' roll and goth shops in Melrose are garden variety reproductions: dyed black pieces of material with safety pins, studs and patches. Marsha found my declining to shop on Rodeo Drive as a sign of someone with serious mental health problems. My request indicated a trip to dress designers who could knock up a piece of old Hollywood glamor with an exotic vivant, a Theda Bara vibe. The dress they would eventually make for me was blood red silk with hand sewn beads.

Frank proudly introduced me to his New York buddies who were in town and basically a collective of Sopranos rejects. I lost count of how many Tommy Two-Tones, Mikey Baby Faces, Jimmy the Sniffs, Johnny Irishes, and Bill the Butchers I met. And the extravagant dinners in prestigious establishments only made this bunch more of an eyesore: above the ping and scrape of crystal and steel, a fug of aftershave, gold chains and perma-tanned alligator skin.

"Did you take care of that thing?"

"What thing—the first thing or the second thing?"

"No, no, that other thing."

"Oh yeah, yeah, Vinny the Chin from Pittsburgh took care of it," was the rhythm and tempo of our table, which was piled high with the rusty exoskeletons of crustaceans cracked open and scraped off on top of rare steak and veal parmigiana, aged whiskey, and red wine. No more taco stands. Within the week I had gotten fatter, my corsets requiring extra room. No more Sunset Strip, either, as I was forbidden from stepping foot there or hanging out with musicians and going to the Rainbow as it would be too disrespectful to Frank. At the restaurants, security men were planted like centurions at the entrance or by windows.

I excused myself to go to the bathroom and Frank had a bodyguard accompany me to the toilet, standing outside the door while I used it as if I were likely to get whacked whilst taking a piss.

Frank cooed over me like a baby, hand feeding me portions of everything on the menu while he placed little kisses all along my arm and gazed at me like a lovesick puppy. He thrust venison in my mouth, which I spat out in disgust—and then he tried it again with veal and foie gras. And even after I'd tried to educate him on animal torture, he went and bought me a couple of fur coats, which made me so fucking enraged that I slapped his aardvark face.

Frank wanted to keep me padded in a little drawer lined with perfumed paper. I was distant to him, fake-polite and snappy. Perhaps this is why he wanted me more and more: because men only want something that's a challenge. He knew I was only enduring him till the Golden Globes, and when he'd come to touch me, I would be mechanical and non-affectionate. Frank Russo: his criminal body against mine. Not a Ray Liotta or an Al Pacino but a sloth man with enormous girth and droopy lids. I made it quite obvious from my body language that I did not like being intimate with him in any way. All he did was sink booze, talk "business" with his associates, take me for dinners in expensive places, and make me dress like an old woman. I was forbidden from wearing anything too sexy; I had to be all covered up in plain grandma clothing. In only a matter of a few days, I was bored. I liked being in close proximity of seedy sunset strip creatures. At least their loserville lives had an edge.

He had taken me out of the roach motel and put me up in a very luxury albeit Gotti hotel full of old white people who played golf. Some nights he'd stay and in the morning take me to his murder and extortion meetings, and I would plug up my basic human receptors from absorbing any information. I would sit by myself in a different part of the room with either Marsha or a bodyguard, away from the talks until he had a break and came to the table for a scotch and veal. There was no chance to get away. I was under Frank's surveillance nearly twenty-four hours a day, and even when I made an excuse to go and see a girlfriend, I would be driven there and Marsha would be told to wait until I was finished so she could drive me back.

Having bodyguards everywhere also made me realize that Frank was always a target which made me a target. I didn't know too much about what exactly Frank did, nor did I want to know too much in case it was used against me. Sometimes I'd hear names of sport players being paid off, sometimes they'd talk about a lawyer and judges being a *gavone* or if someone was a *fenook*, but I tried not to listen too closely. Frank always had stacks of cash on him, and he owned a couple of casinos, strip clubs, and construction businesses, but I'd rather not know whom he had ordered to be killed. Sometimes at night when he came to my hotel, he would sit on a chair just staring into the dark and drinking and not wanting me to be near him, which was great for me but also made it impossible for me to fall asleep not knowing what he would do. Some nights he would mention his father, muttering something about "that night," and his face would darken.

"I want to buy you an apartment in Santa Monica. Would you like that, my Persian princess?" He'd kneel in front of me holding my hand as I, in my pajamas, fucked off and bitchy at my sleep being constantly interrupted, told him to fucking leave me alone and let me sleep and stop singing Frank Sinatra and not to touch me.

"What about a car?"

"Well, I don't bloody drive in America, so how can I drive it?" It wasn't that I hated him; he was just so annoying. Also, I love sleeping, and anyone who disrupts my sleep is a terrorist.

No one had talked to him that way and I'm sure that's why he was intrigued by me, his brain muddling frustration with serotonin. And because I didn't demand the usual material things from him, he wanted to give them to me even more. One night as the bundles of rolled notes were flung on the nightstand and Frank was gurgling in an intoxicated stupor, I decided to count how much was in each bundle. Tip toeing to the bathroom to count out the bills by the mirror, my heart was giddy as I leafed through one bundle of cash. It was one thousand dollars and there were eight or so other bundles on the nightstand. Would he notice if one was gone? Was this a test to see if I would take one? As much as Frank adored me, he was still a mafia guy. I put the bundle back with the rest of the stack.

It wasn't only my dream of going to the Golden Globes that kept me hanging out with Frank; I could eat and stay in roach-free hotel rooms now, and I did not want to go back home to the UK. I was sick of poverty and living hand to mouth, and I was sick of my stepfather's constant name-calling. But I couldn't withstand the cossetting of Frank, either, so one night I told Frank that I was going out and there wasn't a damn thing he could do about it.

I got my friend and bro Zack to take me to a famous rock producer's house. The designated house of unholy activity, where LA's most degenerate cretins hung out alongside box-fresh teen actors. Zack would not touch the place, but Jimmy, the producer. had always instructed me not to bring guys anyway. It was the first time I had gone there alone, and I found it really scary but exciting. The high-powered seemed to be attracted to the scummy energy of low lives as an antidote to their high-octane power roles.

Inside, there was a fountain in the middle of a lobby and death metal blared. Pig-tailed, makeup free girls with Mickey Mouse tops flitted about and biker gang members chatted to an up-and-coming band that Jimmy was producing. People hung off the banisters or pored over scripts in the diner style banquets seating.

I had never known anyone as insane as Jimmy. He was a combination of a biker and a gangsta rapper. A jet-black handlebar moustache and teeth gleaming with gold grills. From a heavily tattooed trunk neck hung a dozen gold rope chains, knuckles dusted with love/hate weighed down with clusters of diamond, jade and ruby hip hop bling rings. To finish the look he wore a Hell's Angels leather jacket and leather biker pants

I passed another room with brocade curtains. A group of people were doing some sort of séance. Feathers and bones and binding dispersed over the table while the necromancer beckoned a famous actor who was leaning against the doorway. He always played terrifying characters with that quiet menace and blazing blue eyes. I had loved him in a Tarantino film. Taking a brazen chance, I took his hand, leading him downstairs and into a quiet booth where I lay my head on his denimed lap and gazed into his eye as he whispered to me in that thick New York accent of his. I swooned, basking in the arousing heat of fame, the dopamine high of this alpha-male movie star. How the tones and shades of mafia are Disney-fied in Hollywood films, I thought; women want to fuck them, and men want to be them. The sexual charisma, the wit, the endearing vulnerability, the torment inside. Funny how as a real mafia guy Frank had *none* of these.

Our heavy petting had spilled into a small party up in the studio with Jimmy, a reality TV star, and a male porn star, and I hadn't even had a drink like everyone else because of my epilepsy so the night for me fizzled out by 4 a.m. I staggered into the dawn, rearranging my features the way you do for your parents when you're past your curfew and know they've stayed up all night waiting for you to get home. I went to a cheap motel to avoid Frank and tried to sleep for a bit. I thought about AIDS. I hadn't used a condom with those people. Why did I always put my life at such risk? I called Jimmy, who was still partying, and then the porn actor. They reassured me that they were clean. I was still terrified of HIV, though, and couldn't sleep. Why had I done it? I shuffled in bed.

Outside the motel door, footsteps approached. Probably early morning cleaners.

Then Frank burst into the room with two massive Samoans.

"You were followed and filmed in that garbage's house," he barked, stumbling, rheumy-eyed.

"Fucking following me everywhere, you fucking freak!" I threw a glass at him, narrowly missing his jaw. "Constantly having your goons follow my every move, how fucking sad. You don't even know how to dress, like a fucking peasant you are! You don't even know how to spell properly, write *English*!" I was incandescent with rage.

"I have the recording from your time in the party and with that faggot actor."

Faggot actor? He certainly had not been a faggot with *me*.

Frank reeled off a list of names, places, and exact times from the previous night. He knew when I went into the party, the exact time I went downstairs to hang out with an actor, and exactly who I had chatted with at what time. The chief executioner reading out the list of the crimes of high treason to the accused. I was dumbfounded and apoplectic with rage. Surely, he didn't have a hidden camera in that party? Or a spy? Doom zapped through my veins, the impending feeling that I was about to get seriously hurt. Frank's feelings for me weren't the soft fluffy kind; but an affliction onto himself. I couldn't believe how my exact movements at their exact times had been logged and noted. I imagined a factory with rows and rows of identikit employees typing and cyber-hacking into the night. Samoan bodyguards at the ready, waiting to pounce in case I tried to get away, I pleaded my case to Frank and lied that I was just drunk and didn't know what I was doing. He just stepped close and said: "Come on, kid. Let's go for a ride."

FORTY

Two big guys were sitting at the front with one of them driving. I was in the back of the car with Frank. I was in last night's clothes, the ones I had fallen asleep in. I thought, if I caught HIV, then it's better that I get murdered anyway. Just make it quick.

On a small camera, Frank was showing me the video footage of everything I had done the previous night. I had been followed and somehow someone had planted cameras in Jimmy's house.

"Do you see how you have humiliated me?" Frank kept saying.

I hadn't understood what I was playing with.

We drove for what seemed like ages, somewhere out of town, and then the car stopped off a highway by a dilapidated warehouse and the two men got out. I was strangely calm, passive. Frank grabbed my face and whispered, "You don't know what you have done. You're not mine anymore. My guys in New York…they know about it. I'm their boss. Do you understand how I look to them now? What am I supposed to do with you now?"

"Frank, please," I appealed to this man I found repugnant. "Let's just talk about it. I know how much you care about me, and I really care about you. I just got wild and carried away." I could hear my voice wobbling, threatening to break.

"How could you choose that over Frank?" Pitbull number one snarled from the front.

"You chose that fuckin' hippy bum over a classy guy who gets you anything you want?" Tony had a gun, so I didn't argue. He was tall and chiseled with an aquiline nose and exquisite suits, a contrast to Frank's gold-dripping greasy Guido chic. He was the type that would overrule Frank's orders just because he got off on the violence, the kind to do a hit less for the money and more to quench his bloodlust. Even if I cut ties with Frank, his subhuman orcs would follow me if I stayed in LA. Street soldiers involved in extortion, fraud, drug and human trafficking, gambling, loan sharking and murder. Individuals hired for their penchant for violence.

Frank had tears in his eyes. "I really did love you."

And with that the door was closed and locked, leaving me alone in the back seat. I looked though the tinted windows and saw him get into the back of another car, watched him drive off. Then two henchmen got back in. Nothing was happening. I sat there for the longest time, none of us saying anything. It felt like an underwater blurb. I checked my limbs. My bones still connected together, my hips spread soft on the seat. I swallowed. My larynx clenched. Everything functioned. The air in the car was creamy. It was dreamy. I was relieved. It had been a warning to scare me, and it had worked.

FORTY-ONE

At the Golden Globes, there was Mark the Jew and brothers Nicky and Angelo. There was Vinnie, who was in his thirties, wore thick glasses and sweated profusely like he would fold under questioning. There was Nicky's girlfriend Linda, who wore swathes of crepe charmeuse and sequin bows cinched together with diamanté flamingo trinkets. The women wore marabou pumps and carried jeweled fruit clutch bags; Tina, a rhinestone watermelon slice, and Nicky's girlfriend a crystal encrusted lemon slice.

What a time to be alive.

Having been waxed, plucked, and moisturized prior to checking into the Beverly Hills hotel, I had then been sent off to get a full MOT in a beauty salon. Technicians hovered around me, scraping off the acne puss and plastering over my acne scars until I emerged like a gleaming marble goddess out of the welding sparks and the crackle and fizz of pyrotechnics. Frank was so proud. He had bleached the rock chick out of me. I emerged from the lab room, blinking into the sun, glazed and laminated, pressed on mute and issued to Frank fresh as a page.

A round of after-parties beckoned after the Kodak theatre. Chocolate rooms, gloopy and glidey with chocolate fountains and chocolate walls and me, just wanting to meet Harvey Weinstein. And there he was under the warm hum of peach lights and his staring bored through me. It felt icky, and I was grateful that Frank in his stalker-y blurry alco-gaze had come to pull me away from him. I could have gone home with one famous actress, but I declined. I admired her acting too much.

The Golden Globes were exactly what I'd wanted, but nothing had really moved me. I had not earned this. I wasn't a film star, wasn't up for an award, and I felt like an intruder, an imposter edging closer to becoming LA fodder—a vacant doll, dead behind the eyes on the arm of a rich old man solid of paunch and leather skin, dripping in gold Rolex with a saggy arse, showering me with gifts and holidays to Bermuda in exchange for my youth and use of my orifices. But now I could be free of Frank, even though he had decided to keep me forever.

Realizing my sense of urgency to get away from him now that the Golden Globes were over, Frank suggested a trip to Vegas with several thousand spending money. My epilepsy medication was making my hangover even more potent, so his offers of gifts and money were even more nauseating and fucked me up worse than usual.

I was literally bundled into a limo by Frank's henchmen as I left my girlfriend's apartment in West Hollywood in the early hours of the morning a few days later.

Frank sat in the dark of the limo, stone faced, staring ahead. He flung a fur coat at me as I got in.

"Here—wrap up, baby cat, we're going to Vegas."

"You're such a walking cliché it's actually painful." I rolled down the window and threw the fur into the highway.

"You break my heart, kid, but you know what? I'm gonna let you make it up to me in Vegas because I guess..." he trailed off. "I guess I'm in love with you and it's killing me," he said redundantly.

"Can't you try to care about me a little?" His bulging cow eyes drooping down and so far apart made him look like Sloth in the *Goonies*.

"Well, you know that I do care about you a lot." I tried to be kind, charitable. I didn't wish the torment of unrequited love on anyone; it's the worst torture possible.

In my haste to slip away from any of Frank's men, who followed me everywhere, I was wearing my sweatpants and hadn't brought any clothes, so when we got to the hotel in Vegas Frank told me to wait in the car for a little while before coming up to the room with a bodyguard. He had a whole thing planned for us with all his New York buddies: mostly a tumult of restaurants and clubs where they would undoubtedly be dropping colossal stacks of cash. Waiting in the car, I honestly didn't know how I would have the energy to sit around day and night with the cast of rejects from the Sopranos and engage in banality. It occurred to me how mind-numbingly dull it was for me and how emotionally redundant it made me feel, this business of staggering into Michelin star restaurants, being fast-tracked into VIP sections of nightclubs, being driven in limos to bleed money in designer stores. But I did need money. I had no savings in England; the tutoring and teaching jobs merely let me eat and have a roof over my head.

Frank was always throwing a lot of cash around, especially if he was gambling and partying, and I would have to take whatever he gave me from winnings.

An hour passed until I was ushered into the suite. Nervously, I knocked and waited. It took a while for Frank to open the door and when I walked in the room, it was dark. The heavy drapery was drawn, the lights dimmed. The foyer decked with columns, fountains, and an indoor garden festooned with begonias and cactus overlooked the city. A kaleidoscope of bars, bedrooms, fireplaces and lounges rippled into focus, a watercolor feast of luxury living.

"Hey, kid." Frank materialized from the shadows like the Phantom of the Opera. He kissed and embraced me. "I got a surprise for you," he gestured around the room. Dangling from lamps and furniture were luxury bags: Chanel totes, delicate velvet pouches, jewel encrusted baguettes dangling by their dainty chains, and lace clutches. A forest of sparkling purses. He bowed, hands clasped in front of him in servitude. "Look around, baby, it's all about you on this trip. Open them—one by one."

I was of course expecting a trap, some explosion, or to meet my demise by some toxic agent hidden in the pouches. But then I saw that each handbag contained a hundred dollars, and there were ten bags, and the money was all for me. Ahh…to be bought. Not only your orifices but your soul, your mental health. In return I was obliged to be not only kind and amiable but legs akimbo. It's strange when someone who repulses you gives you money, and stacks of it. It is kind of like pushing back vomit with copious amounts of your favorite food and drink. To pay me to perform overt gestures of affection and adoration. But alas, that carousel of hanging handbags was the opening act. The main show, the masterpiece, the pièce de resistance was in the master bedroom: a pirouetting menagerie of dresses. Blousy, floral patterned polyester kinds straight out of the museum of 1970s Italian grandmas.

"I got you all these dresses, baby." Frank was giddy, like he'd just scored the winner in a world cup game.

"You got all this stuff in one hour?" I stayed amiable.

"Hey, I had help from the hotel staff downstairs. They know me here." He was proud, adoring.

It was a passive aggressive turn. The cash in the bags had been a honeyed trap to get me to comply, to wear the old maid–style outfits. Ghosts of Italian mob wives past stared back, battered and probably meatloaf stained. What I didn't understand was why the dresses weren't new but musty secondhand ones. Frank was either really thick or just wanted to humiliate me on an epic scale.

I bit my lip to remain pleasant. "Why are they so 1970s housewife-y and second hand?"

"They're class, baby!" Frank beamed. "That slutty rock chick corset look does not make you look like a lady. I want you to be Ava Gardner."

"But surely this would make me look like Ava Gardner's grandmother, and not in a cool vintage way, but in a proper crusty meatloaf way."

"You should wear this tonight." Frank picked up a taupe velour piece buttoned to the neck.

"I can't do that for you, I am sorry," I defied, more firmly this time. "I can't look like someone's dead mum."

"I bought all these dresses for you!" Frank screamed. "Do you want guys looking at you when you are with me? Is that what you want? To be seen as a Vegas hooker?"

"With these clothes, I assure you that everybody will be looking at me… like I have dressed for Halloween!" I flung the dress in his face.

But Frank was determined on forcing me. He reminded me of the money in the handbags, which he would gift me even though he had now put it all in the safe. I could just leave with my dignity and peace of mind, but again I told myself that if I just tolerated this couple of days, I could go back home free from financial worry before I continued my master's degree.

I was lucky. A person from a violent poverty-ridden home was L.U.C.K.Y to get this. I stuck my head under the air con panel. I had never been a fan of Vegas, a gothic hotel somewhere in Scotland or Transylvania suited my temperament more.

Downstairs, Frank's guys congregated looking like they were all about to attend a 1978 wise guy convention. I was just surprised the vat of aftershave they have clearly been dipped in didn't set alight the gallon of oil that slicked back their hair. They flocked to Frank, asking which motherfucking cocksucker faggot should be taken out first, smoking like lab beagles and swigging from whiskey tumblers.

"These guys are something, aren't they?" A wispy blonde not more than twenty swathed in a billowing robe-dress whispered to me. A newbie. Peach-fresh from the mid-west, she was not yet the seasoned mob wife whose years of choking down Mafioso cock had soured her on life, whose blotchy sallow skin was caked in powder and droopy with a cyclops face lift and bad Botox job. Caitlyn giggled feebly: "They don't want other guys to look at us, huh?"

A Monroe blonde, whispery and giggly drinking bourbon. She had doubtless stepped off the bus into Hollywood Boulevard and inevitably met a few bums before being swooped in on by Angelo. I can't believe I have to wear this." She frowned. "Angelo thinks it looks cute on me."

We compared notes on the gloomy attire we wear forced to wear by our men before Angelo grabbed her and took her away.

Our dinner at Eiffel Tower at the Paris hotel was everything I expected. A scaffolding of sea creatures whose delicate pink meat was softly scraped off from their shells before Frank desecrated a plate of steak tartare with baby potatoes and started on a plate of ravioli. Around us teenage demi-hookers on alligator-skinned men's arms made me in some way relieved to be in such a dowdy dress; at least I wasn't so obviously mob girlfriend.

I was hoping Frank would keel over in a sloth-inspired stupor once we got back to our room, but he was bouncing to go to a place called Hyde with the rest of the wise guys. There were guys from another family in Vegas that night and Frank's men had congregated in our room with guns and were planning a hit, so Frank gave me a gun. I had never used one before and wasn't at all keen on carrying one. The guys in our room were planning something, so I dove into the other room and turned the TV on loud not wanting to be a witness to any information. The film was *All About Eve* and its dreamy bleat too gentle to mask their chatter, but in any case, Angelo burst into the room carrying a tumbling mass of platinum ringlets and petticoats and tossed a kicking Caitlyn onto the bed and told me to stay with her. I had this gun and I was scared to even touch it. It made me think though: If I am given a gun and I am staying in the room, then there was a definite possibility that Frank's enemies knew his room.

"Do you think we should go downstairs?" Caitlyn murmured dreamily, one hand fumbling around for her bag until she fished out a rattling vial of pills she struggled to open in her hazy state, her face and body a heap of smeared lipstick and cluttered curls. Purple welts and lacerations like rail tracks travelled from the back of her leg to her spine, her flesh like a bruised peach.

When Frank came up to the suite I was still watching *All about Eve*. The safe was locked so I hadn't been able to get at my money. I wasn't even sure if I would be getting it or whether Frank had dangled it in front of me as bait, to make me stay. He looked exceptionally chipper, slick with the glowing sweat of someone who has just sorted out a killing.

"Here, kid, put your best dress on, we're going downstairs to play cards." He threw another one of the frocks at me. "Wear this. I wanna show you off."

"Is it safe? What about that other family? What happened?"

"Hey, I told you to never worry about that stuff," Frank fixed me a cold stare. Then shifting his gaze, he sneered, "If I tell you my business, I'll have to kill you."

Good, you'd be putting me out of my misery, I mumbled under my breath.

"What was that?" Frank stopped and cocked his head.

"Nothing," I beamed, snickering.

"I have done so much for you. You have to show you're my lady in front of other families."

"THIS," I cracked, taking the pile of cloth in my clenched hand, "will not make me look like a lady; it will make me look like a CUNT. You have absolutely no fucking clue about clothes, fucking peasant." It was liberating talking to a murdering mafia boss in this impertinent manner. I ran to the desk in the lounge and took out the huge pair of scissors I had seen in there and cut the dress to shreds. Then I started on another of the foul dresses cutting it to ribbons.

Defeated, bored with his own atrocities, Frank stood and watched,

To him I was a creature like no other. No matter what I did, he couldn't hate me, he couldn't ever hurt me.

I was horrible to him, so fuck knows why. Furthermore, I had a miserable face on downstairs as we headed to the high rollers table where Frank proceeded to drop hundreds of thousands of dollars.

"You could have given *me* that money!" I said in disgust as he continued his losing streak of hundreds of thousands.

It seemed like there was only two types of female for these guys: hardened peroxide matriarchs draped in gold and fur or pilled-up demi hookers called Destiny or Crystal who had been choking down warty cocks since their teens. I guess I was special if Frank insisted on getting me to cultivate the matronly image. It made sense now: sexually provocative clothing signaled that you were just another ho to the mafia boss, whereas the yeasty old aunt vibe was a signifier that you were held in high esteem.

Frank said he wouldn't "release" the money to me until we were in LA. Probably not even then. It was to keep me around. I had benefited from his money anyway, by being able to eat and stay in roach free hotels. Ditching the bodyguard, I grabbed my handbag and legged it to the airport leaving Frank spunking his money away.

Back in my LA hotel room, I packed my stuff and invited Zack, my baby bro in LA, to stay with me till I got my flight. Zack was a twenty-two-year-old kid from Ohio who had come to LA to make it as a hair metal dude. He had been in a gang in Ohio before waking up one morning and deciding that gang life wasn't for him and stepping into the specter of spandex, eye liner, and big hair, ditching NWA and Tupac for Poison. Then, fearing for his life after gang members discovered this treachery, Zack had got in his car and zoomed out of town toward California, Van Halen screeching from his tinny speakers.

Zack had loved me like a big sister ever since I had arrived in LA, driving me to the Rainbow, keeping me company, picking me up to take me to my beloved Taco Bell, taking me on cozy long late night drives in the twisting foresty lanes of Laurel Canyon, up to vista points where we'd park in the pitch dark and talk about my latest shitty rock star, and he'd put a blanket over me and drive me to wherever I was staying.

Zack was a superb musician with catwalk model looks, but when he tried to audition for hair metal bands, there was a lot of prejudice because he was black. No matter how many re-hashed eighties glam rock bands in LA were looking for talented guitar players, they didn't even consider him, literally taking one glance before he'd played a song and saying no. Hair/glam/sleaze metal is fundamentally a white male blue collar phenomena, its heartbeat knucklehead white working class machismo, so a black band member would be jarring to the showcasing of white working class male identity.

Thankfully, Frank hadn't called after I ditched him in Vegas, but on the second night he did, to say that he had flown back from Vegas for Tony Bennett and I had to get ready to go see the show and meet Tony. My heart sank. As much as I loved Tony Bennett, I no longer wanted to see Frank.

An hour later a Middle Eastern man was opening my hotel room door. Behind him stood Frank.

"That's it? Is that it? You're an amateur, kid!" he beamed at Zack.

I smiled. "Stalking me again, Frank?"

The flunky stepped forward, gun clearly on show from his trench coat. He had leather gloves and the compulsory villain goatee, looked like the token baddie straight out of a straight-to-video mob movie. "You pick this nigger over Frank?"

"How fucking dare you?" I screamed at him. "Get the fuck out of my room."

"This is not your room"—the hitman pointed at my packed suitcase—"and these aren't your clothes."

"Get this nigger out of here," Frank ordered as the man lunged at Zack. "You choose this over me? You are disgusting. I offer you a limo to a Tony Bennett concert to meet him and you choose this thing?" Frank nudged Zack with the tip of his shoe as the manservant emptied the entire contents of my suitcase on the floor, barricading himself between me and all my belongings.

I was left with only my passport and a bit of spare change. The rest of my cash was taken, and just to ensure that I was kicked out of the hotel, Frank called reception and told them I was an intruder in his room. Security kicked me and Zack out, leaving me with nowhere to go. Zack lived in a warehouse somewhere out of town, and every motel Zack drove me to told me they had no vacancies. I was wearing a halter neck dress and as soon as I walked in reception with Zack, they took one look at us and decided we were pimp and ho. I slept at the airport, and as I flew home the next day, I realized that in taking all my belongings, Frank had taken my beloved Dean Martin cassette tapes as well.

FORTY-TWO

Somewhere in the Turkish mountains, 2016

In the end I never contacted Frank for the cash. I preferred to clean toilets, do more web-camming and general selling of my soul to pay the smugglers.

Now, Hassan drives up the winding roads toward the mountains. Rocky terrain winds before us blotted with huts, yard fires smoldering in the distance. A pruned old woman shrouded in black, hands-on-hips stares as we drive past her sheep. It's getting dark and I know I won't see Elijah again.

"Chai?" Hassan motions a cup swig. "Man evim, (my home)," he points to the mountains. The mountains look chilled, blue, ethereal. It's strangely comforting, like being taken to a dreamland on a magic carpet ride even though this man is a stranger and paid smuggler. I have to trust everyone on this journey or I'll go mad. Has it been an advantage to my life that I have already had sex with him? Hassan must have thought I did it out of obligation, as female sexuality or agency and choice clearly has no concept in our world. Just like in the Western world, female sexuality must be placed within the context of duty, sex work, or derived as the result of some background trauma. There can never be female sexuality detached from a reason: it is not allowed to be just purely human pleasure.

My pulse, my wrists, my knee joints, my small pouch attached to my hips: a surge of currents that seize me rigid and blue. The purple sky drawing closer. The van is cold so Hassan puts on a cassette of Kurdish music, village songs about mourning and life's end.

It seems ages later that we pull up outside a hut, where a brood of chickens and a donkey greet Hassan like family pets. I have said nothing in the car, silent in my dread.

This hut is my new temporary home and I try to embrace it. I don't know how long I'll be here, or where I will go next. When I ask him, Hassan doesn't seem to know either. "Later, later…" is all he says. A row of jars filled with sugar, then salt, sugar then salt are sitting on a stone ledge. Inside the hut,

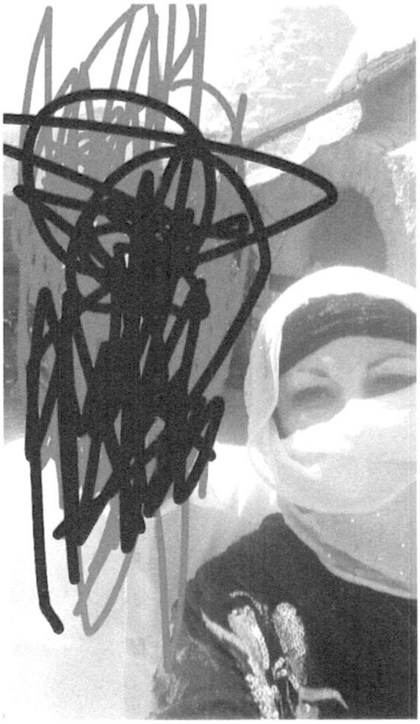

Hassan's wife, so much older than him that I wonder if he had meant mother stead of wife, greets us, head wrapped in multi-colored scarves and thick woolly cardigan over broad shoulders. "Merhaba (hello)," she says warmly, and as she gives me two kisses I can smell stale cooking fat on her lips. How I have betrayed her. I feel bad and wonder if she will alert the authorities out of spite if she finds out I've lain with her spouse.

A plucked chicken sits on a wooden table ready to be hacked.. I offer to give her a hand as Hassan swoops up a small screeching barefoot child running back and forth zooming a plastic toy helicopter. Handmade Turkish and Persian rugs layer the floor, festooning the ground a pool of tulips and huntsmen. Two big canopy beds packed with kilims and cushions in the corner of the hut are lit warmly in the glow of the paraffin lanterns as a peep of chicks run inside, quite bravely I think, since their elder relative just got the chop. I find the toilet outside, where within the heart of the mountains it's still and icy. Wrapped in my chador I find the squat variety of loo specially exerting. To balance oneself in a squat as one pisses and shits for any length of time must surely need a regimen of calf and thigh muscle isometrics and toughened knee joints. How do the constipated fare on squat toilets? Their legs must be made of steel. I am thinking these thoughts to keep worse ones away. I have been mentally prepared for being smuggled illegally into Iran and now I must bear it.

It's ironic, I think, how the moneyed in their Primrose Hill mansions, munching on their organic kale as some "war-torn souvenir" ripped from the charred hands of a child soldier in an African village sits on their mantelpiece, would pay a fortune for this "ethnic chic" hut and its toilet while this poor family only covets shiny plastic trinkets made in China. I wonder how much of the money I am paying for the smuggling will go to Hassan's family.

After the dinner of hacked chicken and Aryan, the salted yogurt drink, I feel a fresh surge of fear jabbing at my guts. I'm hoping to stay in this cozy hut for a while longer. Outside, stars have studded the sky and smoky wood fires gently dissipate into the night. There is the lone sound of a goat bleating somewhere.

"Come on! Come on!" Hassan signals for me to go in. "Tomorrow, tomorrow," he clasps his hands together and rests his head on them in a sleep gesture.

My body perspires profusely but I'm a solid slab of ice, even with the thick chador sheathing me. Hassan's wife is putting out the lamp, having throughout the evening been careful of engaging in conversation with me, her gaze deliberately absent. She points to the corner of the hut where a pile of bed linen, sheets, and quilts are laid out. I am not sure if it is bad etiquette to take off my chador, so I sleep with everything on. Shrouded in the mummifying layers, I curl up to sleep, the smell of meat and paraffin from the sheets overwhelming me. I must be grateful. Inch by inch I am getting closer to my beloved Iran.

I have just fallen asleep when I am shaken awake by Hassan. "Hurry, hurry," he urges me. It's still dark. Hassan's wife and child are nowhere to be seen. Hassan is smoking like a lunatic, jittery, shuffling from foot to foot. He finally gets into the van still in his pajama pants and zips his anorak.

"Where are we going? Hara jedirookh?" I grab my small pouch, grateful that I have left most of my stuff with Elijah.

"Tez ol! (hurry!)" Hassan is agitated, not his usual gold-toothed jovial self. We speed off into the dark, rocks and stones gravelly beneath the tires, jolting and shaking the van, but still he revs the engine as if we are fleeing hellfire. Maybe he knows about my book, I flinch as he zooms round the serpentine paths just narrowly missing the drop from the edge of the mountain.

"Are you all right, Hassan?" I put a hand on his shoulder.

"Sarbaz (soldier)," is all he says.

We must be nearing the border of Iran. Driving together, opposite genders and unmarried or related, is perilous.

He is smoking some foul-smelling pipe now. Opium? Crack?

Whatever it is, it's calming him down a bit.

The van rattles, bumping up and down dizzying black mountains, huts and clouds of smoke mottling the landscape. We must have passed Ozalp, a small town near the border, I calculate. Hassan is on his phone now, speaking in a dialect that sounds Kurdish. The adrenaline has overtaken my tiredness and as we drive through the pitch black, I try and remain tough and calm.

Finally, Hassan stops the truck and tells me to get out at the foot of a hill, on top of which I can make out a brick house with piles of broken concrete, rubble and tarpaulin sacks spilling with wire cables outside it. Walking up the slope a huge torchlight glares into our face and Hassan greets two men; kisses on the cheek ensue, cash exchanged. I pull my layers of hejab tighter around me, as if the more mummified I am, the more invisible and invincible I'll be. Inside looks like a derelict warehouse and the three men are deep in conversation, speaking Kurdish and occasionally pointing at me, then pointing at the mountains, followed by low sniggering chortles-probably saying what an absolute twat I am. Hassan motions me to sit on the hay-coated floor lit by the low flicker of propane gas lanterns. A big white dog, some wretched cross breed of Husky, chain-tied to a pole, growls, a red tag punched into its ear which oozes bloody gunk and puss. For the first time the two men's faces become clear: heavily bearded, densely monobrowed and they wear loose clothing with rain jackets; the older man—in his fifties—sports a fuzzy Russian hat.

"I will leave now," Hassan says. "You stay."

"Why are you going? I don't want to stay alone with these men. I thought you would be with me all the time." I think of my little nephew who purses his lips and says I *want dadda*. And with that he is out the door. I hear his footsteps hasten and then his van revving off into the night.

"You vont viskey?" the older one and wearer of fuzzy Russian hat who I'll later find out is called Ibrahim. grunts to me.

"No, thank you," I shake my head politely to the whiskey and the glass of tea offered to me in case they're drugged.

The younger one, Yusuf, wears a Nike cap with his billowing Kurdish robes and is stacking cartons of cigarettes into a box along with bottles of vodka and whiskey. Later he brings out a pile of neatly folded clothes from a suitcase.

"Inaro bepoosh" he says in Kurdish-accented Farsi. *Wear these.*

In the corner of the derelict warehouse I take off my chador and slip a weighty floor-length turquoise skirt over my jeans followed by an orange floor-length dress and finally a pink scarf tied around my waist, as I have seen Hassan's wife do in Kurdish fashion. A wool cardigan goes over the top, and finally having taken my headscarf off, I put a long white scarf on my head and fasten it with a knot. This displeases Yusuf, who clicks his tongue in irritation and undoes the knot, wraps the long scarf over my head and all over my mouth Kurdish style, so that only my eyes and nose are peeking through. He stares at me, his piercing blue eyes sizzling from a sun-charred face. I feel properly bandaged up like a walking bundle, although it also makes me feel cozy and comfortable. Yusuf tells me that if I want to sleep, I can go in the corner—there is a blanket. Lack of sleep is bad for my epilepsy, and though I decide to stay awake, my epilepsy medication is making me drowsy and I draw the coarse fleece over my heavy clothing.

"Bekhab, bekhab (sleep sleep)," Ibrahim says. "Tomorrow."

I resist it with all of my being, but sleep envelops me. Visions of mutilation and rape, possible necrophilia, are too brazen, too vaudeville. I sit up next to the dog as the men play backgammon and run frothy film strips in my head: *Friends, Sex and the City, Dirty Dancing, Some Like it Hot*, the fucking *Lion King*, but they keep getting interjected by missing limbs, deformed faces, Kalashnikovs, revolutionary guards. The dog licks my swathed face. I cuddle him. If I befriend him, he could be a proper mate if something happens.

Hours pass and I doze off next to the dog. Ibrahim and Yusuf end up falling asleep in the corner on rugs. Somewhere a rooster crows. I walk up and peek my head through the door, to see dawn splintering through over majestic mountains coated in wild heather. I pee behind the hut and for the first time I see how many petrol containers are piled outside. Along with the cartons of cigarettes and whiskey inside, it must be a smuggler's hut. I contemplate sitting outside in the morning air.

Before I do, Yusuf bursts outside. "Nah, nah!!" he hustles me inside hastily. "Nobody must see!" He shakes a finger in front of my face.

Inside, Ibrahim is boiling water on a pan on a butane gas stove. This time I'm grateful for the tea he offers. I watch Yusuf wrap around a turban-like head dress and then he's gone.

"Can you untie the dog please?" I say in Farsi. "It's cruel. *Bichareh*."

Ibrahim nods and I pet the grateful creature, who miraculously hasn't shat or pissed on the ground. Probably too terrified. Unchained, the husky leaps out the door like a demented beast running in and out, chasing his own tail, peeing, howling, shitting. I cuddle and kiss him as much as I can giving it all the love it has been starved of. He licks my face gratefully.

Yusuf is back. Driving some old rattling heap of junk. In the back of the car is an older woman and a child. I go up to the car and we greet each other. The woman is possibly in her early fifties, wearing colorful Kurdish garb. Pruned and weathered, a cluster of moles mushroom her face as she warmly greets me with a gold toothed smile. The small child beside her is raggedy, crusty snot caked on her sun burnt face and soiled Barbie jumper.

"Zood bash, zood bash! (Hurry! Hurry!)" Yusuf motions me inside and thrusts a passport and an envelope in my hand. It's an Iranian passport and the woman, a Neda Gholamzadeh, in the photo looks about twenty-five and shares only a passing resemblance to me. Even though I have brought my own Iranian and British passports, which I am told I must hide in my clothing, this new identity is useful for getting me around, but it's a hazard right now. If found in possession of a fake passport, I'd be tortured and imprisoned as a criminal, a traitor, a spy. Also in the envelope is Iranian money, about two hundred British pounds worth, which is barely enough for a bit of food and some taxi money, such is the severity of the sanctions in Iran, which have sky-rocketed the price of everything from bread to public transport. I have already paid four thousand US dollars to the smugglers, so I am hoping they will give me a bit more Iranian money once we get closer to Iran.

"Bia, bia! (Come on!)" Yusuf motions me to a feast of bread, a block of feta, and the butter and honey he has brought back. We all get back inside and sit on the floor for breakfast with hot black tea in tulip glasses. The dog gets a couple of rooster heads which he crushes in one go—crunching and grinding the coral crests, brains, the beaks, and eyeballs—a flutter of white feathers lodged in his teeth after.

Then we pile back into the orange clunker, Ibrahim driving and Yusuf up front, the little girl between me and Golnar, the older lady, in back. We are a family now. Yusuf gives me a gold wedding band to put on my ring finger before we take off. The ploy must be to stage a family outing and I'm assuming I am Yusuf's wife and Golnar, Ibrahim's—the little girl possibly their grandchild. I drape the long scarf over my face, my eyes peeking through the slit at the cinnamon earth, the coarse gorse and thicket, snow-capped summits powdered like icing. The vast land speckled with the white wool smudges of grazing animals, shepherded by teenage boys.

After an hour or as the men chain-smoke, we stop.

Ahead, surrounded by barb wire and billboard portraits of Khomeini and Khamenei, is the border checkpoint. There are a few porta cabin–style trailers that house the immigration office facilities and a couple of huts that serve as barracks. Turkish and Iranian flags blow in the breeze as lines of people alighted from buses stand waiting to have their passport checked. Armed soldiers inspect the trucks and lorries queued back-to-back.

Yusuf and Ibrahim have stopped the car and are engaged in heated debate. "Nah khoob nist" (it's not good), Yusuf snaps, grabbing the passport from my bag and then my forefinger. "Fingerprint… migiran mikoshan (they'll get you and kill you)." He points at the soldiers. "Fingerprint here," he says in English. "No good."

"The plan wasn't to go through a border checkpoint anyway!" I say angrily. I paid to be smuggled across, not go through an official route, fingerprint or no fingerprint. "I am not going through a checkpoint!"

The child begins to cry. We're out of here. Back up the mountains

I need a piss badly but hold it in, not wanting to anger the men any more than I already have.

We're only a short distance from the checkpoint when Yusuf points to a soldier patrolling the ground ahead of us, rifle hoisted on his shoulder. The car comes to a halt as the soldier walks toward us. Leaning into Ibrahim's window, he talks in a mix of Turkish and Kurdish and I can make out the words "where," "why," and "who."

I keep my head down as he points his rifle into the window.

Whilst Ibrahim talks softly, Yusuf's temper has flared up again and he is now exchanged in a heated argument with the guard. I find myself thankful for my Kurdish garb, which makes me look like part of the faux family. It seems like an eternity till we're finally waved on and there is visible sigh of relief from everyone.

After a while we get to a hut. Outside, a gaggle of scraggly barefoot kids play with rocks, their screeches of delight blending with the loud cackles of adults from inside. Plastic toys, laundry hanging on washing lines, and chickens clutter the courtyard. Golnar and the little girl get out of the car and walk inside. I don't know who they were but I'm grateful that, knowingly or not, they have acted as decoys.

It's early evening and me and the two guys continue driving through the twisted roads and up craggy mountain paths till we reach a dilapidated building sitting alone and derelict, the cold barren land giving it an eerie silhouette in the twilight. There's no life around. Inside is a concrete storehouse with meat hooks and metal chains hanging from the ceiling like a slaughterhouse. Hens and sheep that must have been plodding about in the back follow us inside as Ibrahim lights a gas camping stove. This must be some sort of hideaway for smugglers and fugitives. Suddenly, an array of colorful rugs, blankets, and stuffed cushions are produced from a concealed vault in the ground. I'm exhausted, as I am sure the men are, and curl up into a ball in the corner by some bedding. I am told nothing about the next part of the journey, and so I wait, wanting to be as invisible as possible. The gas stove is lit and as if by magic Ibrahim has produced a sliver of some questionable meat from a plastic container, some feta cheese, and wraps of lavash flat bread. If the bitter cold, the wild animals, or these men don't kill me, I'm sure food poising will, but I am starved and don't have to be asked before I dig in.

The three of us eat as night approaches, Ibrahim and Yusuf no doubt exchanging anecdotal gems, reminiscing with Kurdish words difficult to understand. The barn grows darker. Ibrahim lights candles and with the faint glow of the stove and lamps, we sit and wait. They ask me about my family and life, and I try and give as little information as possible. The hum of the kerosene lamp and the smell of burnt wood and smoke in this dark cold night lull us into a hypnotic trance, taking me back to those nights during the war when there were frequent power-cuts, and with the sound of air raid sirens wailing, we'd sit in deep silence.

We sit there for a few hours, each of us staring into the hypnotic glow of candles. The silence is broken by approaching footsteps. They are coming closer. I hear a donkey braying followed by the neighing of a horse.

A big muscular man, about mid-thirties, comes in greeting Ibrahim and Yusuf. He wears a heavy trench coat and also has a Russian fur hat. The village gangster perhaps? He greets me like a long-lost friend and gives me a slap on the back like one of his bros. Suddenly I miss my mum and for some strange reason I feel a fresh surge of safety and happiness, as if I am protected by some good spirit. I am so excited to be going to Iran, gleeful.

Outside: the frozen night, voluptuous and ethereal, incandescent with clusters of stars, the donkey and horse await me. They'll be my new mates.

Posing for Hustler Magazine, 2011

FORTY-THREE

England, Italy, Norway, 2010–2011

I hadn't slept much that summer of 2010. I had been doing back-to-back publicity in LA and New York and was supercharged to bounce into the UK leg of the publicity tour and braced for a round of interviews in London when my publicists' request to the UK media were suddenly met with refusal after refusal. I was stunned, a real feeling that "you do not belong here" had been shoved down my throat. I continued my publicity tour on the phone with the US, Europe, Australia, and South America.

By 2011 I had moved back into a flat in Bristol and started looking for work. There was a wrought-iron bed and a lamp from Glastonbury. Tommy had slept on that bed of mine for months, all Swedish bag of bones of him complete with ginger beard, sometimes drugged up because I had drugged him with Valium to stop him twitching toward me.

In my flat, I had bleached my eyebrows, whilst he had saturated his uber blonde Swedish locks with raven-black from packets of hair dye to be like Lemmy. It was his presence there in my bathroom full of white cabinets and poverty.

The lady movie star from Titanic who had once hit on me at the Golden Globes when I had gone there with Frank was a reminder of some of my worth, so I also displayed my invitation on my bathroom wall.

"Feel sunny!" I used to tell him. "Life isn't about black metal and Satan, dearie."

"I hate people," he'd snarl.

"Eat some pizza." I'd push food onto him the way my mum did onto me to build a honey bridge through the gap.

"I want beer, I want fags, I want cuddles, I want a blow job, I want to watch *Superman* and then *Superman II*, I want to smoke weed, I want to become famous, I want you to get your saggy tits ballooned up to Lolo Ferrari size, I want you to be Anna Nicole smith."

"All right, Tommy! I'll do it!"

Nothing compared to the horror of Tommy, the pound-shop rock star. I had bought into his mythology of generic black hair dye and smeared kohl, his epidemic of tattoos cobbled together a patchwork of skeleton figures, a Swastika, a 666, and a "Trailer Trash." I had bought into the blazing blue eyes, the toxic wad of angry rape-y semen that he pumped into women to make them yelp, pummeling away at rectums, fannies, and mouths all over London. He had been a fixture in London, with a CV of violence, immeasurable sexual partners, and chronic drug abuse and of no fixed abode. Young girls and middle-aged women alike, creamy at the thought of a pound-shop Tommy Lee giving them a shag in the men's toilets of the local rock bar, bought him his booze and waited around to get fucked by him. He had them in rotation like rotisserie chicken and left a trail of sobbing, sozzled girls wailing and dribbling alcopops on Camden high street in their urine-soaked fishnet tights, battered but aching for him. A patina of semen shimmering between bloodied thighs, desperately adoring him for the soul-shredding orgasms he gave them. For his endgame was to maim, hurt, and fill up holes. To use the human female body as a vessel to defecate his rage into. As a teen it had been the bath towels crusted up with his ejaculate piled high in his cupboard, and in his twenties, men's sex toys-flesh-lights-pudgy with his semen at the sex shop in Soho where he had worked, placing them back in their packaging once he'd filled them. This alcoholic violent junkie who had shredded my bones, my mental health, and my emotions into pulp.

My flat in Bristol in 2010 was on the ground floor, facing a square grass patch where my adopted cat Scampi did its toilet. Scampi was stolen from my mother's communist neighbor. It had mental health problems, and I couldn't even touch it for fear of the viscous bloodshed it would unleash. Its aim was swift and superb. It even growled manically when it ate its food, at war with pate. I was continuing my US book publicity every day on the phone and giving talks at universities when I could and trying to keep Tommy fed and watered, and Scampi would roam the concrete corridors terrorizing the neighbors.

47 Park Street was where we went to hang out with Tommy's favorite type of humans: anyone who fit the description of dregs of society, chronic druggie, or criminal. The place was crusted with fecal matter and the milky phlegm of

humans who were into GG Allin. A band would play a sort of punk "Copacabana" on repeat as Moroccan taxi drivers dropped in to score cheap skunk then lie around telling of their woes of being taxi drivers trying to feed their six kids. Tommy didn't like me talking with humans because he said I gave out pheromones from my head, which made humans want me sexually. It had become a process of making myself smaller so he could become bigger; the lionizing of a lowlife. The more publicity I did for my book, the more beaten I would get; the bigger the audiences at my university talks, the bigger the abuse afterward.

When I had first met him in 2006, I had been drinking and feeling epileptic-y, was trying to get soup to stave off a seizure. It was night. It was Soho. It was a cellar. This cadaverous youth bug-eyed and enraged with speed and coke had grabbed me and tried to drag me into the toilets whilst his girlfriend looked devastated. I love the unwashed natural smell of "I've just got off stage playing in a stadium" or "I've been ploughing in a field," but Tommy's unwashed smell was stagnant, an *I've just been sitting on a sofa for days in my crusty, skid-marked tracksuit watching daytime TV* smell; it lacked productivity, ambition, and crossed the line from "bad boy tattooed rocker" to "I just shat my pants junkie."

Fast forward to 2010, a month before my first book was published, and Tommy had found out where I lived.

I was on the precipice of international publicity and an advance check for my book which made him promptly dump his girl, borrow cash to hop on a flight from Sweden, then a train to Bristol and a cab to turn up fried from a continuous spool of speed and mushrooms at my flat in Bristol.

I saw a rabid dog who had been mangled under a car, starved and gnashing its teeth, and I did what my mother had done for my stepfather when she had felt scared of him: I scuttled into the kitchen and made him food. I had learned how to care-take from a young age, and violent men were my specialty.

From sleeping rough, Tommy had pissed himself and was crinkly with congealed cum.

"More pasta?" I shoveled piles of food onto his plate like my mother did.

"Why don't you go and put on something sexy? You look like my grandfather in your pajamas." Tommy sneered at my cotton pajamas. "And porn makeup!" He banged his heavily chained wrist on the table as he ordered me to my bedroom, where I hastily slipped on a sexy outfit as he wolfed down the dinner I'd made for him.

He stared at my chest. "I wish you had bigger tits. My mum has massive tits. But she is fat, I fucking hate the cunt. She always says I am the biggest mistake of her life." He suddenly started howling, eyeliner mottling his cheeks, a snot balloon blowing out of his left nostril. "I hate her so much. She showed me porn magazines in her bed when I was eight years old."

In the night Tommy had crawled in my bed begging me to have sex. And kind of like trying dog meat in a country where it is a delicacy and you find it repugnant but you have a macabre proclivity for the repugnant, I dipped my toe in the diseased water.

It was sheer bad luck that it was Tommy who matched my sexuality. After so long without sexual intimacy, the orgasmic convulsions he gave me leaned into a sort of religious frenzy. And even though I was repulsed by Tommy, my body had responded against my control. I was aching for a feral sexuality and I felt like a new girl again, never having experienced such all-consuming, raw animal sex.

Unfortunately my downstairs neighbors were old women who didn't like me flushing the loo after 8pm. A letter had been pushed under the door:

Hi there
We could hear EVERYTHING that you were saying and doing until 3.45 AM! We are not adverse to fun but that was a bit excessive, especially the screams of the man shouting "Satan."
Can you keep it down please?

My place was straight out of the catalogue for Sink Estate Chav. I, being in denial of my environment had sugared my world with damask rose wallpaper, stacked my bookshelves with Fellini and Warhol, Derrida and Foucault, and noshed on food bought with Waitrose vouchers that my mother insisted on sending me even though she had no money. I kept my Keppra locked away from the sight of potential friends in case they thought epilepsy made me less cool.

FORTY-FOUR

I landed back in the UK from my US tour pumped up. I'd been on a publicity buzz, rounds of parties and events in my name in New York and LA, and while I hoped for the same in London, I found all doors firmly closed in my face, so I made myself busy with US and European publicity on the telephone.

Desperate emails from Tommy had filtered through. I hated saying no to people especially to a broken addict. My mother always said that broken people needed women like us to heal them.

"I don't want to see my next birthday without you, Roxana."

He talked as if he were dying.

In London, under the lurid red of Soho's rock vaults, middle age boilers, their faces a real forty fags and bottle of vodka a day, would wink and nudge Tommy: "All right, luv, fancy anovver?"

Goth girls, hippy girls, fetish models, and milk and cookies girls, scouse mums, rock chicks, dominatrixes, and boarding-school girls fresh from mum and dad's chalet in Gstaad. By the end of the night, I had gotten a warning from all of them: "Be careful, babes, he's fakin scum who'll kick your head in." They would warn me of violence, nipples tautening pleasingly, chewing on a stand of hair, still missing the animal-fucking.

Tommy was only happy to talk to pat-a-cake friends whose collective attitude was just short of idolatry: rows and rows of identikit youths in uniforms of black denim with Motorhead patches from Camden market and black hair dye, dangling with oodles of waist chains. Whose brand of "anarchy" was to dress in exactly the same black clothing, have the same black dyed hair and get fucked up. They hero-worshipped Tommy for his violence because it made him more "rock star" and Tommy, feeding his inferiority complex notched it up more. I watched him glug bottles of whiskey, pop, snort, and smoke whatever was floating about on the street which was passed in rotation to be heaped onto him to keep the circus monkey act churning.

And now he had someone with a bit of "fame" to bolster his status. His attraction to me was, of course, my bit of "fame" and the potential money that would bring with it. He didn't know this was the reason. He thought it was love.

"Why don't you love me, Roxana?"

"Love" was my jaw. My aching jaw.

I was hemorrhaging money on hotels and restaurants in London. We went back to my flat in Bristol, and then to Wales—my friend Stuart Cable, the drummer for Stereophonics, had choked on his vomit and died. The night before the funeral, Tommy watched the Superman films back-to-back and wept. "Come *on*, baby, I am feeling sad here! Suck my cock." Tears and stringy mucus drooled out of his nose, and he pushed my head down as I'd exhaustedly, mechanically, deep-throated him as he cried through the credits.

But most of all it was me wearing pajamas in bed that would unleash a torrent of violence. "Why are you wearing pajamas, Roxana? Don't you want your skin to feel mine?" he snapped later that night.

"I am so cold," I whined.

"You don't give a fuck about me. You are so self-obsessed and selfish," he hissed. "If you really cared about me as a human, you wouldn't wear pajamas. It's the worst thing a girl can do to you."

Mr safe sterile Henry was beginning to seem very appealing in those times. But I was slowly healing Tommy by giving him money, a laptop, food and shelter, comfort and patience and so for now, had to tolerate him. It was not his fault he had these issues. At the age of thirty he had no job, money, or home, and I gave my publicity interviews quietly in other rooms so he wouldn't feel emasculated.

Tommy stood in front of me glaring as I did my phone interviews.

"Dumb hooker," he guffawed loudly so the interviewer on the other side of the line could hear. I motioned with him to be quiet, curling up into a ball in the corner of the room to continue the interview. But he came closer and sat in front of me, glaring at me when I gave the interview.

"You think too highly of yourself. Get in that room and spread your legs. Make yourself useful."

I called rehabilitation places, but every encounter with therapists was filled with real or imaginary belittlements for Tommy.

I was soaring with joy. A top university in London had asked me to give a guest lecture on sexual politics in Iran, and I busied myself with books and research material for the lecture. The hotel in London was booked and I gave Tommy some money to go to the pub while I prepared notes, slides, and visual materials. I wanted him to come to my lecture so he could see that I was more than just a conduit for his rage and sperm, that I had something to say.

The hall was packed, and I looked at the audience nervously—a mix of students and lecturers—until my gaze found Tommy sitting in the middle of them all. Instantaneously he slid his index finger across his throat mouthing "you're dead."

I froze with fear and my heart sank. Dazed, I followed the lecture with a Q&A and signed my book.

Now, he grabbed me and marched me out of the lecture hall.

"Do you like making me feel like a failure?" he cried.

"How?" I stared at him. "I don't do anything to you."

"I feel like a failure when you do all your career stuff. What do I have? Nothing. I am thirty. I don't have a job, money, home. You are supposed to be my girlfriend. You are supposed to love me. What do you make me feel so worthless?"

"I don't mean to. I love giving lectures at universities and writing. It makes me happy."

"It's all about you you you, isn't it, Roxana?" he screamed. "Worthless hooker." Tommy hocked up a fat loogie and spat it into my eyes in front of everyone.

He then picked up a metal bar from the ground and was about to smash it into my skull, when somebody from the audience stopped the metal bar just short of meeting my head.

"That guy nearly crushed your face with that metal bar!" the guy said. "If I hadn't stopped him in time, you would have had a broken jaw and nose!"

"Guys like that are scum." The guy looked so shaken up and upset that it was me who had to give him a reassuring pat on the back.

"Waiting to get your pussy stuffed with his cock, are you?" Tommy raged at me.

"No, no. I am upset," I said pathetically. "He is just being kind."

Afterward, Tommy filled up a bathtub and tried suicide by dangling a plugged-in hairdryer over it. I was terrified he would die because of me.

Henry was oblivious to the carnage in my life. He didn't know that I had been bred from a young age to love men who hurt me. I had learned how to care-take. To "fix." I functioned by what was familiar to me: harm, chaos, pain, sabotage and pouring love and care into harmful men. I could only get turned on with men who were violent boys in dangerous situations, because the adrenaline rush was linked to the danger of soldiers around me as a child. Dangerous men and sexual pleasure was enmeshed within me and "fixing" them was a learned behavior from watching my mother's normalization of my stepfather's abuse and violence to her.

When Henry visited me, I would be so grateful of the sex break my body got, the silence, the non-sexual contact, the gentle hum of day-time TV and wearing my pajamas. Tommy would be in London, waiting for me to end it with Henry.

"If you don't break it off with him, I'll kill you, then I'll kill myself," Tommy had threatened.

"Okay, I'll tell him this weekend," I lied.

That weekend Henry helped my mum and stepdad buy a new kitchen for their home. Then he helped them put it together, made me dinner and gave me a massage. He backed away when I reached out for intimate touching and said he wanted to watch a car show on TV instead. It hurt me. But I could never be without Henry. I would relinquish sexual intimacy blithely if I could stay by his side and make him feel loved and warm. I was getting in deep into a double life and I didn't know how to get out of it. I wanted to look after Tommy and Henry both to make them feel loved. I couldn't leave these two wounded and desecrated child-souls alone; it would be a sin. I split myself in two, playing two different roles and a life of deceit. The cancer in me grew, of guilt and shame, as I juggled a daily routine of which one I was meant to see and whether the other one might call whilst I was in the middle of a movie or dinner with the other; devising rosters for each boy.

Emotional cutters, masochists; somewhere, we enjoy the degradation, the humiliation… either because we have known it all our lives and the familiar feeling is part of us, or because we need a project to triumph over the past.

When I went to Italy in September to do a book signing in Venice, my belly was full with fetus.

I got jowly whenever I was pregnant. Stuffed chipmunk cheeks made my face look rounder and dumber, and when I did a book interview photoshoot I looked like a sad, abused Iranian chipmunk. Tommy had knocked me up on the pill. His sperm had found a way to break through the cladding. I had visions of this thing turning up nine months later, viciously punching its way through my flaps, a bug-eyed, bony-foreheaded demon entity, made from some mad alchemy of Tommy's radioactive load and me, the gibbering wreck. It would be so entirely imbued in Tommy's angry energy that none of my personality traits would have seeped through.

When the positive result had come up on the test, Tommy had wanted to get a last dose of heroin from his friend. He was ecstatic, except now he'd have to go back to slaughtering salmon to earn a crust for his progeny. He had always been desperate to be a father. But I also knew that wanting to become a father was just to fill a void. It was pollyfilla to fill in all the cracks of the wretchedness inside.

Photo by Beki Cowey

Posing for Hustler Magazine, *2011*

FORTY-FIVE

In Venice, a fan had gotten my face tattooed on her leg and I signed limbs and books whilst looking like the Pillsbury dough boy, wobbly tummy spilling through my white lace corset, deep pouches swinging from under my eyes. I had been getting so much love and support from fans around the world, but I felt so lost in life. I felt compelled to flush down luck, opportunity, love and to self-sabotage. I was terrified of Tommy, so frightened that he would kill me. He had been calling me to scream at me, to beg me to keep his child. He even threatened to cut me if I didn't. He desperately wanted me to have it.

I was going to get the thing scraped out of my body. The damn contraceptive pill hadn't blockaded the fish; like those blades of grass that push through concrete, life had miraculously begun to grow.

Pregnancy scans don't test for cruelty, psychosis, and brutality. If they did, I wonder how many fish women might throw back. So for the abortion itself, it was a wicked thing going through it, no matter how much you have come to dislike the father of the baby.

Tommy showed up at my home a day after the abortion and gave me a list of demands.

"Suck my cock. If you really love me, suck my cock," he ordered me as I lay in bed, curled up with a hot water bottle and painkillers. "Come on, baby, I have been so lonely. Can't you at least give me anal?"

He pushed my head down into the pillow while I screamed in agony.

"Stop feeling sorry for yourself!"

He bashed my skull and only got off me because I gave him my email and social media passwords, which he used to angrily delete things, shaking me awake in the middle of the night to interrogate me about something he had taken a dislike to on my computer.

I would never tell my family that I had made yet another horror decision with another horror man. Because the real war zone was my mum. She had always refused to take any of her medications for blood pressure and epilepsy, hiding the pills in tissues or under the bed and making it a life-long mission to lie to every doctor and specialist she ever saw.

"I am so ill, I am suffering, I have really high blood pressure, I feel very seizure-y," she would tell us all the time throwing us into terrifying high alert of an imminent heart attack or an epic screaming seizure.

The response from her loved ones was always the same: "Please take your medication, please mum, you'll have another stroke or crack your head on the ground again with another seizure,"

She'd snap and get upset. "It has nothing to do with you. It is none of your business why I don't take my meds."

That had been the pattern since my siblings and I were kids, and we braced ourselves every minute for an episode. I had been used to them. So when a stranger called my phone from her phone, I knew what they meant by "your mother has had a fall."

My mother lay in the middle of the fruit and veg section of a supermarket, a huge puddle of red seeping out around he. Her ponytail was soaked in blood. In the past, if by chance I had been near her, I had managed to catch her body right before she had gone into a seizure to cushion her fall but I couldn't always be there. People gathered round, gawping at her twitching, blue, with her tongue hanging out of her mouth, her eyes rolled back, her breaths gurgling in her throat. I cradled her in all her bloodied clothes, her gashed head seeping. We were taken to a hospital, where when she came out of her unconsciousness, the first thing she did was to bitterly scold me for having snitched to the doctor that she was not taking any of her medication. She was heartbroken at my betrayal.

But weirdly, she was obsessed with nourishing her kids with a wide variety of super healthy foods and juices, going to extreme lengths to find all sorts of exotic fruit and spending hours in the kitchen preparing a festival of Persian stews, rice, salads, and desserts every time she saw us. Then she'd harangue us about the harmful chemicals entering our body, getting enough sleep, and even how much damage I had done to my hair. "Every wreckage and destruction there is, you have meted out to your hair. All those hair extensions, wigs, and the constant bleaching and dyes, straightening, chemical sprays…" She nearly had another stroke in 2009 when I got a nose job.

I went to see a therapist, an Irish Catholic mammy who sat there gawping, my story not quite in the same stratum as her middle-class housewives with social climbing woes. The therapy was funded by a Christian/Catholic charity, so I didn't have to pay the full fees, but it was like putting a band aid on a bullet hole, and the therapy left me tired for days, feeling achy. Instead, I started working for animal charities and campaigning against cat and dog fur in China. I went to the theatre with Henry and tried to talk to him about my obsessions: Bette Davis and Joan Crawford, Christine Keeler, John Waters. I tried to make things click.

But Tommy had begged me to go with him to Oslo so he could get help with his addictions. He had been doing heroin and wanted to be amongst his friends whose social hangout was a creative/recording space for the city's creative homeless addicts.

The Scandinavian winter splintered my skull. Gothic darkness blanketed the winter city in the arctic cold as we marched briskly to the bar where Tommy worked, ice and snow crunching under our boots in the eerie glow of the yellow streetlamps. Me with my head down, not allowed to glance at anyone. I had called many rehab centers to get him in but he had refused, insisting that my presence in Oslo was all he needed to come off the junk.

At a friend's flat where Tommy had a section partitioned off with sheets we had a thin mattress next to a small electric heater, its shallow breath rising feebly as we slept. Nick was a black metal musician who was in the middle of transitioning into a lady as he had always felt like Nicole rather than Nick. Genteel and graceful, being a Nicole Kidman type lady was more becoming of him than a savage black metal fiend, although the human and animal skulls and part of Tommy's ear he kept pickled in a jar on the shelf–it had been sliced off in a fight-were emblems of his black metal proclivities and a preview into his lifestyle.

There was Hilda Frankehooker the frontman of a glam metal band, a dragged-up fishnet-stockinged man in his fifties with dagger-heeled PVC stilettos and chalk-white face powder. Blood-red gloss dripped from his lips as a luxuriant weft of hair attempted to disguise his bald patch. Although of delicate bones and slender build, a massive sagging gut spilled over from a crop top Barbie t-shirt which he teamed with a micro mini skirt held together with tracks of studded belts. He looked like an old 1980s hooker fallen on hard times.

Bjorn the Bastard was an ex-army dude who had done unspeakables in Bosnia and never wanted to talk about it so he self-medicated a lot. And there was Jorgen the Bear, a silent schizophrenic who was prone to losing his shit if you touched his stuff. Within the creative/addict shelter complex there was a rehearsal room they hung out in, rehearsed, ate and slept and did hellish amounts of Norwegian-grade speed. Along with instruments, the room was littered with CDs and mirrors flecked with powder, heaped ashtrays and a bucket of warm piss which I periodically contributed to as I couldn't be bothered to trudge it all the way to the courtyard and upstairs through a maze of offices to the small toilet. Copies of serial killer digests lay scattered on the floor keeping me entertained as Tommy hung out with the guys, with intermittent bitch fights and storming out episodes: Hilda shrieking and whacking Bjorn the Bastard with his handbag when he got too fresh, threatening to never come back as he marched out in his black stilettos, Jorgen being reduced to rocking back and forth in a corner covering his ears, chanting *no, no, no* knowing that one tiny trigger would topple him over the edge, and Nick/Nicole in full black metal mode having shed the genteel Victoriana lady part of him for the Rotting Christ church-burning one for the rehearsals.

With them, I felt protected from Tommy. Like a ring of orcs, who at my behest would crush Tommy if he hurt me in front of them, they planted themselves in-between us when he got nasty, leaving me free to scarper to another space in the complex to do my publicity interviews on the phone. It felt scary leaving them each night from the rehearsal room as Tommy and I walked back to the flat. At night I waited till he fell asleep and sneakily put on my pajamas and took them off as soon as he woke up.

Still, he'd catch me some nights:

"You really don't give a fuck about anyone but yourself do you Roxana?" he'd hiss close to my face, fists clenched.

When I explained to him that I loved sleeping in my pajamas, his hands squeezed around my neck. "You look like my dad in pajamas! Why would you want to do that to me? Why don't you want your skin to touch mine? Take them off NOW!"

In this city full of trams, Tommy affronted any Somali and Arab immigrants who crossed our path, spitting on the ground as we walked past them with a *svartskalle*-a Swedish racial slur for a person of color, his abhorrence for anything darker than beige always vocal and proud

In his little sweet innocent voice Henry kept asking me what was taking me so long to get back to England from helping "this poor addict Tommy" in Oslo. I had told him that I had a friend who was in trouble with his health and that I was helping him find rehab places.

"Why are you helping this guy?" Henry kept asking innocently. "Why are you giving him so much of your time sweetie?"

I trashed the loving, the adoring, the respecting, the healthy and glugged down radioactive waste, the carcinogens, the bash in the skull.

"You're always doing nice things for others. Taking care of them, helping them. Well, be careful with this guy. Make sure he doesn't try it on or anything."

The guilt, this evilness that was me, gashed my jugular and to myself I was worse than a pedophile for doing this to Henry. I was a dark entity and I deserved every bad thing that was coming my way. So I took punches and being spat on by Tommy unflinchingly, feeling that I deserved it. I started doing copious amounts of amphetamine, smoking heroin and doubling my epilepsy meds so I wouldn't have a seizure from the booze and drugs. Self-harm was on an epic scale, just the way I had wanted it. I would whisper to Henry that I missed him which I did so much. "Who the fuck are you talking to?" Tommy would bark at me, and I'd have to tell him that it was my mother.

"Tell her to pay for you to get your tits done," he'd snort.

After Tommy had fallen out with Nick/Nicole we had switched to staying in the spare room of a mousy hausfrau drug dealer named Annie who was a "furry": someone who is interested in creating and wearing life-sized animal fur costumes whilst exhibiting animal characteristics with human personalities. A brightly lit Moulin Rouge themed bedroom with candelabras and baroque mirrors held boxes of amphetamines as she sewed and stitched, hot glued, trimmed and embroidered manically, nose streaming and jaw grinding. Huge furry animal hats and man-size fur suits for human wear and play lay all over the place. Great hulks of foam cut-outs, faux fur, glass eyeballs and giant stuffed paws piled high on her shelves as she agitatedly but intricately made animal suits for sale to fellow furries. She'd rush to her bedroom door when Tommy knocked, compliantly dishing out freebie speed whenever he demanded it. Swathes of fabric, buttons and scissors were flecked with powder as a revolving door of customers dipped in and out for their drugs.

To pay for all of Tommy's food, bills, booze and transport I dipped into my book advance money which I was meant to be saving. In return, Tommy pummelled away at me like a trafficked sex worker and the more I rejected his advances, the angrier he got that I didn't love him.

Up the dark winter streets we marched to the bar where he worked, where I would sit on a stool, head down until he finished work, even asking his permission when I wanted to go to the toilet handing him my phone. I was to be in his eyesight in the corner of the bar until he finished work.

One night I suddenly felt the onslaught of an epileptic seizure. Like tectonic plates shifting, you feel a sudden shift in your aura as if your surroundings are flat and not real and feel paralyzed as if a giant tsunami is about to engulf all of you and it's the point of no return.

Instantly I took off my thick coat in the snow, burying my wrists deep into the ice, to snap my senses out of it, biting my fingers and arms to feel deep pain to release fast adrenalin to shock my brain into reversing its decision to have a seizure. I ran in the street with pain, whacking chucks of ice against my face to shake me out of the seizure feeling. It had been six years since my last one and I normally bit my tongue to shreds and was bedridden for months. Tommy ran after me with raised fist: "dumb hooker," he screamed trying to get to me for a beating. I pleaded with passers-by and a few guys stopped him from lunging at me. Still, Tommy couldn't help hocking up the phlegm to spit into my face, shouting "you're dead." One man grabbed me and shoved me into a cab and I went straight to the airport where I slept till I was able to get a flight to England. When Henry picked me up from the airport I had a seizure in his car.

A couple of months later, Tommy had tried to push me out of a hotel window in London. And it was only when he had gone to prison that he was finally out of my life.

Photo by Beki Cowey

FORTY-SIX

Somewhere in the Turkish mountains, 2016

It is peace here. Clean. Silent. I feel like a newborn.

I am standing outside the hut looking at my new mate who will transport me across the mountains.

"A donkey is better for you, not horse. It is small. You can ride better," the trench coat gangster dude says in English. Good point. The horse is a magnificent beast and I'm sure I wouldn't be able to handle it even though I learned to horse-ride as a teen. Yusuf gets on the horse and I put my foot in the stirrup and get on the donkey. Poor thing, having to lug around my lard ass. I truly feel sorry for it. I kiss it and tell it how sorry I am for my enormous girth and it looks depressed. The saddle is adorned with a small coarse kilim, and I grab the saddle horn on top of the pommel for support, my layers of skirts keeping me warm as the howling icy mountain wind gashes at my face like a razor blade.

"Khodahafez, tamoom (goodbye, finished)," Ibrahim says, brushing his palms together. He has been very kind to me, and I am sad he does not come with us. He was a fatherly protective gentleman. I bid him goodbye, stretching out from the donkey for a semi embrace. We ride in silence and make slow progress on the cold dark land, the new guy grabbing the donkey's bridle and marching next to us and Yusuf farther ahead on another horse.

The icy air clamps onto my face, the biting wind whipping my eyelids as we trudge along in this dark craggy silent land, the hollow of the mountainous valley ricocheting my guard's vocals as he barks out something, triggering echoes, possibly alerting any guards or smugglers that are operating in the vicinity. We stop and listen for any hint of response. Thankfully there is none and we continue in silence. After a while we come to an almost vertical mountain and the donkey's contractual obligation to this assignment, a journey broken into it since infancy, sees it immediately lodge its footing with care and precision on specific dents and ridges at the mountain base.

Poor creature.

"No, no, it's cruel. I'm too heavy," I object and try to alight from the animal as it's still trying to haul up its little body. Yusuf and the man titter at my concerned gesture but help me get off. I say no to getting on one of the horses with the man or Yusuf and manically begin the trek up the mountain by foot. Midway, I am utterly exhausted, and so I get on all fours, continue climbing on my hands and knees. The long and heavy layers of Kurdish dress trip me up and I keep stumbling back down the clusters of rocks. At the peak of the mountain I see my hands are gashed to shreds, my bloody wrists slashed by rocks and shrubbery. I collapse and the donkey sniggers at me with his giant tombstone teeth. Inside, my layers of clothing and fabric are soaked with sweat.

"Please, can we just rest a bit?"

A firm "NO!" snaps back from Yusuf. I have no choice but to get back on the donkey for the drop-down slope. Suddenly the beast lunges down the slope like it's been pumped full of steroids, dementedly galloping down the plummeting corrugated terrain, past Yusuf on the horse. My body judders up and down on the saddle. My legs grip and squeeze the donkey's rear and my bloody hands grip the slithery saddle horn as the donkey, unhinged, plunges down like a bat out of hell.

"Oh my God, oh my God, fuck fuck….I'm gonna fall!!" I shriek, terrified I am going to fall on the sharp rocks and crack my skull. I'm fucked. My hands, slick with blood and sweat, slip off the saddle horn and I grip the donkey's mane, which is more like short tufts of hair. I pull with all my might, which makes him bray and gallop and slide down the mountain; he's probably hoping I'll fall off.

Yusuf's horse whizzes past us and the new guy who is now riding with Yusuf grabs the donkey's bridle and forces the animal to slow down.

"Fuck, I'm gonna fall. It's been going so fast." I pant, terrified.

"Don't say fuck, it is bad word!" the new guy guffaws.

"What the actual fuck…" I recoil getting off the donkey.

"Ohhh, you say it again. Fuck. It make me so horny."

Christ. I'm not sure what to fear most: the deranged donkey, the threat of the Iranian military shooting at us, or Mr. Rapist here.

We reach the bottom of the mountain and what appears before us crushes me: silhouettes of panoramic mountains, foreboding like giant tombstones look down on us. We could still be hundreds of miles from Iranian soil and going up and down mountains for several more hours, I don't know.

Yusuf has already gone to check for any signs of military guards or soldiers. I have heard the stories of how they shoot anyone crossing the mountains on sight as so many Kurds smuggle fuel, cigarettes, booze, and humans through here. The mountains shield us, but the dark freezing wasteland is open.

We trudge up and down more mountains, sometimes with me on the donkey and sometimes crawling up on my hands and feet, my face whipped with the icy wind, my fingers numb and my arms and legs in a state of paralysis. I am sporty but not a mountain climber, and my skull and jaw and eyelids are frozen solid. I feel as if I am in a dream, an underwater burble.. Nothing seems real; the cold, the climbing, the landscape, being smuggled. I laugh hysterically, my body flopping about like a rag doll as I piss myself, drenching my Kurdish rags and sodden to the core.

"Ssssss," the man shakes me hard to stifle my laughing, which reverberates it even more and makes me sound like a cackling hyena, and so he slaps me. I now become infantile, pursing my lips and stamping my feet and crossing my arms as I plonk myself down on the mountain slope and sulk, silently willing my smuggler to pick me up and carry me. He grunts and in one fell swoop picks me up in his embrace and carries me up, urine soaked and giggly.

After a while I see Yusuf, who has been ahead of us, sprint down flapping his hands and motioning for us to cower down. We halt our movement and hear muffled voices ahead crackling against the crust of the land. The man climbs up stealthily to investigate, leaving me and the donkey to contemplate our fates. At night, various gangs operate in the area: other smugglers, Kurdish militant groups, lone criminals, cattle thieves, and who knows who else.

Me and my donkey sit down, and I cling to its warm body, its smell giving me a strange sense of life; a mix of hand-made wool kilim, potent dung and fresh soil. Minutes pass and the guy doesn't come back.

What if they have deserted me? I am alone on this vast mute land.

I think of our house in Tehran. I am sitting under the mulberry tree, looking at the stars. The lizards keep scraping their warm soft bellies on the gravelly wall and my friends have circled around me, proffering hugs and dollies. I see my grandmother telling me I'll be okay, not to be scared. I miss Iran so much that if they chuck my dead body over the border, at least I'll be physically in it.

It seems as if hours have gone by when I hear "Bia, bia! (Come on, come on!)"

Wearily I reach out to pull the donkey up by the reins, but my limbs don't budge. I tell my brain to send a message to my limbs to shift but they don't bloody listen. I blink. My lids and lashes cooperate, anyway. I contemplate sleeping on the slope and continuing the trek up the next day. I wonder if I'll have a seizure, but it is too cold for epilepsy as if it, too, won't emerge.

Yusuf looks down on me from the summit: a fluttering pigeon who dipped her beak in where it shouldn't and is now twitching in her fetal position from the mad alchemy of exposure to the elements and the terror of being caught by the revolutionary guards. He seems to be dragging me up by my arms, a dead weight full of piss and snow, apathy and delirium, eyelashes frozen. I am such an asshole. He drops me on the ground and points at an alcove gutted in the belly of the next mountain. "Khooneh, berim oonja, (House, let's go there)," he says.

When I feel a bit thawed out, we ride down. This endless night. I lie face down on the donkey in a semi embrace letting it just carry my dead weight regardless of whether I slip off or not. Thankfully the next climb is a small slope and we reach a rocky plateau with an entrance to a small cave. Deep caverns in the belly of the mountain make rest-stops and shelter for people passing through. The jagged rock formation of the cavity shelters a muddy bedrock where a boy of about thirteen is trying to force bottled liquid into the mouth of a donkey. Two men tending to horses greet us warmly and hand us flasks of hot tea.

"Are we in Iran now?" I ask.

"Na! Na Hanooz (Not yet)," says Yusuf.

I slump down in the cave and attempt to thaw out my bones. I am exhausted and close to giving up. The tea warms me up and I am handed dried scraps of lavash. In half Farsi the young Kurdish boy tells me he is a shepherd and as head of the family he is in charge of one hundred sheep. His skin is charred, his adolescent teeth already rotting away. A crudely handwoven jumper clumped with food matter and hay barely keeps him warm and his feet are bare and raw. He waters the donkey till the bottle is empty. "Up there" in a "nice" place, he lives with his mother and three sisters, and he is very keen to show me where their home is, that I be a guest of honor and served early morning breakfast with his mother and sisters.

I peel off the soggy wet layers, and as raw and blotchy as my piss-stained flesh is, I unload the prissy princess attitude and prepare to continue the journey with new horses and donkeys. We leave Yusuf's horse and the poor creature that has been carrying me for hours in the cave to recuperate and continue with the new animals. Yusuf hands me over to two new smugglers and I anxiously bid him goodbye and thank him for everything.

These are new smugglers and I have to renew my trust.

Will they be good people? Will they attack me?

They must have already been paid, so why would they care whether I live or die?

Suddenly the young shepherd jumps behind me on the donkey. This new animal will have to carry the two of us. Once again, one of the men rides ahead as his friend rides next to me and Rasoul.

The boy is cheery, as if we are off on holiday.

"Do you have WhatsApp?" he asks in English.

"WhatsApp?" I laugh, amused by the bizarre question and somewhat freaked out by the weight of both of us on the donkey.

"I can take you to my family home, up there," he says in half-Farsi/half English, his hand coming out from behind me, pointing to the right.

"You stay the night, have food. My mother and my grandmother, they make dinner. You live with us. It is good home. You give me your WhatsApp and I will call you."

It's all very surreal.

As we near the bottom of the mountain, I hear water. The sound of a gushing river or stream babbling over the clink of rock shards. I'm not sure how deep it is or whether we can cross on horseback. The stream isn't too wide but the current is robust and vigorous.

Rasoul and I dismount the donkey. One of the guys from the cave is the first to cross the rocky stream, leading his horse slowly across. At times he is wading knee deep, stumbling on the rock debris at the bottom, and I step in with the other guys. The water is freezing and I let out an involuntary squeal, quickly stiffening for the fear of Iranian guards is still very real and we could be shot right here crossing the water. The rapids pull my body to the right as I hold the reins of the donkey with Rasoul and the guide helping me. I suddenly hit a dip and plummet down deep into the gushing chest-level current, losing my grip on the donkey's reins and getting pushed downstream. I grab the edges of the rocks to stop myself bashing my head into their sharp edges. The freezing water crushes my chest, halts my breathing and swiftly I am dragged back up by the men who continue to carry me to the other side of the stream.

I grab onto bunches of shrubs, tree roots and weeds to pull myself up onto a grassy knoll. The first man pulls a blanket from the back of the horse. My layers of Kurdish skirts, my dress, and my headscarf are soaked. My bones feel heavier than ever but still we traipse on along the flat land, the two men strong and lithe, me and Rasoul, a batter of smushed bones, muscle, and sinew. I am having serious thoughts of setting up camp here on this lovely grassy knoll and living on berries and field mice when through blurry vision I see the mammoth hulk of a towering mountain before me.

"Iran! Iran!" one of the men whispers excitedly pointing at the mountain.

From some deep reserve I muster enough strength to dig my claws into the earth at the foot of the mountain. Drenched with heavy wet fabric clinging to my body, brain fuzzy from hunger and fatigue, I think of the mountain as chocolate cake and not Darth Vader as it looms before me. Hours have passed and I have become detached from my soul. I am just a hollow shell clutching at life. I think I will collapse and die here. The guys don't even help me, each lost in their own private struggle. After a while I feel I have lost consciousness, blacked out. I don't remember how I got to the top of the mount.

When we ride the beasts down to the bottom of the mountain, we have reached Iran.

And suddenly all memories of the past few years evaporate, the toxins and radioactives that have contaminated my being dissolve. It's just dirt beneath my feet but I feel different, my life in the West and the aftermath of my memoir now little more than an unpleasant aftertaste.

FORTY-SEVEN

Inky dark dissolves into misty dawn and luscious meadows materialize into focus. Over the valleys, we observe the faint glow of twinkling lights down in the gorge. Homes. A village maybe?

"My house," our leader says proudly.

We sprint down the pasture with renewed energy at the sight of shelter and warmth. In the mist, a scattering of sheep, incandescent, warm puffy clouds, graze by the huts, and as we edge closer I notice a little waterfall crashing down onto the rocks below at the village entrance. An assortment of T-shirts and boys' trousers hang on tree branches near it. The village deep in the gorge is made up of little huts, multicolored rugs draped over their rails, smoke from a morning fire rippling up. The little hamlet is stirring. A woman on a balcony, chador bunched under her elbow tends to a clay oven.

Me and Rasoul follow the two men up a cobbled path which swerves up through the mountain and past the maze of houses. Unexpectedly, the man who rode beside me and Rasoul in the mountains turns sharply onto a wooden bridge and crosses over to one of the houses without saying goodbye. We continue until we reach a bend, and the main guide then takes us farther up the cobbled mountain steps to his home. The balcony next door is filled with his neighbors having breakfast, chattering in a language that I gather is Kurdish, men grouped together on one side and the women at the other end all sitting on layers of Persian carpets and pillows. Jam, slabs of feta, and fried eggs lying next fresh baked lavash. A couple of samovars brew tea. From up here on the stone courtyard, the sun crinkles through, brushing my face, and exhaustion hits hard.

The guide takes the horse and donkey and lets them rest in a yard, leaving them food and water. An old lady wrapped in bright Kurdish dress comes out and greets us warmly. It's the guide's mother. She has bright green eyes, and her white and gray hair is streaked with henna.

She motions me inside and the hut looks similar to the beehive houses I visited on the border of Syria, which naturally maintain frigid air in the summer and warmth in winter. Oil lamps and a kaleidoscope of hand-woven rugs hang from the walls. I am ready to collapse, and the kind lady knows this. She has already prepared a bed and starts hugging me and talking to me in Kurdish and broken Farsi. I can't believe how kind these people have been to me. So welcoming and protective all through this journey. In a small, cool room, she helps me peel off my now crinkled-dry heavy clothing and dresses me in loose linen sleepwear. The bedding is soft and woolly and warm. I gratefully accept the bread and cheese she gives me, gulp down a bit of tea, and collapse into bed.

It's dark when I wake up. There is no one around and for a moment I panic and wonder where I am. Have I been dreaming? The donkey, the mountains, the cold, the men. Was it all a dream? I have trusted so many. I just put my life into their hands eagerly and heartily without letting the barbs of suspicion puncture my faith.

I'm in Iran! I can't believe it. Finally.

But the initial elation is soon overshadowed by the reality that I must now constantly watch my back, not tell anyone my real name or where I am going.

I open the room door and hear voices, and look outside to see folk having food on a flat rooftop next door. Kurdish music is played on a goblet drum and oboe by a couple of men as a few women young and old dance with kids clinging to their legs.

"Salaam, did you sleep well?"

It's the main guide holding a pile of clothes for me. I don't even know his name.

Sirwan, turns out.

I thank him warmly for everything he has done for me. Hassan, Yusuf, Ibrahim…all of them. And where is the boy, Rasoul?

I leave the Kurdish clothes behind and wear the regular Islamic dress. Not the conservative look of chador, the tent-like billowing sheet of synthetic material that shrouds and engulfs you head to toe, and not the contemporary look the girls in Tehran have for years displayed as a *fuck you* to the compulsory Islamic dress code they have been enforced to adhere to since the revolution. A display that is a "barely there" piece of cloth on peroxided bouffants form-hugging mini red and pink manteaus and drag-queen makeup layered on. Their version of "Islamic" attire is a display of anarchy, a counterattack to the compulsory, baggy, shapeless, dour-colored overcoat code of attire designed to cover the curves of a woman's shape, to de-feminize. I think that just a simple navy head scarf and manteau will do me and then realize that I will stand out as a sore thumb, a peasant, amongst the gaudy doll-like ladies. I also realize how long it's been since I washed. I smell like the donkey. And moldy cheese. And piss and shit. Fuck knows what my underwear must smell like. My pouch bag buckled to my waist lies crumpled. My spare top, leggings, and underwear is a mouldering heap.. I have carried my medication, soap, a toothbrush, my passports, and some cash.

Sirwan tells me that he must now take me to Tabriz before the neighbors start getting suspicious. He tells me to continue wearing the wedding ring I have been wearing and waves a fake marriage certificate to show as proof that he and I are married. I have been told that a girl can't really travel alone in Iran and is not allowed to stay in hotels on her own. Everything a girl does in Iran needs to be approved by a man: her father, her brother, or her husband. And because the Iranian intelligence bugs phones and intercepts emails and social networking accounts, even with my fake Iranian passport, I am still not "all-clear." I must remain inconspicuous and publicly pretend to be someone else —a woman called Neda.

Massive credit to the smugglers: they are a very well-oiled machine, thinking of everything, even a new identity and fake marriage certificate.

I have a quick wash in a small washroom, scrubbing with loofahs and a pumice stone. The hot steam relieves me of the stress and cold. My body is covered in cuts and bruises, but I am happy, I feel alive. I really do love this beautiful village and wish I could blend into its watercolors and landscape, the muted pastels of its doors, the magnificent rock of its mountains and brilliantine gushing hues of its local dress. But we must leave the shire and all its magical twinkling night lights.

"Don't forget to tell your mother thank you from the bottom of my heart," I tell Sirwan as he leads me down a steep cobbled stone alleyway to an old mustard car.

Sirwan offers me a cigarette. I have missed having a fag, but this cigarette is like no other; so coarse and harsh is the multiple chemical additives packed into the unfiltered tobacco that it tastes like petrol. It's rough but I consolidate it into the narrative of my adventures.

We seem to have been driving for ages when I see a sign for the famous Lake Urmia, one of the biggest salt-water lakes in the world, an archaeological site going back 12,000 years ago. When I was a child, everybody came here, like the Dead Sea in Jordan, to bathe in its salt waters to heal aching joints like arthritis and treat skin conditions. Everyone would bathe in its mineral rich mud giving themselves face and body masks and holiday on the beaches of its hundred or so islands. Hundreds and thousands of pink flamingos lived on the lake and were part of its setting.

"Are we going past Lake Urmia?" I ask excitedly. I would even bathe in the saltwater lake at night.

"So bad now." Sirwan shakes his head. "Everything is dead."

And sure enough, as we approach, I see a vast salt white barren land with moored boats. Lake Urmia is about ninety miles long. Once, hundreds of species of birds, including its famous 50,000 odd flamingos, lived here. Now Sirwan tells me that eighty percent of it has shrunk and disappeared and the lake is practically extinct because of the government's excessive dam and weir construction for big businesses and the building of a causeway starving the lake of water and making it a slaughterhouse for thousands of its mammals, with carcasses of dead and dying deer and flamingos strewn all over it.

Sirwan tells me about how this once natural wonder of the world is now a desiccated exposed lakebed, causing salt storms which kill local agriculture and vegetation. Everyone's livelihood has been affected by it and the health of domestic and wild animals have been ravaged with respiratory illnesses, eye problems, and throat and esophageal cancer. The lake's food chain and ecosystem has collapsed. It is an ecological disaster zone, an environmental catastrophe, and the Iranian government will not do anything about it. They love to shit all over their country's natural and archaeological beauty.

Sirwan is so angry and passionate when he talks about this that I tell him he should join current activists urging action. This huge tragedy crushes me. The rape and murder of Iran's stunning natural beauty is soul-destroying especially in a country with such rich history and culture. I feel like I want to see more of the land before I go to Tehran.

It suddenly dawns on me that when we get to Tabriz, Sirwan's job is done, and I'll have to go my own way. I am not sure how to feel about that. Naked, exposed, vulnerable. But Tabriz belongs to my mother. Its streets are etched into my lineage; its language—Azari—woven intimately into the fabric of my childhood. Strangely, I will not be defenceless. The city itself, ancient and unyielding, shall serve as my guardian, a protector both boorish and motherly.

We stop at an all-night roadside café for tea and snacks. In Tabriz all I will need to do is a get a train or bus to Tehran. But right now, it seems Sirwan has other plans for me. Before he drops me in Tabriz, he wants to take me to the eight-hundred-year-old troglodyte village of Kandovan, where homes have been carved into the natural formation of rocks on top of one another like layer cake, the whole village a sculpture in the belly of the mountain. Then a place of natural hot springs, too, and he even wants to take me to Palangan, another ancient village a long way away. The whole of Persia is a world heritage site. Such an ancient land, such breath-taking natural beauty. I decide that before anything happens to me, before I get found out and prosecuted, I must see Persepolis, Shiraz, Esfahan, the Silk Road, the ancient bazaar of Tabriz, the palaces and caravanserais and mount Damavand, the iconic mystical strato-volcano that last had an eruption around seven thousand years ago.

Urmia, our current refuge, is itself a living museum—a sprawling testament to four millennia of history. This ancient Christian enclave brims with churches and cathedrals, adorned by echoes of the Safavid, Ottoman, Assyrian, and Qajar dynasties. Its population pulses with diversity: Armenians, Jews, Christians, Kurds, and Azaris, each community adding layers to an already overwhelming sensory tapestry.

I agree to Sirwan taking me to Kandovan, but only if we stay in separate hotel rooms on our pit stop. He drives us to a hotel, our fake marriage certificate allowing us to stay even though we raise suspicion with our request for two rooms.

I am alone for the first time in a long while. I grab the raw mastic soap I have been given and scrub out the toxic history traffic-jammed in me.

FORTY-EIGHT

And in the morning breakfast is served on carpets in a café inside a mountain. I feel like I am actually on holiday, albeit a fucked-up, hazardous one. Kind of like the bitter-sweet concoction of dread and wonder if I was to venture on my own into the Amazon forest.

Sirwan insists on driving us all the way to the village of Sarien, to the thermal hot springs and volcanic pools, even though Kandovan is closer. He has friends he wants me to make a connection with. I am hesitant as I want to get to Tehran and this is already feeling like a tourist tour, but I go along anyway. This could be the only chance I get to see the ancient wonders.

There are nine natural hot springs sprouted around Sarein, some hot, some cold and carbonated. It's a busy place with tons of tourists and we wait till late at night to be let in by Sirwan's friend who works there. It is late and the steam rising from the boiling waters creates a dense fog. Wearing a borrowed old shirt and sports pants I dip my body in the mineral-rich water and float on my back, thankful that we have avoided the crowds. The water is heated by Sabalan Mountain and people come here for its curative aspects, like increased blood circulation from the waters' calcium and sodium bicarbonate and relief from joint pain and tissue damage. The hottest spring has a maximum temperature of sixty-seven degrees.

Sirwan chats to his friend, Keyvan, and I am grateful that thus far every man I have met on this journey has treated me with such care and decency. I am lucky. It could have easily gone the other way, especially with the smugglers.

I wonder if I should call my family in Tehran to let them know that I am in Iran, but I am scared that their phones will be tapped. I am excited, but also terrified. It's insane that I have had to sneak into my own country illegally just because I wrote a book. It's insane that my human story makes me a person of moral turpitude. I am a human being and my life is in danger just because I wrote a book about my life.

Sirwan hands me a towel. "Bia, bia, let's go to another place."

Hopping and jumping all over the place in the thick steam with no visibility feels like I am lost inside another dimension. When I emerge, I see we are at the base of the Sabalan Mountain by the ski resort. Green meadows and bedrock on the flanks of the mountain circle the springs where I submerge my body, my aching joints melting in the thick soup of the water. In the cool crisp air of the mountain we hear voices; Keyvan's friends, two guys and two girls. A soiree at natural hot springs at the foot of a mountain is so much sexier than your average booze and drug fueled vom-fests in Camden on a Saturday night.

But it is death we are smearing ourselves with; that yummy fetid excrete of possible prosecution and flogging if caught by the morality police or the Basij. Mixed genders, especially in this context, is illegal and punishable by flogging and imprisonment. I am nervous, especially as the couples are here to hang out and probably drink alcohol—also illegal and also punishable unless, like everyone else, you bribe the authorities with stacks of cash and gooey schmooze.

The girls greet me like a long-lost friend, and I'm covered with tumbling manes of hair, crimson cushion pouts, and fragrance bombs. Thick-thighed and blue jeaned, they wear the shortest manteaus, and a teeny patch of silk scarf perches like a tea cozy over their hair. They're surely taking the piss with this faux Islamic get-up, which is a fusion of Essex girl and drag queen, though their savagely arched eyebrow tattoos place them in a whole new category. The patchwork of pop subcultures is a look that a lot of Iranian women have adopted in Iran as pushback, a mockery of the forced veiling. Years of torture, of having the state take legal ownership of their bodies, bodily functions, autonomy, and human behaviors has pushed these women to do the opposite: layers of pantomime make up with giant collagen lips over severely chiseled down button noses, Iran being the nose job capital of the world.

Settareh (which means Star) and Roya (which means Fantasy), both common Iranian names, are from Tehran and here for a holiday. They have had to do a "temporary marriage" contract with their boyfriends just so they can travel and holiday together legally. *Sigheh,* a temporary marriage ranging from one hour to ninety-nine years, allows men to have as many sexual partners as they want and up to four temporary wives under sharia law. A man and a woman can obtain one for a fixed period of time and for an agreed fee that the man pays the woman by undergoing a verbal or written private contract in front of a Muslim cleric. The man can end the *sigheh* at almost any time, but there is no divorce rights for women in temporary marriages. The restriction for women also includes that fact that after each *sigheh*, she must wait two menstrual periods before marrying again. And because the man must pay a pre-determined sum to his short-term wife for every temporary marriage (more if she is a virgin), it is basically legalized prostitution and a legal and accepted form of adultery in Islam. Many traveling businessmen take advantage of this law by taking in a two- or three-hour wife for sexual pleasure. Girls and boys who want to date and have sex use this law as a loophole to go on holiday together, stay in hotel rooms, and have sex legally. A certificate to say that they are in a temporary marriage is the best way of avoiding the religious police. Widows and divorcees and women who are struggling financially also take advantage of this for financial gain.

With Settareh and Roya and their boyfriends Peyman and Reza, I hear about alcohol and drug-fueled parties in Iran, where casual sex is openly flaunted. Opium is seen as an old man's drug and associated with the working classes, so cocaine and meth are the rich kids' high. In beauty salons uptown, crystal meth is even sold as a weight loss supplement because they don't think that it could be addictive like opium or heroin. They just think it's chic. There is designer brand alcohol and cocaine and ecstasy for the rich uptown kids of Tehran doing it in mansions with butlers and for the downtown poor kids there are derelict hovels with opium and *aragh sagi*, cheap moonshine vodka made from raisins. Aragh means sweat and sag means dog, the harshness of the homemade brew earning it the name "dog sweat."

Everyone drinks alcohol in Iran and no mixed gender party is complete without a stack of bribery cash at the ready to keep the morality police from prosecuting everyone there. There are three million Basij, a volunteer paramilitary group operating under the command of the revolutionary guards and the supreme leader Ayatollah Khamenei. They cruise the streets of Iran in cars and stalk the pavement looking for any "un-Islamic" dress code and behavior, arresting, hassling, and imprisoning anyone displaying anti-Islamic activity.

The Basij, who are considered the "army of the guardians of the Islamic revolution" and government watchdogs, are in reality a network of armed thugs who stop and beat up whoever they please in the name of Islam. They carry out violent attacks and physically assault anyone protesting or being critical of the regime. They spy on the population, stop cars to check for music, seize music and satellite dish antenna, and stop women for use of makeup, burst into weddings and arrest guest for mixing genders.

A voluntary force, being in the Basij attracts social benefits and material perks, so recruitment is especially targeted at deprived families. Teenage boys are enticed with day trips, summer camps, food, and higher chances of gaining places at university, and because the official age of enlisting is eighteen, deprived families even pay to forge birth certificates for their underaged sons. The Basijis are not there because they are ardent devotees of Islam but for these material reasons along with the power to be legal thugs.

Gashte ershad, literally meaning "guidance patrol," are the morality police. They harass females showing hair under their headscarf or wearing too tight a manteau or too much make up and boys who wear "Western" style clothes or have "Western" hair styles (long hair or "emo" styles). Or anyone listening to music in their car too loudly, especially if it's Western music. Both morality police and the Basij take it upon themselves to do as they please.

I know all this. I know, I know, I know, I have known. But I can't fully love my country if I don't feel its pain. I can't fully embrace the streets and the humans if I don't experience the verbal and physical thrashing and the fury, the harassment, the rumor and suspicion. It is the dirt I am here for.

I have heard this town is fully of honey and I yearn for some as I watch the bodies melting in that hot pot of thick swooshing water. I leave them to it. To them "freedom" is MTV; for me, freedom is the consequences.

FORTY-NINE

The 800-year-old village of Kandovan owes its existence to geological mayhem. Long ago, some volcano cracked open and spewed forth its ash and ruin, and over the years water erosion, cool and soft, chiselled it into cone-shaped domes and beehive homes. The result: dwellings have erupted from the earth's crust rather than been built on it.

Ancient wooden doors are wedged into crannies that pass for thresholds. Balconies are less scenic add-ons than opportunistic hollows in the rock face, doubling as ceilings for the rooms below. The rock earns its keep: it insulates, keeping the house cool during summer and warm during winter, which means that heating or air conditioning is not required.

Steps don't rise so much as sag and dip, dented by bare feet and old sandals, the kind that carry buckets, babies, bread. Six hundred souls call this arrangement home.

Most of the cave houses are two to four stories in height, some maintaining their natural cave formations while others have extra rooms and larger spaces that have been tunneled through the rock, all interconnected like a beehive.

We are met in Kandovan by Parvaneh (or "Butterfly," another common Iranian name), a family friend of Sirwan's from Tehran and studying to be an engineer. We walk up the rutted stone steps sculpted into the mountain. Donkeys carry traders' wares up and women with rouge scarves and arabesque dresses dry sour cherries on top of the balconies, laying out fruit leather to dry. Tourists sit inside the cave cafes that disappear inside secret pathways. Balconies and bridges all interconnect to a network of homes, cafes, vaults, and boutiques. It is no wonder tourists come from around the world to stay here in the cave hotels.

Parvaneh is having her hymen sewn up as she needs to be a virgin on her wedding night. She tells me as we eat a dinner of pureed aubergine with crushed walnuts and whey at the restaurant on the mountain plateau. She is excited because she has found a doctor who can also insert a red capsule into her vagina to make the illusion even more authentic. Even in well-educated, liberal families, a non-virgin bride can bring embarrassment and shame, so many women undergo hymen reconstruction just before their wedding, some even going so far as having red ink capsules inserted in their vagina. In the old days, some from lower traditional classes in the provinces were even forced to display the bloodstained sheets after consummating the marriage.

A long running joke in Iran is that girls ought to get zips in their vaginas because of the amount of times they keep getting their hymen reconstructed only to have sex again. The consequence of all this virginity nonsense is that a lot of girls in Iran only have anal sex, not wanting their hymen re-torn or the hassle and expense of reconstruction.

Parvaneh and I talk for hours late into the night, bathed into a fold of purple and orange hue smudged into the black. The stone houses, so brash in sunlight, blur into soft silhouettes and lanterns glow behind wooden doors. The stars hang low—too many to count, as if the sky has cracked open just above the roofs. I want to stay one more night and one more again; Sirwan's family want us to stay for parties and barbeques.

But I keep thinking of Tehran. The big city. Crumbling mansions uptown. Morality police. The Basij. Hezbollah. Sex parties. Crystal meth trends. Opium. Hymen reconstruction. Flogging for unmarried sex. Poetry nights under the stars and families at the bazaar. Mulberry trees in the street. Sleepy alleyways and bakers working in chain gangs. Underground theatre. Black metal rehearsed illegally in barns. Dinky nose jobs, even on the shop mannequins. *Bazaaris.* Drug addled sex workers walking the streets with their children. A wealth of fresh foods and fruit. Pomegranates. Love. Oppression. Dictatorship. Poverty. Everyone obsessed with education and becoming a doctor or lawyer or engineer. Getting abused on the street by the morality police. Bribery. Clothes. Oppression. 1970s Mercedes.

I think of my father. His hands, his face graying and cadaverous by years of opium. I don't feel a connection to him but feel obliged to be there for him and my grandmother. I feel an obligation to myself to be in my childhood neighborhood. To heal. To find that girl who died in August 1984.

Kandovan

FIFTY

I curl up on the bus, and beside rugged mountain views from the window, I watch Iranian films on a tiny TV screen. I don't know how to feel about seeing my father again, whom I have met briefly back in 2004. I am his only child, and he has never remarried, unless you count opium. From what I gather, his life has been countless trips to rehab or going cold turkey after being locked in rooms by his sister-in-law.

Back in 2004 I didn't feel that sense of danger that I do with my stepfather. I saw a mellow-natured man with a slow drawl and love for poetry and literature. Very old school rock 'n' roll spirit.

After the long bus journey, I finally arrive in Tehran. Naturally, I am met with astonishment and elation- which is stupidly hazardous to my father and grandmother's elderly nerves and hearts. They have never comprehended how much my book makes it risky for me to be in Iran or the gravity of what could happen to me. Because they haven't read my writings—and I really, really wouldn't want them to—they don't understand why a memoir would be so incendiary. I don't explain. It is better they don't know. What I do tell them is that I didn't get here on a plane, that I came another way.

My grandmother is in her eighties and my father who is unwell, doesn't go anywhere. My grandmother burns rue seeds in a brass incense resin bowl swinging from an ornate chain, and with popping and crackling, the seeds smoke furiously, the sweet pungent whiff strongly resembling weed as my grandmother circles the smoldering container around my head to ward off the evil eye. The burning *esfand* reminds me of when I had scarlet fever as a child and the neighbors gathered round me in prayer.

The streets are, infuriatingly, exactly as I remember them when I was ten: children scattered like thrown dice across alleyways and public squares, shrieking with a joy I can no longer access, while persimmon and mulberry trees preside over the commotion. Sycamores line the boulevards, their branches weary, bowing down to the smog and motorbike exhaust, their leaves catching the sun. Somewhere in the din: a Citroën 2CV—a relic rolling past.

In the afternoon, as the sound of Azan laments through the neighborhood, I am lulled into a trance and I sleep deeply wishing I had a religion. The sort that devours you. I wish I could wrap myself willingly in a soft cotton chador—not for ceremony or show, but out of deep conviction, the kind that would make me kneel five times a day and feel relief in the denial of food. I wish I could go to the mosque and believe and cleanse.

I queue outside the neighborhood bakery after the siesta, watching the choreography of the sangak men. Their rhythm is both mechanical and balletic, slapping dough onto stone, then heaving it onto a bed of searing river pebbles. The bread—triangular, blistered, impressively inconvenient—is what everyone waits for, fingertip burns included.

In the corner shop, strained yogurt is sold in plastic buckets too large for any reasonable fridge, thick and sour and homemade next a radiator. I carry one home, swinging it like a child pretending it's a lantern, passing stalls peddling tamarind that could pucker your entire face and roasted beetroot that stains everything it touches with the color of dried blood.

And then it happens: that traitorous sensation. As if I've slipped sideways into time. And I want, idiotically, to freeze this moment. Not because it's perfect, but because it's mine.

Back in 2004 when I had visited Iran, I retraced my steps back to my childhood home in Narmak, and a lot of neighbors and childhood friends that had lived there in 1984 were still there, and as if by magic, they had emerged from their homes to greet me in the square. It had been an on-the-spot exorcism. Everything bad that had happened to me had dissipated; my humanity was reset.

And now I am here again, and word has got round. *Fuck it, if I get caught, I get caught, let's just embrace it.*

I am utterly dumbfounded that these old friends and neighbors are still here after so long, more so that they recognize me. So much of the neighborhood comes to greet me, cooing and gushing over me. My friends, now mothers with grown up kids, are still living in the neighborhood, making gossip and feasts, radiating affection and kinship.

I am smothered with puddings and watermelons puking seeds, with quince and pistachio and cake. Old neighbors give me gifts of belly-dancing hip chains, jeweled mirrors, pearls, and Persian miniature handcrafts. I genuinely don't give a fuck if anything happens to me now.

"I am so happy you got a nose job, finally!" a neighbor I haven't seen since 2004 beams. Not only are Iranians obsessed with nose jobs, but Iranian people who are older than you, whether strangers or family, feel it necessary to loudly blurt out an instant assessment of your physical "flaws," doing you the kind "favor" of proffering advice on how to "correct" them.

Inevitably, scarily, relatives find out I am in Iran and insist on showing me a good time. I am quickly made aware that I look like a peasant, an old maid from the provinces, as a cousin and I drive through traffic-jammed night streets and past grassy knolls with giant families. Women and girls sift through crowds, sunglasses atop bleached hair. Their tight short dress-coats pinching their meaty curves and their faces incandescent with bronze.

I watch them; the new brave, the new punks of the twenty-first century. Boredom combined with pushing the limits, defying the regime and risking arrest and prison. Guys, too, resist the Islamic regime with sartorial weapons: tight jeans and spiky haircuts, pierced brows, tattoos.

The regime has cottoned on to the tactic that by turning a blind eye to the heavily made-up faces, tight short dress, and mixed-gender parties, they are creating a perception of "liberation"-keeping the masses pacified, neutering any seeds of revolt. Making young people believe that "dress code laws are lax now and you have so much freedom" gives them the illusion that they are actively participating in revolutionary resistance, thus suppressing true revolt, and helping to dampen social and political unrest and protests.

I just want to drink some pomegranate juice and see my streets, but I feel like I am in the middle of a mating game. I walk with my male cousin around the street shops and a girl walking past hoots and whistles at him, sucking air through her teeth and hot whispering "what a piece!" as we pass. Another girl sticks a piece of paper with her number into his hand. I glance up at my cousin—surely he can't be *that* hot. But then I see him in a new light. He is tall, very alpha, with a solid frame and thick hair and the high cheekbones and chiseled jaw that all the men on my dad's side have. This is the first time I have ever met him, and I can see the attraction. Many Iranians marry their first cousins, and though I am grossed out by the thought of cousins that I have grown up with all my life, it is different when it is someone I had just only met.

All this aggressive mating calls make me feel I'm in the jungle. Guys and girls exchange flirtations from their cars and throw bits of paper with their phone number through each other's windows, slowly cruising past, holding up traffic behind them as they pass phone numbers to potential dates. It's like mobile clubbing, and it is all done somewhat covertly, in case the morality police are around, though it's obvious that no one gives a shit about any law. In fact, promiscuity and sex parties are the only outlet from this tyrannical pressure cooker.

Huge billboards of Khomeini and the current supreme leader Khamenei etched with revolutionary slogans scowl down at us as my relatives and I drive at night to mehmoonis. Most of my mother's family live in the north of the city, the chic wealthy part of town, and driving from my father's home all the way uptown through the traffic jams can be exhausting. No one observes traffic laws in Iran and driving is done by gut reaction. Traffic lights, signs, and lane markers are disregarded in the haphazard web of lorries, trucks, cars, and motorbikes, none of which yield to pedestrians. The traffic thus whizzes fast in an "each man for himself" fashion in every direction to create a spaghetti web of pileups at junctions, vehicles squeezing past one another by mere millimeters, reversing in the middle of motorways, driving through red lights, straddling all lanes at the same time, suddenly reversing in the middle of zooming traffic, and doing U-turns and maneuvers with no signaling or warning. The car horn is used incessantly to warn of the next maneuver.

We sail past huge billboards of Iraq war martyrs, garland-festooned murals of bearded uniformed war heroes airbrushed with crimson cheeks and rose-bud lips in paradise, white doves galore and etched with Qur'an verses. Young men who were martyrs of the war and now have a key to paradise. I choke on the mid-town fumes till we get to the fresh clean air of uptown, past billboards for new Iranian films, a poster for AIDS with a man coming out of the sea and praying to God, animated sketches of veiled women with speech bubbles blurting out the message that: "Those women who wear makeup and expose their hair from beneath Islamic hejab are deemed to be psychologically damaged by doctors."

Uptown, mansions amongst mountains beckon. Swimming pools in lavish Persian gardens with towering fruit trees and mosaic ponds and servants. My dad, penniless and shy, declines the offer to join me preferring to avoid questions like: *What work are you doing now Nasser? What part of town do you live in? Any plans to go on holiday?* Even his daughter who lives abroad has nothing; no PhD, no job, just sexy photos on the internet.

He drives all the way back to his apartment, where he will sit with my grandmother and watch satellite TV while they eat the food she has prepared with wobbly hands. I feel bad that I am left in this mansion. Persian carpets swathe the floor, marble columns and baroque furniture a little nouveau riche. A throng of people lunge towards me, suffocating me with bear-hugs and smooches, stuffing jewelry and art miniatures into my hand and at the same time pushing me toward a giant buffet.

"Ooohhh, wow, you've gotten so fat, darling Negar," my aunt warmly greets me. "Why haven't you been on a diet? Your face has got very round. Here, I made lamb and all your favorites."

Some old random neighbor of my aunt's, Shirin Khanoum, comes to my "rescue," to tell me, "Tomorrow, I'll take you to the beauty salon, they'll give me a good discount, they know me there. You stick with me."

"Shirin jaan, do they do eyebrows there too? Negar jaan, your eyebrows are so Western. You need to get them done properly and your hair is very thin. I know some doctors, they are single. I am sure you can find a good husband."

I pout and arch my brows haughtily, hoping to settle into the resting bitch face stare Persian women are supposed to have.

We all dance and afterward someone sings a folk song, with one of my uncles reciting Persian poetry and playing the santoor. My uncle is a famous poet and songwriter in Iran, another is a well-known sculptor and ballet dancer, and another, a well-connected film producer.

No one talks about my book but they all want to know how I got into Iran illegally. I give as little information as possible.

I light the samovar with my cousins and aunties, and we gossip about boyfriends or *khastegars*—suitors who visit with family to ask the girl's family for marriage. The dowry is negotiated by the two families. A few of my cousins are dating guys secretly, and some are firm on the rule of no sex before marriage. Nevertheless, my aunts have an open mind about these things despite their illegality. Some of my cousins' friends have had hymenoplasty to be re-virginized for their wedding night.

Everyone at the party invites me to their house so I have a packed schedule of parties, mountain outings, and dance and poetry nights, but I am just not sure if it is *taa'rof*, the Iranian custom of persistent offers and polite refusals.

The practice of *taa'rof* in Iranian culture is a pre-requisite fake pleasantry; an empty offer. Often, the person inviting you to dinner at their home or offering you their seat on the bus and so on is doing it as a pleasantry and the receiver is required to refuse this offer multiple times. You must not say yes immediately and keep saying "no thank you" multiple times to the offer of cup of tea, dinner invitation, gift, house party, a seat, the door being held open for you. This "no, thank you" does not in any way mean that you are refusing the offer; it is a ritual that must be carried out for a few minutes in order to appear polite. Without it, one is perceived as uncivilized and rude.

So when I am invited to parties and trips, I fake-refuse multiple times before I "give in" and accept. That's why every exchange in Iran takes hours. From inviting friends and relatives over to paying for a cab ride, to going through a doorway at the same time- "no, you first," "no, you" etc. Even the shopkeepers will initially refuse to quote a price for an item, saying: "*ghaabel nadaareh*" (it's not worthy of you) obliging the customer to insist on paying before the shopkeeper finally quotes a price. Same with cab drivers who will initially refuse payment saying: "It's not worthy of you, you are worth much more." Under no circumstance does that mean you don't pay. Rather, the driver is making a gracious statement in order to be polite and respectful.

The complications arising from this can lead to one performing a task that one does not want to perform. For instance, if you have offered a friend a lift only as a way of *taa'rof* and being polite, you can become stuck in the situation if the friend actually agrees to take the ride. Or when you're trying to pay for something and are in a hurry, it's hard to get away when the shopkeeper is *taa'rofing*: a constant *it's not worthy of you, no, you shouldn't pay* ensuing.

Taa'rofing is also bound in heavily florid rhetoric:

"I have made you suffer so much." (Dinner guest to host).

"My life is not worthy of you." (Dinner host to guest).

"I hope your hands don't hurt." (Guest to dinner host).

Ta'rofing is part of me; my Iranian-ness, so decided to engage heavily with the theatricality and mind-fuckery of it all.

My cousins and their friends cannot wait to tell me of all the wild parties they want to take me to and don't get that I have come to Iran to get away from that. All I want to do is go to the night bazaar, the mountains and rivers, bath-houses and old parts of town, and be with my grandmother and father, but I am also mesmerized by this secret life, this underground living. This subterranean subversive world crawling with miscreants, the dejected; a product of the Islamic Republic dictatorship.

FIFTY-ONE

When my film producer uncle finds out I've trained in acting, he connects me with a film director shooting a film about a woman's prison as he is locking for actresses. I am delighted and excitedly take the details for the next day's meeting.

I call my friend Azadeh, with whom I gave a talk at a women's conference in London in 2003, and ask her to come to the film audition with me. Azadeh is a photographer and underground filmmaker, constantly documenting real life events and the following day, we rehearse not just my Iranian accent for the scene but learn how to cross the road.

You launch your whole body into a hailstorm of cars bulleting toward you in the utter firm belief that they will swerve, screech, or brake to avoid collision. Other pedestrians gawp and laugh at my attempts.

"Just plunge your body *into* it," Azadeh instructs me, giggling at my distress. "They'll have to stop, trust me."

I grimace. "What do you mean *into* it? Cars are literally going forty miles an hour!"

"They'll stop, they have no choice," an old man snaps impatiently like I am special needs, and Azadeh looks embarrassed from the other side of the road.

We yell our destination to the orange taxis whizzing by at a busy junction. Moving cars jam up the pavements and take up every inch of space, revving outdated emission controls, spitting contaminated exhaust fumes as their continuous honking doesn't let up, reversing in front of oncoming speeding cars, veiling the city in a jaundiced haze.

We take a weird detour in the cab and alight to encounter downtown sex workers getting into punters' cars with their kids as Azadeh hands out condoms, food and kids' toys. I wait in a soup kitchen and rehearse my monologue from *Death and the Maiden* for my audition and try to translate it into Farsi but alas, my Farsi is a bit elementary, so I will need to do the audition in English. The downtown women are addicts—meth, heroin and opium. Most of them are runaways from the provinces, young kids who do a few hours of *sigheh* with old men for the cash.

The sex workers take their kids along in punters' cars to the booking location whilst the punter and his friend(s) take turns it in turns to have sex and alternate between waiting in another room with her kids.

Azadeh tells me about the porn girls, and one in particular who was executed in 2001 when the authorities discovered her identity by reading the serial number of her electricity meter in one of the scenes. The execution took place in Evin prison, where she had been held for eight years. No punishment was ever handed out to the men in the film.

Since I was a little girl, I have heard about stoning, the sentence given for adultery and moral corruption. The body of the person is wrapped in white shrouds, made ready for the grave, then placed upright in ditches—the men up to their waists, the women up to their breasts—as a crowd gathers around them to throw stones, small ones so that they die a slow death. It usually takes about thirty minutes. The law states that the condemned can go free if they manage to rip off the shrouds and climb out from the ditch, an impossible for the women as they have no way of using their arms, the "logic" of them buried up to their chest being that if the cloth is ripped from that area as the crowd throw the small stones, the breasts would be exposed. It's a slow and very painful death, the white shrouds" first gush of red seeps through, speedily escalating to a drenched shredded red pulp.

Yet everyone I see here is obsessed with sex, having it outside of marriage or committing adultery, breaking the law and wiping their arses with the legal codes imposed on them. Everything in Iran is a secret life, bound in danger; it is audacious, blood-thirsty and on the precipice of death.

At the audition, I test for the role of prison guard. The director knows my uncle well and he lets me have a couple of hours going through the scene. The film is about a women's prison, yet it has to remain apolitical. Filmmakers can't risk making films too political, so the script is mainly about the female prisoners' crimes and social problems, which is political anyway. I approach my monologue with a delicate composure that's charged with rage, anguish and revenge. Then I am given a short Farsi scene. After it, I look at the director, and he weeps.

"You have been through so much, haven't you? I can see. It's coming out in your eyes. But when you do the Farsi monologue, your accent is so English."

He sighs, shaking his head. "Too English. Come back again for the recall when you have practiced your Farsi accent."

So English.

I am a bloody foreigner in England and a bloody foreigner in Iran. I have a foreign accent in England and a foreign accent in Iran. *You belong nowhere, you dim-witted oaf.* I take the script and start practicing my Farsi accent with Azadeh. I have to sound like a scummy prisoner with a tough street Tehrani accent, but the genteel English accent is too ingrained in me for it to dislodge and loosen easily, never mind merge into loutish Tehrani I need.

The streets are abuzz with this accent, me mimicking its components: guttural vows and leathery diphthongs, snappy syllables and sing-song intonations. I walk in boulevards under the rows of sycamore trees, skipping over gushing *joobs*, deep gutters by the pavement streaming with water sourced from the mountain north of the city, to flow down through the city, transiting whatever is thrown in it along the way, through the neighborhoods and districts, its boulevards and squares so by the time it reaches the slums south of the city, it's heaving with garbage, scum float, dead rats and sludge. I hop over them, some too wide and some mere arteries.

It seems on every corner street corner vendors offer fresh honeydew melon juice with milk and crushed sugar, fresh banana milk and pomegranate juice. Instead of the generic fast-food chains on every street corner, there is fruit juice for pennies, herbs and cheeses, rices and homemade stews. It is only those seeking something "trendy" and "hip" and "Western" that seek shopping malls and pizza, lattes and fast-food.

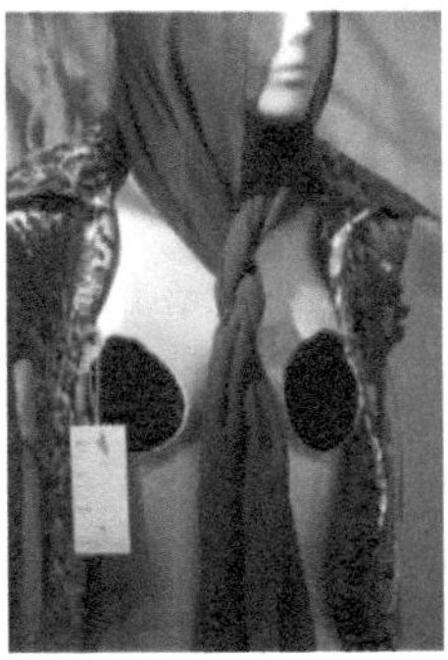

"De-feminized" Mannequin in Tehran shop window.

In a midtown ladies' shop in a small mall, girls are haggling over the price of lingerie. Fashion magazines are strewn over a glass table and Muzak plays in the background. Women talk in lowered tones as the sales lady flogs sex toys from under the counter. Suddenly, at the panicked signal from the designer shop opposite hers, the saleswoman switches off the music, hides the fashion magazines, and dumps the sex toys into a huge plastic bin, concealing them with dresses. The female customers swiftly lower their headscarf and dab at their lipstick as they scram. A gang of morality policewomen have arrived with an elderly chador-clad woman pointing at my feet and shrieking at me, "Khanoum (lady), what is THIS?" Her face is distorted in rage as I look down, perplexed. "Aren't you embarrassed? Don't you have shame or honor to walk around like this? How do you live with yourself?"

She wags a finger in my face.

The jig is up.

They have spotted the infidel.

But it's my ankles they have an issue with, the offending strip of bare skin, bone, muscle, and sinew peeking outrageously beneath the cropped jeans I've teamed with kitten heels and which basically brand me as an enemy of God. I may as well have flashing neon arrows pointing to a sign on my head that reads WHORE.

Azadeh tries to diffuse the situation. "Sorry, sister, she is from England, she made a mistake. Please forgive us."

"What the hell does she think she's doing? Aren't her family ashamed?" The morality policewoman is spooked.

Swiftly, we leave the store.

I am shaken and bemused. This dramedy scene that transpired from the white meat of my ankles was escalating into a Greek tragedy. I've never thought of my ankles as pure sex—not enough to inspire such lasciviousness and societal chaos, anyway. I wonder how all the Tehrani women with their makeup and attire fare daily with the morality police. I get a private cab, not wanting to stand on the corner of the street shouting my destination at orange taxis, and head home to my father and grandmother.

"No, I'm not worthy of you, madam. You don't have to pay. I simply did not do enough for payment."

"Yeah, yeah, WHATEVES," I snap at the cab driver.

"No, no, it's my honor."

For fuck's sake. This goes on for about ten minutes.

At home, my grandmother is making *ashe reshteh* for me and my dad, a traditional thick noodle soup with herbs, lentils, beans and fried mint, onion, and kashk—liquid whey—poured on top. She lights the samovar and pours tea into glasses, my dad watching TV all the while. Then she draws me into her lap and tells me stories of her life, tales matching those of my maternal mother as a child bride. It was the norm then, tradition.

"I was about twelve when they gave me away for marriage," she says softly, drawing her chador closer to her shoulders. She looks away, her tranquil nature and exalted composure having conquered horror, damage, and the band of marauders that robbed her of childhood and innocence. "The husband's family—all the women, my new in-laws—had to hold me down on my wedding night so that I would lie still and he could have sex with me." There is a trace of bitterness that blights her otherwise serene and buoyant temperament. Her eyes, always bright and mischievous, are a piquant mask to the horror of the event and its aftermath.

She tells me that many girls her age ended up with gynecological problems and internal hemorrhaging in those days from undergoing childbirth at such a young age. Like my maternal grandmother and many other pre–1940s women, she also had many babies, all raised within the large community of relatives and neighbors. A lot of children died at infancy from childhood illnesses. And she tells me stories of jinns and spirits she saw seen as a young woman when she and her husband and young family had lived in a remote village. Jinns climbing out of the well and their bloodcurdling malevolent face that would freeze your soul if you looked directly into it. Tales of folk legends and old superstitions.

My best life is shutting the world out and being in the warmth of my father and grandmother and relatives from their side of the family who are so much more down to earth, funny, affectionate and open-minded than my mother's side. It is the night shrouded in a pewter cloud of my dad's cigarettes cuddled up with my grandmother on motakkas as we all snuggle in the dark lit only by the stark white glare of TV. Their shabby flat, poor and meagre in a traditional neighborhood with street traders and chain gangs of bakers and people sitting on their doorsteps is my best life.

I used to think it was dating rock legends or being tour with bands, even after I went through all the cirrhotic-livered rehabbed and now anodyne American rock stars and experienced Rammstein.

"Yoo vill valk this vay. Single line only please."

Rammstein's modus operandi had been to get roadies to scout the crowd before the show and give out backstage passes to girls who would then be herded in typical German fashion and marched in an orderly queue to the side of the stage to view the fire and chainsaws, dildos, and explosions on stage. The fire would sizzle my skin, warming my eyelids and thawing me out from the freezing cold of the festival night. There would be tons of girls standing on the side lines, but not all of them would dare to enter the sex lair. And those of us who did would sprawl on sofas and nibble on fruit platters waiting nervously, rouged and powdered, glancing at the other stock, discreetly checking body odors and crotch hygiene, wet-wiping and stuffing sponges in our vaginas if we were having a period—although from my experience, Till liked blood sports; all rock stars do. With Rammstein there was so much fucking insane sex. Fire, sex, sexual deviance. My friends and I would get the room keys from Til's manager and meet him in London hotel rooms filled with champagne and flowers and wait for him to show up and devour us. It was the kind of bestial and profane fucking that left crimson streaks and albumen taints all over the sheets. In the morning we would fall asleep next to him under a big blanket.

Now my best life is different. It's how my skin chafes from the coarse, musty blankets my dad and grandmother tuck me into, the bruised bandaged night pricked by the paraffin lamp of night traders. It's how the eternally black-clad war widows swish and sway in bazaars, and how my grandmother and dad tell dirty jokes that only the Shirazis know how to tell. It's how we snack on salted cornelian cherries as my father smokes death cigarettes, the coarsest chemically enhanced fags I have ever seen. It's the smell of having nothing and having the earth, having the vivacity to make poverty a piquancy. It's the smell of rosewater and scorched pavements and hearts. It's my grandmother shimming her hips to Arabic music in front of an audience. This is real.

I cuddle my dad as we watch old Persian films at night, leaning against the motakkas, both of us smoking those cheap Iranian cigarettes. My grandmother sleeps on the floor of the living room in swathes of bedding, and I join her while my dad sleeps in the spare room. Early morning my grandmother and I fold up the sheets and bedding and leave them in their corner of the living room as she kneels in her first prayer of the day, facing mecca with a mohr on the floor. The murmur of street vendors below echoes into the living room as we sit on the floor to breakfast.

Here is a man next to me and we are biologically related, but I don't think of him as a parent because I don't have that bond with him. I don't know what it feels like to have a dad, a male parent figure. It feels icky to me, having a male who can love you unconditionally and not for sex or what you can give him in return. Henry did, on some level but I found it too weird, too uncomfortable. It is too late now, I am too old to have a male come into my life and love me unconditionally, because I'll scream: "what the fuck do you WANT????"

One thing that has stayed the same is the squat toilet. Man, how I hate squat toilets. I deduce that everyone in countries that has squat toilets must have Olympian thighs and calves of steel. What if you are intestinally challenged? You're going to need to squat for a good while, which means you're gonna have had a few good rounds at a gymnasium daily. You can't exactly stop for a few minutes for a break and squat back down again, can you? And no toilet paper, just a sad little dribbly hose coiling from the wall.

There is something more insufferable, though: illegal satellite TV.

Although illegal in Iran because it is "depraved" and Un-Islamic, about ninety percent of the population has it as state TV is just an endless loop of prayer and propaganda. A sea of dishes outlining the skyline offers ample opportunity for the morality police to detect, raid, dismantle, and demolish before fining the owners. Iranian channels broadcast from LA are a dime a dozen due to LA's densely populated Iranian community and are mainly vacuous fodder. Trashy talk-shows and vapid game-show bonanzas ding-ding-ding into Iranian homes in the Islamic Republic and Iranian singers showcasing their latest saccharine love songs clogs the airwaves. Forced bonhomie amongst LA-based diaspora presenters matches their bungeed face lifts and it is all escapism to beat the oppression and tyranny of the regime.

Satellite TV inevitably blares into my dad's little apartment, and I realize with sadness how badly needed these tacky shows from LA are, how much of an escape it is for him from the poverty and addiction and absence of his child. Never having seen the world, my dad and grandmother stare mesmerized at the kaleidoscope of colors beaming at them as some presenter drivels on.

How I love their sweet innocence and humility.

My dad takes me to the shanty towns, the slums, the bazaar, and cafes by the mountain waterfall on night rides because he also has a penchant for the rhythm of human life—for the kids selling rocks, for the workers of Iran—and a revulsion of the phony. He shows me people living away from the glamourous ski pistes of north Tehran and the designer boutiques. He takes me where the pollution guarantees respiratory problems, and people make do with cardboard homes and soup kitchens, where people sell their kids for sex and young boys sell bricks instead of going to school. He doesn't want me to romanticize Iran; he wants me to see it for all it is.

We drive through the city, me squeezing shut my eyes and holding onto the window ledge for dear life as cars, motorbikes, and humans zoom toward each another as if on one vast collision course or playing some mad game of "chicken." We get to the Grand Bazaar, a centuries-old labyrinth of narrow alleyways and corridors six miles in length split into arteries—a city within a city holding guest houses, mosques, and banks. Along a maze of beehive arches are tucked-away vaults where vendors sell carpets, spice, copper and gold, textiles, and hand painted miniatures and crafts. We push our way through the heaving throng of bodies, and amongst the Persian gems and artifacts we come across an old man at the end of a shoe alley ladling out asheh reshteh from an enormous vat for pennies, a charitable gesture to bless all with the nectar of goodness and purity.

I buy jeweled anklets, handcrafted tea glasses, antique lamps, blood red silk shawls with gold threading, saffron, belly dancing chains, and sour plums. The haggling and taa'rofing, which my dad does in Farsi, takes about thirty minutes.

Some nights we find ourselves in Darakeh, a mountain village just outside Tehran, gushing with streams and waterfalls. Nestled in the foothills of the Alborz Mountain, the cool air, the woods and hiking trails attracts locals and tourists. Tea houses and mountain-side restaurants serve barbeques and snacks, as people lie back on canopy cushions, dipping their feet in the cool stream. A storyteller recites tales of Shahnameh.

Vendors dotted around walnut trees, rock outcrops and wildflowers, sell every type of fruit, fresh or leather, sour or salted or left to ferment in the sun. Apricots the color of rust. Lavashak that pulls your mouth inside out.

Families sprawl across layers of kilims under the lantern-lit sky. Conversations unravel. Secrets slip out like loose change. Humans begin to act like one family as we bind together like glue, sharing the silent broken sorrow and torment for our motherland; ceaselessly she is choked, maimed and mutilated. And still her body nurtures us, nuzzles us.

I don't miss pub culture at all.

I don't feel the loneliness.

FIFTY-TWO

My film character is a streetwise hustler who is a newbie in jail and has become a snitch. I am on the last three shortlisted at my audition recall, and excited that I might be in such a big film but my accent is well, dodgy—part English private school girl and part Amy Winehouse. It is nowhere near a real Iranian accent. The director really wants me to have this part but is holding back; under no circumstances can she have a foreign accent, especially not like mine.

I am practicing my Farsi accent for the next round of film auditions when my cousin Anahita calls to invite me to a party. My grandmother has made me my favorite pudding— *shole zard*, literally meaning yellow flame, a rice pudding with saffron, cinnamon, rose water and crushed almonds on top—and we are about to cozy up alongside my dad. She's even spelled our names on top in cinnamon powder, And while I want to see everything in Iran, I get the biggest rush from cuddling up to my father and grandmother, both of whom I am really getting to know properly for the first time in my life. But all my relatives think that because I was from the West, all I want to do is get pizza, go to shopping malls, and do "Western" shit.

The party is obviously an illegal one—mixed genders, alcohol. My cousins are determined to initiate me into a secret world with the potential to be each attendee's personal apocalypse, and I have a compulsion to self-vandalism, so I agree to go. The consequences of this type of partying are so dire if raided, that I don't understand why it is such a thrill for these girls. Mixed genders in a room is illegal by itself. The bribery money on the side for the inevitable raid by the morality police, who are not raiding because they actually give a fuck about the Islamic "ethics" of the party but because they want the loot, is not going to help them much in a party such as this, I fear.

Iran has a rich erotic past detailed in Iranian literature, poetry, and paintings. Like India's legacy of Kama Sutra, the depiction of sexuality and erotica in Persian art features ambiguous sexualities never labeled as lesbian or gay. Without a label attached to them, courtships between two women in the past involved an exchange of gifts bound in elaborate rituals. Tradition dictated that one who sought another as "sister" approached a go-between, who would take to the beloved a tray of sweets in the middle of which lay a dildo (made of wax or leather), and if she agreed to the proposal, they would then take vows of sisterhood, drink fruit juices, and on Friday evening spend the night together.

And it is with the most traditional girls that I now attend the most erotic. These girls and their side-eye over arched brow, the jet black of lash over huge almond peepers, the rosebud lips. What is it about Iranian women? These sensual creatures sashaying into night, shrouded in secrets.

Afsaneh, Anahita's pretty twenty-eight-year-old friend, is from a bazaari family. Bazaaris are the merchant classes, a traditional and conservative class of people whose family histories are rooted in business and commerce in the marketplaces of Iran. A bazaari is from a lower to middle class background and seen as new money with old-fashioned religious values as opposed to those of intellectualism, academia, and modernism. In her family, a twenty-eight-year-old unmarried woman is practically an old maid left on the shelf. Yet she has secret boyfriends and gives a loquacious performance of her sensual awakenings. Like most Iranian women she is very sensual and I find it a travesty that as such she must block the tsunami of desire inside of her.

Afsaneh's family is different to my friend Azadeh's, whose relatives are intellectual academics and let their daughter be free with her choices. But with all the class of person I meet in Tehran, one thing is clear: every Iranian lives life with the intention of their children becoming a doctor, dentist, lawyer or engineer, utilizing these professions as the filter with which to evaluate the humanity of others.

"Did you hear what happened last week at Kiaroosh's party?" Elie, a film student, asks. "Gasht raided it. Everyone got handcuffed to each other and taken to the police station to have blood tests for alcohol and drugs. They were in cells for a few days and their families were called."

"What happened?" Anahita asks.

"Even Armin whose parents are super rich couldn't get him out of jail. He was in a cell with junkies and murderers for days and just about avoided getting the hundred lashes as his dad offered the judge a massive bribe."

The problem with this forceful "Islamification" of the Iranian people—Islam being used as a political tactic—is that it drives people to behave in as much of an un-Islamic way as possible. There is a saying that before the revolution people prayed at home and drank in public and that now, after the revolution, they drink at home and pray in public. The deliberate hyper-visibility of nightclubs and discos in the Shah's time had been his desperate attempt at showcasing how "liberated" and Westernized he had made Iran, with praying very much a private affair behind closed doors, whereas now it had to be a public act of loyalty to Islam and the Islamic regime and the partying that was hidden and underground. The Iranian people have lived with a double life since the Shah and this is now a natural way of life for them, subterfuge and secret identity becoming part of the Iranian identity.

So we are in this big house outside of Tehran belonging to a bazaari family whose son, Siavash, has organized the party. Designer brand spirits and wine provided by Armenians (Christian by birth, they are allowed to drink alcohol in private in Iran) flows freely, as do meth and coke. Girls in silk chemise and bright gowns float by, having already slipped out of the conservative attire they'd wore in, hence the pile of hejabs on the floor.

Everywhere, bodies twist and crawl in a heap of limbs, heels and heads. People make out. A girl with a pageboy bob, tasseled pearl body necklace and a pair of shiny black Mary Janes, reclines on a pile of cushions with two guys.

I have been throwing the remnants of what appears to be the carcass of a chicken dinner to this crying cat and her litter, all of whom have found their way to the garden, and I'm thinking about how there are so many stray animals in Iran, how most people cannot have the capacity for empathy toward animal welfare when they are too busy with human right atrocities, when Yasmin, mono-browed and black braided, comes over and pulls me to her voraciously.

"You are so nice, such a nice girl," she says in broken accented English, laying me down. She smells like the outside, like parks and match sticks.

Right there in the garden by the trees and a craggy wall etched with calligraphy, she acts like the typical timid Iranian girl, but secretly ravenous for the hardcore. She goes down on me and I reciprocate. I have gone down on girls all my life and they seem to taste like the foods they eat, even after deep bathing. With Iranian girls it's like Iranian food flavors are so strong that it oozes out of their pores, their pussies, their lips and hair, hours, days after consumption.

Afterward, she shudders silently, twitching like a wild animal caught in the grip of a snare, and she gets up, slides off her bracelet, and gives it to me. It is a multi-strand freshwater pearl cuff. I can't take that kind of gift, I tell her. No, you are our guest, you must, she replies, smiling shyly. Then she tells me that if I am not drinking, there is caviar and fruit in the kitchen, that I should help myself.

The pretty girls of Iran glide and float, kiss and swoon in smoldering heaps. And then there's me: not quite as pretty, not as goddess-like, more like a potato from a council estate. I can't compete with Iranian girls.

Late night after the party, girls and boys in cars all seem to be coming out of parties to cruise around, loud music blasting.

The Basij and morality police super vigilant at this late hour stop cars with young people in them frequently. Stationary in traffic, I see Basijis by the roadside clipping off the long hair of a young guy and screaming and punching him.

"They've cut his hair off. Look at them punching him, motherfuckers." Mahtob says.

"He probably had booze on his breath as well," Anahita adds.

"These teenage Basijis have a fucking chip on their shoulder, because they come from poor families and now have the power to beat up and arrest the rich kids who have everything they don't have," Mahtob says.

As we roll along I watch as two girls with heavy makeup getting dragged out of the car with the two young guys. A pair of Basiji guys who look barely out of their teens are screaming obscenities at them:

"You fucking whore! Your hair is out, make up like a whore. Wipe it! I bet you would spread your legs for own dad if he paid you."

And with that one of them takes a cloth and is scraping and slathering her face with such ferocity it looks like he is exorcising the Satan out of her.

The definition of moral corruption and anti-Islamic behaviour is ad hoc; improvised.

Those arrested with un-Islamic dress or behaviour will be taken before a committee of revolutionary guards, humiliated and interrogated and kept in without food or contact with family. If they don't have the money to bribe the officials that is. The revolutionary committee will contact the person's family to ask for the title deeds to property as bail depending on the severity of the crime. The more severe the crime the higher the demand for money.

We have arrived at a late night/dawn café packed with lorry drivers and laborers getting ready for the day ahead to eat sheep's head and hooves, the literal meaning of Kalleh-Pache, the traditional breakfast stew of sheep's head and hooves. A bit like Haggis. It has suddenly become hip for the young crowd of hard party-goers to eat this to soak up the booze after binge drinking. It is seasoned with turmeric and cinnamon and even though traditionally eaten at dawn, it is also good for hangovers as it is very fatty. High in cholesterol and full of calories it gives men with hard labour jobs enough energy for the whole day and the cool kids, a new trend in curing hangovers. My memory of this dish is of a 4am car ride packed with my mum's activist friends going to visit someone in prison. It was too heavy for my palate and I gagged, confused by animal trotters floating around in my tummy.

I have my final audition call-back in the morning, so I sleep for a bit, then practice my accent a bit more as I walk around my old neighborhood, go to a bathhouse, read poetry and let my whole self be saturated and soul soared by the sound of the Azan from the mosque; not because I am religious but because it is a celestial blanket to tuck the whole nation into bed at night; a celestial cradle that locks us in.

My father has been gone to meet someone since early morning and I have been trying to get hold of Azadeh, who has wanted me to come watch her theatre piece being staged at a secret house, but her phone line is dead and after calling her family I find out that she has been arrested for writing the play. Her crime: anti-government activity and propaganda, mocking Islamic practices and Islamic sanctity.

She will be kept in prison.

Early evening arrives and I am sitting with my grandmother till my dad comes back for dinner. We call his phone, but he has left it at home. I walk up and down the alley and look around the neighborhood square, but he isn't around.

FIFTY-THREE

In the summer of 1988, one of the biggest crimes against humanity occurred in Iran, and to this day no one has been held accountable for it. It was a genocide, a "cleansing" of the country from those who either followed a different version of Islam or didn't believe in god. The war with Iraq had just ended, and Iran's Supreme Leader Ayatollah Khomeini issued a decree in July 1988 to annihilate the enemies of Islam immediately. Beginning in July and continuing for several months, the extermination of at least thirty thousand political prisoners took place in Iran with most of the executed being either high school or college students who'd committed the "crime" of holding different political or religious views to those of the Islamic Republic.

The majority of those killed were supporters of the People's Mujahedin of Iran, who were deemed Monafeq (hypocrites) and supporters of other leftist factions, referred to as Mohareb (enemies of God) and their "crimes" could be as minor as having passed around political leaflets. A three-member "Death Committee" "tried" the prisoner in a minute or two, deciding whether the prisoner was mohareb or a mortad and then sending political prisoners who refused to abandon their beliefs to execution.

Every day, hundreds of political prisoners were hung in batches- hanging didn't mean death by breaking of the neck or drop through a trap door but hanging the victim to choke slowly, which meant that many took twenty minutes to die. Documents smuggled out of Iran reveal that prisoners were loaded onto forklift trucks and hanged from cranes in half-hourly intervals. Sharia mandates The reason for mass slow hangings and not the use of firing squads was because Sharia mandates hanging as the execution method for apostates and enemies of God. It is possible though that hanging was a quieter method than gunfire, preserving the secrecy of the extermination. The Islamic Republic refused to provide information about the whereabouts or fates of the prisoners, and some families began their own search, which resulted in the discovery of Khavaran, an unmarked cemetery located in southeast Tehran, its mass graves deliberately void of markings on them to further torment the victims' families. The section of the cemetery in which the political prisoners are buried is known as Lanatabad, which means "place of the damned." More mass graves would be discovered in the area throughout the rest of the year with families discovering and photographing body parts of partially buried victims.

The authorities then began to destroy hundreds of individual and mass unmarked graves in Khavaran, to destroy any forensic evidence for investigation by human rights groups. So many family members still tend to Khavaran to ensure the site remains intact despite repeated attacks by the authorities, which locked the gates to the cemetery and in 2009 demolished the grounds, removing any sign of mass graves. They continue to destroy any photos or notes marking the graves in any way, even dowsing the land with lime to prevent families from planting flowers at the cemetery. Today, the Islamic Republic security forces still harass and threaten with arrest those who continue to seek information about the disappeared or attempt to gather or mark the anniversary in any way.

The perpetrators of this genocide continue to enjoy impunity.

It is night, and my grandmother and I are still waiting for my dad to come back. He would have been here now, legs crossed on the cushions, smoking his death cigarettes. Gazing at me in his gentle, meek, timid way, telling me how much he loves me, the glare of satellite TV reflecting on his thick glasses.

What beautiful horror is this portion of the planet. Iran, one of the world's greatest ancient civilizations, the mighty Achaemenid Empire of Cyrus the Great and Darius the Great, with their majestic palaces and paradise dream gardens in Persepolis before Alexander the Great burnt the cities to ashes and stole its treasures on twenty thousand mules. Then it was the Arabs who burnt our books and tried to erase every trace of Persian culture and brought Islam to Iran, tried to force Iranians to devote themselves only to Islam instead of their own ancient Zoroastrian religion. Iran is like a beautiful maiden who has been repeatedly raped and violated, but she is still smiling, spirit unbroken, giving us all a wink to say, "I am all right, loves, nothing will break my spirit."

Azadeh has disappeared. The authorities won't release any information about her as she is "an enemy of god." I haven't heard back yet about the outcome of my final audition recall. I am bovine and more unsightly than the actress with the green eyes and porcelain skin who is also in line for the part, so the role of a rough con is probably more suited to me, but she has the natural Farsi accent, so I don't think I will get the part.

In the morning my neighbors and I put out flyers and stick posters around the neighborhood for my missing dad.

FIFTY-FOUR

My epilepsy medication is canary yellow. It is oval and fluorescent in its blister pack. It makes me drowsy and deeply fatigued, which means that if by some happenstance I ever smoke opiates—like weed—the state of zombification takes affect to turn me into a proper Nurse Ratched job. Hence why my mother has been rejecting epilepsy meds all her life, preferring the split skulls on concrete and the botched face after crashing down flights of stairs at the onset of a seizure to the sluggish fatigue of medication.

So I don't get my father's lifelong embrace of opium. However cheap as chips in Iran, it is still a zealous commitment to lethargy and an all-encompassing state of sedation and dulling yourself to the world.

The sheets are clean and the bedspread is plain, and the matrons coo and fuss. The carpets reek and the windows frames leak, and the lights tend to flicker, and the rotary corded phones give an air of 1960s institution to the place.

My father is strapped down to a bed and shrouded in bandages as nurses administer shots and dab at glops of ooze from his gauze. He's been in rehab before, but this is calamitous. My father had left home in pursuit of his drugs, mid-morning, before the lunch time rush, and the neighborhood mosque brought out the usual pre-noon prayer social hub of men drinking tea and hanging out in its yard. Men who were husbands, fathers, grandfathers, bakers, teachers, and clerics—community elders. And he had walked past them into the kamikaze roads, snaking his way through street vendors and mums with kids and shopping bags to score and disappeared.

Two weeks later and after a stack of missing posters and police reports, a feeble scratching at the door late at night shook my grandmother and me from our slumber.

My father lay slumped by the door, his face crushed into a bloodied pulp, his skull caved in and splinters of his eyeglasses dented into his eye sockets. His teeth had been knocked clean out of his mouth and what remained was a hollowed, slumping, broken jaw popping out. Blood and viscera encrusted his clothes. The fact that he'd been kidnapped and beaten by a gang of drug dealers to whom he owed money had never crossed my mind, but it seems both my mother and father have a propensity for self-harm, and now I see why I am who I am, why I do what I do.

I hold him only as I can and let him float away.

My father passes away a few weeks after. His sense of awareness was gone and his broken body and catatonic state was all that remained of him. He didn't know how to speak. He didn't know how to walk, go to the bathroom, eat. He was no longer there. Years of loneliness and abject poverty, years without family and a useless daughter who had brought him neither financial stability nor grandkids had resulted in this, this end of life, this wretchedness.

What was I? Was I born a demon? To destroy Anneh, Henry, friends, and now my own father?

I know I am dark. I bring ill omen and suffering to those around me. I can't rid myself of it.

FIFTY-FIVE

I have made my way to Tabriz and am waiting at the bus depot to get the bus. This town, 1500 BC, with its skull crushing winters, is my mother's ancestral home.

As a child she lived in a three-hundred-year-old decrepit house with antique doors and overgrown orchards. Her family, all eight of them, slept in a large assembly hall even though the three-story house had nine different rooms all cluttered with rubble and mice. The only toilet was a hole in the ground in the far corner of one of the orchards. And the only water for drinking was drawn from a well in the cellar.

Under this old house were vaults hiding antique coins and treasures left by past residents. My mother, as an eight-year-old child, found them all one night while playing with the mice in the subterranean recesses of this catacomb and was told to stop playing with old trash and throw them away.

Anneh and her family: my mama is in the back

My maternal grandmother Ashraf who as a child-bride had been married off to a man twenty years older had been lucky that my grandfather, a landowner who had been born in that house out of respect for her had never taken any other wives. This was very unusual as his brother and the other prosperous men in the nearby villages normally had more than one wife. Being of an educated nature, he had acknowledged Ashraf as a child, treating her more with the loving tenderness of a father than a wife, even accompanying her to the doctor's when she had first started her periods.

After the death of their babies and especially the youngest girl, blue-eyed Nahid they had all gone a bit mad with grief that summer night. Another child dead.

When my mum became a teen, she got her own room filled with mice and scorpions. Giant beetles and insects would crawl under her pillow and upon waking she would lift her pillow to find a squirming black floor. And she would feed every creature, especially the scorpions. Her parents thought her odd, so at nights they sent her down to the cellar to draw water from the well for the household's cooking and cleaning. Hundreds of stone steps led to a cavernous cellar where, in the dark, shelves held rice, pickle jars, meats, cheeses, quince, and jam. Some winter nights the temperatures would drop to minus-thirteen. She would carry the bucket of water up to the house for her siblings, going to sleep only to wake up at dawn to go down the cellar again to free the mice from their traps. She would dangle half-dying mice into a basket and let them loose again so they could feed from the sacks of rice and crumbs of nuts and cheese. Her love of animals continued with rescuing stray cats until there was twenty-three of them roaming the house.

As I get on the bus in Tabriz, I look up at the driver. He speaks Azari, his breath like onions. I get on, ready to go to the next city. Whatever happens to me in Iran, at last, I have tasted my own freedom.

Epilogue

Somewhere in Europe. Summer 2025

I write this somewhere in Europe, as bombs rain down on Iran. My homeland faces an unprecedented attack from Israel, a genocidal regime already engaged in the annihilation of Palestinians in Gaza. I cry for my country as I sit at dinner with the Rock Star, who I have not seen in a long while. The conversation staggers from Iran to the impending Yulin festival—a grotesque bacchanal of cruelty during which dogs are flambéed alive while children laugh. Then to my mother.

She faded away suddenly, in 2021, just after she got her first shot of the Covid vaccine. Her kidney levels plummeted, and her heart gave up. After a second vaccine a few weeks later, she fell into a coma and was not able to walk again. I stared at her face as she gasped her last breaths like a fish too long out of water and then stopped, her ravaged face in an instant evaporating into a younger self—that of a twenty-year-old girl.

Death was what she always wanted. Not in a suicidal way, just in that way certain people do—those who never quite belonged here. She was otherworldly, her divinity incompatible for this earth's soil.

I left Iran as quickly as I had entered it, getting back to Turkey with the passport given to me, and then to England with my British passport. I didn't want to leave, but I felt I had to; it was getting too risky.

I lived in the oldest city in the world: Yazd. The wind catchers whispered above me and the mud walls glowed like burnished honey. The fire temple had been burning for 1,500 years, and my home had thick stone walls and a blue door that stuck in the winter rains. The desert air held me close, dry yet gentle, a tender embrace from a country that bruised me deeply but never let me go.

I had learned to move softly through the ancient city. My hejab was loose but respectful, a subtle negotiation of visibility and invisibility. My presence there was as fragile as it was defiant; I had returned to the place from which I was torn, reclaiming quietly what was taken from me amidst the scent of saf-